L·9 95

Bundeshauptstadt

Berlin

Capital City

D1312785

Für Christine

Ulf Meyer

Bundeshauptstadt

Berlin

Capital City

Parlament · Regierung ·
Parliament · Government

Ländervertretungen · Botschaften ·
Federal State Offices · Embassies

Vorwort von Peter Conradi
Foreword by Peter Conradi

jovis

Editorial:

Dieses Buch führt den Leser zu allen relevanten Schauplätzen der Politik und Diplomatie in Berlin. Kurze Texte auf Deutsch und Englisch beleuchten die wichtigsten Aspekte der Architektur und Entstehungsgeschichte der Alt- und Neubauten. Sie sind nach Nutzungsart und innerhalb der Typologien nach Orten geordnet. Karten erleichtern die Orientierung. Infokästchen (▭: Adresse; ✎: Architekturbüro; ⚒: Bauzeit) geben nötige Informationen und Register helfen beim Finden. Abkürzungen waren notwendig (BM: Bundesministerium; LV: Ländervertretung). Im Architektenregister finden sich nur die Architekten der Neu- bzw. Originalbauten und die des jeweils letzten Umbaus. Mein Dank für die Mitwirkung an diesem Band geht an meinen Co-Autoren Hans Wolfgang Hoffmann (hwh).

Ulf Meyer

Editorial

This book takes the reader to all the relevant sites of politics and diplomacy in Berlin. Brief texts in German and English illuminate the most important elements of the architecture and origins of the old and new buildings. They are classified by the type of usage, and within the typology they are classified by locations. Maps help you to find the way, information boxes (▭: address; ✎: architectural office; ⚒: construction period) provide necessary information and indeces help you to find items in the book. Abbreviations were necessary (Fed.Min.: Federal Ministry; FSO: Federal State Offices). The index of architects includes only the architects of the new or original buildings and the most recent alterations. I would like to express my thanks to my co-author Hans Wolfgang Hoffmann (hwh) for his cooperation in this book.

Ulf Meyer

Übersetzung / translation: Victor Dewsbery
Redaktion / editing: Yamin von Rauch
Recherche / research: Claudia Arnold, Sabine Isensee, Ina Steffan, Timo Strauch
Korrektur / proof reading: Wolfgang Gottschalk
Umschlagfoto / cover photo: Udo Meinel
Umschlag / cover design: sans serif/Lisa Neuhalfen, Berlin
Gestaltung / design: grafikkugel, Berlin
Satz / types setting: Kooken Unlimited, Berlin
Lithografie / lithography: Satzinform, Berlin
Druck, Bindung / printing, binding: DBC, Druckhaus Berlin Centrum, Berlin

jovis Verlagsbüro
Kurfürstenstraße 15/16
D-10785 Berlin

ISBN 3-931321-98-3

Inhalt / Contents

Peter Conradi
Vorwort / Foreword

In seinem oft zitierten Vortrag „Demokratie als Bauherr", den Adolf Arndt, damals „Kronjurist" der SPD-Bundestagsfraktion, 1960 in der Akademie der Künste zu Berlin hielt, fragte er, „ob die demokratische Gestalt des Gemeinwesens sich als eine Besonderheit auf das Bauen auswirken, ob das Bauen in der Demokratie andersartig sein müsse als innerhalb einer nichtdemokratischen Ordnung…". Architektur zeigt den Zustand einer Gesellschaft, ihre Probleme, ihre Werte, zeigt, wer in einer Gesellschaft was zu sagen hat und wie eine Gesellschaft leben will und das deutlicher als Literatur, Musik oder Malerei. Adolf Arndt meinte, „daß jedes Bauen eine Vorstellung von der Weise des Lebens verkörpert, als auch, daß Demokratie ein universales Prinzip ist, das sich in einer Weise des Lebens verwirklichen soll, mithin die politische Gestalt eines Staates mit einer Gesellschaft und die im Bauen zu schaffende Gestalt menschlichen Bleibens nicht unverbunden nebeneinander, nicht gegenseitig gleichgültig voneinander sich abwenden können". Architektur zeigt geistige Bewegungen, sie schafft nicht autonome Formen und Stile, sie spiegelt wider, was in einer Gesellschaft vorhanden ist. Manchmal weist sie in die Zukunft und zeigt, was kommen könnte. Bei uns gibt es zur Zeit ein Nebeneinander, zum Teil ein Gegeneinander, manchmal ein Miteinander unterschiedlicher geistiger Strömungen. Die bequeme Parole „anything goes" tut so, als sei es belanglos, für welche Architekturformen, für welche bauliche Sprache sich der Architekt entscheidet. Das Gegenteil ist richtig: Weil wir keinen übergreifenden geistigen Konsens haben, der wie früher einen für alle verbindlichen Baustil hervorbringt, muß sich jeder Architekt fragen, in welchem geistigen, politischen, sozialen und ökonomischen Kontext seine Architektur steht. Ge-

In his often quoted lecture "Democracy as a client" which Adolf Arndt – then the leading law expert of the SPD parliamentary party – held in 1960 in the Academy of the Arts in Berlin, he asked "whether the democratic form of the state community should have a special effect on building, whether building in a democracy needs to be different in kind from building in a non-democratic structure …". Architecture shows the condition of a society, its problems and values, it shows who has what to say in a society and how a society wishes to live, and it does so more clearly than literature, music or painting. Adolf Arndt considered "that every act of building embodies a concept of the way of life, and also that democracy is a universal principle which should be realised in a way of life, therefore the political form of a state with a society and the form of human habitation created by building are not unconnected and separate, and can not turn away from each other in mutual indifference." Architecture shows intellectual movements, it does not create autonomous forms and styles, it reflects what exists in a society. Sometimes it points to the future and shows what might be. At present we have a juxtaposition, to some extent a conflict and sometimes a cooperation of different intellectual streams. The comfortable motto of "anything goes" pretends that it is unimportant which architectural forms, which structural language the architect decides to use. The opposite is true. Precisely because we no longer have an overriding intellectual consensus which leads to a building style that is mandatory for all, every architect must ask himself in what intellectual, political, social and economic context his architecture is set. Buildings live longer than the intellectual movements to which they give form. Anyone

bäude leben länger als die geistigen Bewegungen, denen sie baulichen Ausdruck geben. Wer plant und baut, muß wissen, welchen Werten, welchen Ideen er/sie damit bauliche Gestalt gibt. Die Bauten der Demokratie gehören und dienen der Gemeinschaft und lassen deren Zustand erkennen. Die Diskussion über „demokratische Architektur" ist unsinnig: Beton ist nicht undemokratisch, Glas nicht demokratisch. Die Forderungen an die Architektur des Bauherren Demokratie sind inhaltlicher Art: Sie sollen weder von Willkür noch von Gewalt geprägt sein. Das Gebaute soll Vertrauen und Selbstvertrauen deutlich machen und Rücksicht nehmen auf Menschen, auf Gebäude, auf Stadt, auf Landschaft und Natur. Öffentliche Bauten in der Demokratie sollen offen sein, ohne falsches Pathos. Sie sollen den Menschen nicht kleinmachen.

Der Bauherr Demokratie baut mehr als die historischen Bauherren Fürst und Bischof. Sichtbar wird der Bauherr Demokratie eher in Schulen, Kindergärten, Altersheimen, Krankenhäusern, Wohnungen und in den Bauten für die demokratischen Institutionen. Mit dem Beschluß des Bundestags, Parlament und Regierung sollten von Bonn in die Hauptstadt Berlin ziehen, begann eine lebhafte Planungs- und Bautätigkeit der öffentlichen Hand. Neben Neubauten für Bundestag und Bundeskanzleramt wurden zahlreiche Altbauten – so das Reichstagsgebäude, daneben andere für die Bundesministerien – modernisiert. Die Neubauten für Bundestag und Bundeskanzleramt geben Zeugnis von der Baugesinnung des Bauherren Demokratie. Aber auch die Art, in der die Altbauten für neue Aufgaben umgebaut wurden, sagt etwas über unser Selbstverständnis, diese historischen Bauten nicht zu rekonstruieren, sondern sie uns mit den architektonischen Mitteln unserer Zeit anzueignen. „Denn ein jedes Ding – so auch Staat und Politik – hat seine Erscheinung. Nichts anderes heißt Ästhetik. Was ist eine Republik? Ein Staat, in dem die Bürger die öffentlichen Angelegenheiten als ihre eigenen begreifen… Deshalb bedarf der demokratische Staat einer Ästhetik, die dem Bürger das Gefühl der Verantwortung für seinen Staat ermöglicht. Ein Staat, der darauf verzichtet, wird seinen Bürgern verächtlich – und daraus entsteht gewiß keine republikanische Haltung." (Stephan Speicher, 1994)

Die öffentliche Beteiligung an Planungen und die kritische Bewertung des Gebauten sind unverzichtbar. Beim Bauen in der Demokratie ist das Verfahren so wichtig wie das Ergebnis: Beteiligung der Betroffenen, öffentliche Diskussion, Transparenz der Entscheidungen, nicht zuletzt eine Öffentlichkeit, die sich dafür interessiert, wie sich unser Gemeinwesen in Rathaus und Parlament, in Gerichtsgebäuden und Universitäten, Krankenhäusern und Schulen baulich darstellt.

who plans and builds must know what values and ideas he/she is giving architectural form to. The buildings of democracy belong to and serve society, and they show what condition society is in. The discussion about "democratic architecture" is senseless. Concrete is not undemocratic. Glass is not democratic. The demands on the architecture of the client democracy are related to the content: they should be neither despotic nor coercive. What is built should clearly express trust and self-confidence, it should pay due consideration to people, buildings, the urban setting, the landscape, nature. Public buildings in a democracy should be open, without any false pathos. They should not make people feel small.

The client democracy builds more than the historical clients duke and bishop. The client democracy is mainly visible in schools, kindergartens, old people's homes, hospitals, dwellings and in the buildings for democratic institutions. With the decision by the German Bundestag that the parliament and government should move from Bonn to the capital city of Berlin, lively planning and building by public authorities began. In addition to the new buildings for the parliament and the Federal Chancellery, numerous old buildings have been modernised – including the Reichstag building and the buildings for several ministries. The new buildings for the parliament and the Federal Chancellery bear witness to the attitude to building of the client democracy. But the way in which the old buildings have been converted for new tasks also says something about our self-concept, the way we did not reconstruct these historical buildings but rather took possession of them with the architectural means of our time. "For each and every thing – even the state and politics – has its appearance. That is all that is meant by aesthetics. What is a republic? A state in which the citizens regard public affairs as their own. Therefore the democratic state needs an aesthetic concept which enables the citizen to feel a responsibility for his state. A state that does without such a concept becomes despicable to its citizens – and that certainly does not lead to a republican attitude." (Stephan Speicher, 1994)

Public participation in the planning process and critical review of what is built are essential. In building in democracy, the process is just as important as the result: participation of those affected, public discussion, transparency of decisions, and not least a public which is interested in how our state community presents itself architecturally in town halls and parliament, in courts and universities, in hospitals and schools.

Hans Wolfgang Hoffmann
Das Festival der Demokratie / The Festival of Democracy

Am 1. Juli 1999 trat der Deutsche Bundestag zu seiner letzten Sitzung in Bonn zusammen. Artig und nicht ohne Wehmut verabschiedeten sich das Volk und seine Vertreter am darauf folgenden Wochenende von dem Residenzstädtchen, das ihnen ein halbes Jahrhundert als Dienstsitz diente. Ab dem 5. Juli brachten dann 24 Güterzüge der Deutschen Bahn und unzählige Möbelwagen 70 Tresore, 1300 Computer, 56.000 Kartons und rund 120.000 Einzelstücke vom Rhein an die Spree. Seit dem 7. September finden hier alle Sitzungen des Bundestages und das Gros der Regierungsarbeit statt. Damit findet zumindest ein symbolisches Ende, was neun Jahre zuvor am 30. August 1990 mit der Unterzeichnung des Einigungsvertrages begann: Das wiedervereinigte Deutschland hat Berlin zu seiner Hauptstadt gemacht. Der Weg dorthin verlief nicht ohne Hindernisse. Doch hier soll es nicht darum gehen, den Prozeß nachzuerzählen. Am Ende vieler hundert Exkurse könnte dann nur ein „Es ist vollbracht!" stehen. Die Zeit ist vielmehr gekommen, Bilanz zu ziehen: Was hat das Hauptstadtprojekt Berlin gebracht? Und – noch wichtiger – wie verändert der neue Dienstsitz den Bund?

Das hauptstädtische Berlin

Als am 20. Juni 1991 der Deutsche Bundestag mit einer Mehrheit von nur 17 Stimmen die Verlagerung von Parlament und Regierung vom Rhein an die Spree beschloß, knallten in Berlin die Korken. Die Erfüllung eines Traums, der knapp zwei Jahre zuvor in der Sektlaune des 9. November 1989 geboren worden war, schien gesichert: Berlin würde wieder, was es zuletzt bestenfalls noch in

On July 1st 1999, the German parliament met for its last session in Bonn. The following weekend, the people and their representatives meekly and regretfully took their official farewell from the residence town which had served as the political centre for half a century. Starting on July 5th, 24 goods trains and innumerable removals lorries then transported 70 safes, 1300 computers, 56,000 packing boxes and about 120,000 individual items from the Rhine to the Spree. Since 7th September, all sessions of the German parliament and almost all government business have been conducted here. This at least symbolically completes the process that began nine years earlier on 30th August 1990 when the reunification treaty was signed: the reunified Germany has made Berlin its capital city. The path up to this point has not been without obstacles. But this is not the place to narrate the whole process: at the end of a host of explanations it could then only be declared "It is finished!" The time has now come to consider what the capital city project has done to Berlin. And – even more important – how does the new seat of government change the Federal Republic?

Berlin as a capital city

On 20th June 1991, when the German parliament voted by a majority of only 17 to move the parliament and government from the Rhine to the Spree, there was celebration in Berlin. The fulfilment of a dream that had been born almost two years earlier in the heady night of 9th November 1985 seemed to be assured: Berlin would again become what it had only been in memory: a met-

der Erinnerung war – eine Metropole. Nicht nur in Meyers Enzyklopädie des Jahres 1972 war der Begriff untrennbar mit dieser Funktion verknüpft. Selbst die Berlingegner hatten diese Hoffnung unbewußt angestachelt, die nordrhein-westfälische Staatskanzlei vergeblich versucht, mit dem furcherregenden Pleonasmus „Hauptstadt-Metropole" die Abgeordneten umzustimmen.

Heute, da die Regierung die Stadt leibhaftig betritt, macht sich Ernüchterung breit. Am deutlichsten fällt das Urteil aus, wenn man auf einen Aspekt blickt, der zwar nur ein Teil des Hauptstadtprojekts ist, der die zukünftige Entwicklung aber schon jetzt erhärtet: Stadtstrukturell haben die politischen Zentralorgane des vereinten Deutschlands Berlin weit weniger umgekrempelt als alle Staatswesen, die hier zuvor Heimstatt fanden. Erinnert sei nicht nur an die gigantomanische Vision einer die ganze Stadt durchpflügenden Nord-Süd-Achse, die Albert Speer im Auftrag des Nazi-Regimes entwickelte. Obwohl die damals projektierten Neubauten nicht Wirklichkeit wurden, ließ die Planung das Diplomatenviertel entstehen. Das Viertel am südlichen Rand des Tiergartens bekam ein Gepräge, das zu den charakteristischten der Stadt zählt und das auch heute wieder aufgenommen wird. Noch deutlicher formte die DDR Berlin: Mit erstaunlichem Durchhaltevermögen errichtete sie über vierzig Jahre lang nicht einfach nur Regierungsbauten. Mit dem Fernsehturm, dem Palast der Republik und den dazugehörigen Freiräumen entstanden populäre Orte, welche bewirkten, daß die Stadt nicht allein in administrativer, sondern in jeder Hinsicht das Herz des Landes darstellte. Zudem vermochte das Zentrumsband zwischen Spreeinsel und Alexanderplatz die bis dahin von der Entwicklung abgekoppelten Ostbezirke an Berlins Mitte zu binden.

Vergleichbare Impulse hat das aktuelle Hauptstadtprojekt Berlin nicht gebracht. Von stadtstruktureller Relevanz ist allein das „Band des Bundes". Seinen Standort freilich findet es nicht auf der Spreeinsel, die seit Jahrhunderten den Mittelpunkt des Staates repräsentiert und die seit dem Zusammenbruch der DDR-Institutionen Impulse bitter nötig hat, sondern im Spreebogen – einer Fläche, die seit der Zerstörung des Alsenviertels im „Dritten Reich" urbanes Niemandsland darstellt, was das Projekt dem Risiko aussetzt, zu einem gar künstlichen Gebilde zu werden. Eine Befürchtung, die die Bundesbauten an seinem westlichen Ende bereits bestätigen. Das Bundeskanzleramt und die Abgeordnetenbüros, die im Spreebogen entstehen, sind zugleich die einzigen Neubauten. Alle übrigen Institutionen kommen

ropolitan city. It was not only the Meyer encyclopaedia of 1972 that saw an inalienable connection between a metropolis and a capital. Even the opponents of Berlin unconsciously stimulated this hope, and the North Rhine-Westfalian state chancellery tried in vain to sway members of parliament with the horror of a "metropolitan capital city".

Now that the government is actually moving into the city, reactions are rather more sober. This is especially so when we consider one factor which is only part of the capital city project, but which already gives an indication of the future development: the central institutions of the unified Germany have had far less impact on the structure of the city than all state systems that the city has ever seen. This applies not only to the monstrous vision of a gigantic north-south axis through the city which Albert Speer developed on behalf of the Nazi regime. Although the new buildings envisaged in the scheme were never built, the plans still led to the creation of the diplomatic district. The area on the southern edge of Tiergarten thus acquired a structure which is one of the most characteristic in the city and is being revived in the present. The GDR formed Berlin to an even greater extent. With astonishing persistence over forty years, it built more than mere government buildings. With the television tower, the Palast der Republik and the associated open areas it created popular locations which meant that the city was not only the administrative centre of the country, but its heart, too. And the central ribbon of buildings between the island of the Spree and Alexanderplatz created a link from the city centre to the eastern suburbs, which had previously been isolated from the city's development.

The present capital city project in Berlin has not provided comparable impetus. The only element with relevance for the urban structure is the "ribbon of government buildings", although this is not located on the island of the Spree which was the centre of the state for centuries and urgently needed new impetus after the collapse of the GDR institutions, but rather in the meander of the Spree – an area that has been an urban wasteland since the destruction of the Alsen district in the "Third Reich". As a result, the project is in danger of becoming a merely artificial structure - a fear which the government buildings already confirm at the western end of the ribbon. The Federal Chancellery and parliamentary offices that are being built there are the only new buildings. All other institutions are moving into existing buildings, and the reconstruction and, in some

in bestehenden Gebäuden unter, deren Rekonstruktion und teilweise Erweiterung natürlich nur einen bescheidenen Gewinn bedeutet. Da sie außerdem stärker als jemals zuvor über die Stadt verstreut liegen, hält ihre prägende Wirkung zudem im Zaum. Insgesamt hat Michael Mönniger (*Berliner Zeitung*) zweifellos recht, wenn er das Hauptstadtprojekt weniger als Politisierung der Stadt denn als Verstädterung der Politik beschreibt.

Die Resignation geht freilich viel weiter: Prognosen, die Berlin nach der Hauptstadtentscheidung einem Wachstumsschub vorhersagten, haben sich bislang als falsch erwiesen. Von ihr erwartete beispielsweise die regierungsnahe Berliner Bank noch im Jahr 1991 eine „Initialzündung für einen wirtschaftlichen take-off der Region". Das Geldinstitut rechnete allein durch die nach Berlin kommenden Parlaments- und Regierungsinstitutionen, Verbände und Medien sowie des Diplomatischen Corps mit 45.000 zusätzlichen Arbeitsplätzen, infolge mitziehender Haushaltsangehöriger mit einer vielfach höheren Zahl von Neu-Berlinern und mit einem Anstieg des regionalen Bruttosozialproduktes um drei Milliarden Mark jährlich.

Heute stagniert Berlin jedoch. Die Arbeitslosenquote ist selbst für Großstädte überdurchschnittlich. Seit 1994 sinkt die Bevölkerungszahl immer stärker, allein 1998 um 50.000, woran die gut 11.000 Bediensteten des Bundes, die jetzt in die Stadt kommen, kaum etwas ändern werden. Selbst wenn man Brandenburg mit in die Betrachtung einbezieht, das infolge der Stadtflucht zum einzigen Bundesland mit Einwohnerzuwachs avancierte, steht die Region längst nicht so gut dar, wie es die Prognosen nach der Wende vorhersagten. Freilich konnte das Ergebnis nicht anders ausfallen, beruhten die Erwartungen doch auf einem Denkfehler. Für Berlin ging es 1991 nicht darum, Regierungssitz zu werden, sondern zu bleiben. Während die alt-bundesrepublikanisch geprägte Sprachregelung mit dem Begriff „Umzug" Hoffnungen auf den Gewinn von etwas Neuem weckte, ging es in Wahrheit nur um die Fortschreibung des Bestehenden. Berlin war bereits fünfmal Hauptstadt und Regierungssitz – erst von Preußen, dann des Deutschen Reiches, der Weimarer Republik, der Nationalsozialisten und zuletzt der DDR. Historisch betrachtet, stellen die zehn Jahre seit 1990, da Deutschland allein von Bonn aus regiert wurde, den Sonderfall, der Umzug dagegen die Rückkehr zur Normalität dar.

Zudem veränderte sich der Staat, seit Berlin zuletzt Hauptstadt eines einheitlichen Deutschlands war. Von dem alten, zentralistisch-totalitären Nationalstaat ist

cases, extension of these buildings is naturally only a moderate gain. And they are more widely distributed through the city than ever before, so they are not so striking in their effect. The journalist Michael Mönniger is undoubtedly right when he suggests that the capital city project represents an urbanisation of politics rather than a new political dimension in the city.

But there is even more cause for resignation. The forecasts that predicted a surge of growth in Berlin after it had been declared the capital have so far proved to be wrong. In 1991, for example, the "Berliner Bank" predicted an "initial impulse leading to an economic take-off in the region". The bank anticipated 45,000 new jobs just from the parliamentary and government institutions, associations, media and diplomatic corps moving to the city, a far higher number of new Berlin citizens with the family members and a rise in the gross regional economic product by 3 billion DM per year.

Instead, Berlin is now stagnating. The unemployment rate is above average even for big cities. The population has fallen at increasing speed since 1994, with a loss of 50,000 in the last year alone, and the 11,000 or so government employees who are now moving to the city will hardly make any impact on this figure. Even if the consideration is widened to include Brandenburg, which has become the only federal state with a growth in population because of the tendency to move out of the city, the region is still far from the position that was predicted after the Wall came down. But this result was only logical because the expectations were based on wrong thinking. The aim for Berlin in 1991 was not to become the seat of government, but to remain so. Whereas the language used in the old Federal Republic, with the term "relocation", aroused hopes of gaining something new, the real concern was to continue the existing situation. Berlin had already been a capital city and seat of government five times – in Prussia, the German Empire, the Weimar Republic, then under the National Socialists and in the GDR. Historically, the ten years from 1990 onwards in which the whole of Germany was governed from Bonn were a special case, and the relocation is a return to normality.

But the city has changed since the last time that Berlin was the capital of a unified Germany. Nothing remains of the old, centralist and totalitarian national state – this can be seen most clearly in the fact that the GDR needed four times as many government personnel to administer an area that was hardly a fifth of the present territory of Germany. Even the old Federal Republic decentralised a

nichts mehr übrig, was seinen deutlichsten Beleg darin findet, daß die DDR einst viermal so viele Bedienstete brauchte, um kaum ein Fünftel des gesamten deutschen Territoriums von Berlin aus zu verwalten. Schon die alte Bundesrepublik hatte einen Großteil der Macht aus ihrer Hauptstadt in die Provinz ausgelagert. So wurde etwa Karlsruhe Sitz der Dritten Gewalt im Staate, um durch den Standort die vom Grundgesetz geforderte Unabhängigkeit des Bundesverfassungsgerichts zu unterstreichen. Im geeinten Deutschland wird die Verteilung sogar noch föderaler sein: Der Umzug wurde damit erkauft, daß von den heute nur noch 14 Ministerien gerade acht ihren Hauptsitz in der Hauptstadt haben werden. Zwar werden alle Minister an der Spree residieren, doch die Mehrzahl der Bundesbediensteten verbleibt infolge des Bonn-Berlin-Gesetzes von 1994 am Rhein. Als Konsequenz des Beschlusses von 1991, der unter dem Titel „Vollendung der Deutschen Einheit" eine generelle Neuverteilung gesamtstaatlicher Institutionen vorsah, werden einige der früher hier ansässigen Behörden, wie etwa das Umweltbundesamt, in die neuen Bundesländer übersiedeln. Insgesamt verläßt Berlin nahezu die gleiche Anzahl von Bundesbediensteten wie hinzuziehen. In Zukunft werden europäische Einigung und Globalisierung den Stellenwert einer nationalen Hauptstadt wie Berlin weiter verringern.

Gleichwohl glaubte sich Berlin mit der Regierung im Rücken auch auf dem Weg zu einer Art von Metropole, die gemäß neuerer Definition nicht mehr Zentrum des Staates, sondern der Wirtschaft ist. Tatsächlich erwies sich das Hauptstadtprojekt als Katalysator der Modernisierung Berlins. Insgesamt wurden in den letzten zehn Jahren rund 100 Milliarden in öffentliche Infrastruktur und dreimal so viel in Privatimmobilien investiert. Freilich wurden diese Prozesse vom Termindruck der Regierungsverlagerung nur beschleunigt, nötig waren sie mit dem Ende der Teilung allemal. Vor allem – und da sind sich inzwischen alle Experten einig – werden weder die Chancen, die die Bauleistungen der Stadt eröffnen, noch die Regierung allein sicherstellen, daß Berlin eine „global city" wird. Zwar entstanden mehr als zehn Millionen Quadratmeter neuer Büroflächen, die für eine Dienstleistungsmetropole nötig sind. Doch derzeit steht ein Zehntel des Gesamtbestandes leer – mehr als selbst bei günstiger Konjunktur in einem Jahrzehnt bezogen werden könnte. Hauptniederlassungen von Großunternehmen, die nach Berlin übersiedeln, lassen sich an einer Hand abzählen, Allianz, Daimler-Benz, Sony, die Deutsche Bahn AG. Insbesondere die Protagonisten der Geldwirt-

large part of its power from the capital city to provincial centres. Thus, Karlsruhe became the seat of the third power in the state to underline the independence of the Federal Constitution Court demanded by the constitution. In the unified Germany, this distribution of powers will be even more federalist. The relocation to Berlin was bought at a price: of the 14 ministries in the national government, only eight will have their main headquarters in the capital city. And although all ministers will work from offices by the Spree, most of their civil servants will still be in Bonn. And as a result of the decision of 1991 under the heading "Completion of German Unity", which envisaged a general redistribution of the overall tasks of the state, a number of institutions that were based in Berlin are now moving to the new federal states, such as the Federal Office of the Environment. In total, almost as many federal employees are leaving Berlin as are moving to the city. And in future, the unification of Europe and the general globalisation trend will further reduce the importance of national capital cities like Berlin.

Nevertheless, Berlin thought that with the support of the government it was on the way to becoming a new style metropolis which would be not so much a centre of the state, but a centre of the economy. And the capital city project has acted as a catalyst for the modernisation of Berlin. Over the last ten years, well over 100 billion DM have been invested in public infrastructure and three times this amount in private property development. But these processes were only speeded up by the relocation of the government – they were necessary anyway when the division of Germany ended. However, the experts now agree that the opportunities created by building activities in the city and the presence of the government will not, on their own, ensure that Berlin becomes a "global city". Although more than ten million square metres of office space have been built – which are necessary for a service metropolis – a tenth of this space is actually vacant, which is more than the space that can be filled in a whole decade even in a positive economic climate. The headquarters of major corporations that are moving to Berlin can be counted on the fingers of one hand: Allianz, Daimler-Benz, Sony, Deutsche Bahn AG. Especially the protagonists of the financial world, who play a key role in a "global city", are remaining in Frankfurt am Main, which has strengthened its role as the monetary metropolis in Europe by becoming the location of the European Central Bank. The capital city is left with branch offices instead of headquarters.

schaft, denen in einer „global city" eine Schlüsselstellung zukommt, bleiben in Frankfurt am Main, das durch die Ansiedlung der Europäischen Zentralbank seine Stellung als monetäre Metropole Europas weiter festigt. Statt Zentralen blieben für die Hauptstadt nur Filialen.

Auch diese Entwicklung kann kaum überraschen. Schon die praktische Politik hat sie unbewußt unterstützt: Das Entstehen bedeutender Einzelprojekte wurde durch die Förderpolitik des Bundes, die in erster Linie auf dem Instrument allgemeiner Steuernachlässe aufbaute, nicht eben unterstützt. Weit wichtiger ist jedoch, daß Staat und Geschäftswelt im geeinten Deutschland nicht – wie noch in der DDR – direkt miteinander verflochten sind. Für letztere ist Lobbyarbeit der einzige gangbare Weg der Einflußnahme. Dafür muß nicht die gesamte Unternehmung Staatsnähe suchen, sondern nur das entsprechende Segment der Managementetage. Die allumfassende Standortgemeinschaft mit der Regierung, auf die Berlin hoffte, ist also schlicht nicht notwendig. Und das gilt nicht nur für die Wirtschaft, sondern für den größten Teil des privaten Sektors, letztlich für alles, in das der Staat nicht direkt hineinregiert.

Statt dessen entfaltete das Hauptstadtprojekt eine viel näherliegende Sogwirkung: Die Stadt zog jene an, die Umgekehrtes im Sinn haben – Lobbyisten, Vertreter, PR-Berater, Öffentlichkeitsarbeiter, Marketingstrategen und Medienmenschen. Berlin wurde zur Stadt der Repräsentanzen. Freilich liegt es in der Natur dieser Exponenten, daß ihr Mengeneffekt beschränkt ist, sie allein also all die Büros kaum werden füllen können. Bedeutsamer sind die qualitativen Veränderungen, die sie dem gesellschaftliche Klima der Hauptstadt angedeihen lassen. Mit den Repräsentanzen kam eine Kultur der Repräsentation nach Berlin. Von dem der Regierung am nächsten gelegenen Quartier, der Friedrichstadt, in dem sowohl im Kaiserreich wie in der DDR ganz andere Nutzungen die Oberhand hatten, hat sie regelrecht Besitz ergriffen. Alles, was im Stadtzentrum geschehen ist, war unbewußt auf sie gerichtet.

In Zahl und Ausgestaltung übertreffen die Repräsentanzen alles, was man aus dem politischen Zentrum Westdeutschlands kannte, aus dem Ostdeutschlands sowieso. Was dort nur Briefkastenadresse war, mauserte sich nun zu einem eigenen Bauwerk, manchmal sogar zum Kulturzentrum, wofür die Dependance des Guggenheim-Museums das prominenteste Beispiel ist. Wie die Allianz in Treptow stellen sich Unternehmen selbst an nicht unbedingt dafür geeigneten Standorten durch Kunst zur Schau. Am deutlichsten wird die Entwicklung bei den re-

This development is also not surprising. Even practical politics provided it with unconscious support. The development of major individual projects was not exactly helped by the subsidy policies of the national government, which was mainly based on the instrument of general tax allowances. But a much more important factor is that the state and the world of business are not directly linked – as they were in the GDR. For the business community, lobbying is the only practicable way to exercise any influence. But this does not require the whole enterprise to be close to the state, only the appropriate segment of the management. The shared overall location with the government that Berlin hoped for is simply not necessary. That applies not only to business but to a large part of the private sector – in the last resort to all areas which are not directly governed by the state.

Instead, Berlin developed a far more obvious attraction: the city drew in those with opposite intentions: lobbyists, representatives, PR consultants, public relations staff, marketing strategists and media specialists. Berlin became a city of representation. It is in the nature of these sectors that they only have a limited quantitative effect, which means that on their own they will not be able to fill all the offices. But the qualitative changes they bring to the social climate of the capital city are more significant. These representative bodies brought a culture of representation to Berlin. This culture took possession of the Friedrichstadt, which was dominated by completely different forms of use in the Empire and the GDR. Everything that happens in the city centre was sub-consciously directed towards this cultural identity.

In their number and design, these representation offices exceed all that was known from the political centre of West Germany, and they surpass East Germany even more clearly. Where there was only a letterbox address, there is now an entire building and sometimes even a cultural centre, the most prominent example being the auxiliary premises of the Guggenheim Museum. Like the Allianz insurance company in Treptow, companies present themselves with art even in locations that are hardly suitable for the purpose. This development is clearest in the institutions closest to the government: the embassies. The embassy complex of the Nordic countries is a prime example of the fact that it is not only the superpowers that have built veritable festival halls in Berlin. Hardly any other seat of government has diplomatic institutions which are so conscious of their public image. Thus, the capital city project enriches the city in

gierungsnahsten Einrichtungen: den Botschaften. Die Gesandtschaft der Nordischen Länder bezeugt prototypisch, daß sich in Berlin nicht nur die Supermächte regelrechte Festspielhäuser leisteten. An kaum einem Regierungssitz geben sich die diplomatischen Vertretungen derart öffentlichkeitswirksam. So bereichert das Hauptstadtprojekt die Stadt gerade dort, wo Berlin schon früher den Rang einer Metropole einnahm: auf dem Sektor der Kultur.

Das Gesicht der Berliner Republik

Die Politik verband mit dem Beschluß vom Juni 1991 nicht weniger Hoffnungen als die Stadt. Daß sie in Berlin normaler, nach innen den Problemen der Menschen und nach außen den östlichen Ländern näher sein, daß das Hauptstadtprojekt insgesamt die deutsche wie die europäische Einheit vorantreiben werde, waren Erwartungen, die nicht nur Bundestagspräsident Wolfgang Thierse bei jeder Gelegenheit wiederholte. Natürlich ist es noch zu früh, über ihre Erfüllung zu befinden. Sprechen lassen kann man allein das Gesicht, mit dem sich das geeinte Deutschland präsentiert. Hier sind in der Tat gravierende Veränderungen sowohl gegenüber der ehemaligen Deutschen Demokratischen wie gegenüber der alten Bundesrepublik zu konstatieren.

Kaum zwei Kilometer liegen zwischen dem Reichstag und dem einstigen Sitz der DDR-Volkskammer, und doch liegen Welten dazwischen. Überraschenderweise ist der Kontrast zwischen dem Bonner Bundestag und dem Berliner Plenarbereich sogar noch größer. Die Unterschiede springen ins Auge, lange bevor man in den Kern der Gebäude vordringt: Hinter dem Palast der Republik thronen Karl Marx und Friedrich Engels mit Blick in den Osten. Demgegenüber ist der Vorplatz des Reichstages frei von derart eindeutigen ideologischen Anspielungen. Und doch hat der riesigen Repräsentationsrasen mit seinen begradigten Busch- und Baumrabatten ebensowenig mit der zwanglosen Laubenpieperidylle gemein, die man im Gartenhof des Bonner Bundeshauses antraf.

Daß sich das Erscheinungsbild des Staates derart wandeln würde, galt 1991 alles andere als ausgemacht. Als der Bundestag für die Verlagerung von Parlament und Regierung vom Rhein an die Spree votierte, war damit eigentlich nur die Dienstadresse Deutschlands neu bestimmt. Eine Debatte über das Gesicht der Berliner Republik gab es damals nicht. Klar war nur das Ende aller Provisorien – eine Vorgabe, die im Bundespräsidialamt der Architek-

the area where Berlin was metropolitan in earlier times: in the cultural sector.

The Face of the Berlin Republic

Politicians placed just as many hopes in the decision of June 1991 as the city did. It was not only the parliamentary speaker Wolfgang Thierse who frequently expressed the hope that they would be more normal, closer to the problems of the people and to the eastern federal states and that the capital city project as a whole would advance German and European unification. Of course, it is still too early to pass any judgement on whether these hopes have been fulfilled. But we can comment on the face presented by the unified Germany. And here there really have been radical changes, both compared with the German Democratic Republic and with the old Federal Republic.

It is hardly two kilometres from the Reichstag to the former seat of the People's Chamber, but the two buildings are worlds apart. Surprisingly, the contrast between the parliament in Bonn and the plenary chamber building in Berlin is even greater. The differences are obvious long before the visitor enters the building. Behind the Palast der Republik are statues of Karl Marx and Friedrich Engels looking east. The parliamentarians exchanged looks with the intellectual founders of the state before they entered the debating chamber. The area in front of the Reichstag is free from such ideological references. But the enormous lawn with its geometrical bush and tree gardens has just as little in common with the informal weekend garden atmosphere in front of the parliamentary building in Bonn.

It was by no means clear in 1991 that the appearance of the state would change in this way. When parliament voted to move the parliament and government from the Rhine to the Spree, this merely changed the official address for Germany. At the time there was no debate about the form and design of the Berlin Republic. It was only clear that all provisional arrangements would end – a goal which was most directly reflected in the Federal President's office by the architects Gruber and Kleine-Kraneburg which has an elliptical form that will be as effective in thousands of years as it was thousands of years ago. Beyond that, there were merely two rather diffuse expectations that were voiced: first of all the hope that the political scene could be simply transported from the Rhine to the Spree, and secondly the fear of a restoration

ten Gruber und Kleine-Kraneburg am direktesten Gestalt fand, dessen Ellipsenform geometrischen Gesetzen folgt, die noch in Jahrtausenden so gelten werden, wie sie vor Jahrtausenden galten. Darüber hinaus hörte man allenthalben zwei eher diffuse Erwartungen: Erstens das Hoffen auf eine einfache Verpflanzung der politischen Landschaft vom Rhein an die Spree und zweitens die Furcht vor einer Restauration der nach Weltgeltung strebenden Hauptstadt, die Berlin vor 1945 gewesen war.

Tatsächlich legten die Beschlüsse unbewußt bereits das Fundament dafür, daß diese Vorahnung genau nicht Realität werden konnten: Ein Finanzrahmen wurde fixiert, innerhalb dessen eine Hauptstadt nicht neu erfunden werden konnte – eine Perspektive, die durch die erwähnten retrospektiven Erwartungen ohnedies aus dem Blickfeld gedrängt worden war. Zudem legte man sich auf eine Stadt fest, die um so vieles mächtiger war als die Bürgerresidenz Bonn und die alles außer einem hermetisch abgeschlossenen Regierungsviertel wollte. Schließlich entstand die Kapitale hier anders als in Bonn, wo die Bundesrepublik erst rund zwanzig Jahre nach ihrer Gründung eine Hauptstadtplanung begründete, von Anfang in einen systematischem Prozeß, bei dem nur eines fehlte – ein allumfassender Masterplan. Der Bund stritt mit Berlin um Details. Institution auf Institution fand ihren Platz. Die Hauptstadt wurde erobert, nicht im Handstreich, sondern Stück um Stück. Jede Entscheidung mußte zudem vor der Öffentlichkeit gerechtfertigt werden, mehr als das selbst in gestandenen Demokratien bisher üblich war. Ein großer Wurf konnte dabei nicht entstehen. Der Bund mußte Kompromisse machen, vor allem hinsichtlich seiner Sicherheitsbedürfnisse: Während er sich am Rhein noch hinter Stacheldraht und Abstandsgrün hatte verschanzen können, mußte er an der Spree hinnehmen, daß Eingangskontrollen in die Gebäude gedrängt wurden und sich die Bonner Bannmeile in Berlin zu einem deutlich kleineren und weniger reglementierten „Befriedeten Bereich" wandelte. Im Ergebnis operiert die Politik hier anders als am Rhein nicht mehr in einer Raumstation.

Ein entscheidende Weichenstellung erfolgte 1994 aus Kostengründen: Das Kabinett beschloß, für die Bundesorgane mehrheitlich nicht neu zu bauen, sondern sie in Altbauten unterzubringen. Fortan war man gezwungen, sich mit der Stadt, wie sie war, und mit ihrer Tradition als Dienstsitz deutscher Staatlichkeit auseinanderzusetzen. Die Aneignung der Monumente und ihrer Geschichte erfolgte – gemäß dem Arbeitstitel fast aller Umbauten – durch „Herrichtung". Diese Methode erlaubte sogar wie-

of the capital city Berlin was before 1945 with its striving for global renown.

The actual decisions taken unconsciously laid the groundwork to ensure that this foreboding could not become a reality. A financial framework was fixed which made it impossible to create a new capital city – a prospect which had in any case been displaced by the retrospective expectations. The decision favoured a city which was far more powerful than the bourgeois residence of Bonn and which certainly did not want a hermetically sealed government district. And the development of the capital city was different from the procedure in Bonn where the Federal Republic only began to draft plans for a capital city about twenty years after it had been founded – and although these plans were developed in a systematic process, they were not based on an all-embracing master plan. The national government argued with Berlin about the details. One by one, the institutions found their locations. The capital city was conquered piece by piece and not in one fell swoop. Every decision had to be justified before the public – to a greater extent than is normal even in established democracies. It was not possible to create a great overall design. The national government had to compromise, especially with regard to its security needs. Whereas it had been able to hide behind barbed wire and strips of vegetation in Bonn, on the Spree it had to allow the guarded access points to be moved into the buildings, and the protected zone in Bonn became a far smaller and less regulated "pacified zone" in Berlin. The result is that political life here will be less like a "space station" than it was on the Rhine.

A decisive step was taken in 1994 for cost reasons. The cabinet decided that most federal institutions would be accommodated in old buildings instead of creating new buildings. From then on, politicians were forced to face up to the city as it was and its tradition as the centre of German state history. The listed monuments and their history were "altered and adapted", and the renovation work for almost all old buildings was described in these terms. This method meant that it was even possible to use buildings that were historically compromised in the National Socialist era. Besides the extension of the former Reichsbank, which is designated for the Foreign Office, the Reich Air Travel Ministry is the most prominent example. Its facade once appeared as dark and overpowering as the "Third Reich" itself. But now that the building has been brightened by sandblasting and the scars of time have been repaired, nobody is worried by the fact

der in Betrieb zu nehmen, was durch den Nationalsozialismus historisch belastet war. Neben der Erweiterung der ehemaligen Reichsbank, in die das Auswärtige Amt einzieht, ist das Reichsluftfahrtministerium das prominenteste Beispiel. Dessen Fassade erschien einst so dunkel und übermächtig wie das „Dritte Reich" insgesamt. Nachdem sie per Sandstrahl aufgehellt und Narben, die die Zeit geschlagen hatte, ausgebessert sind, stört niemanden mehr, daß ein demokratischer Finanzminister in dem ersten Regierungsbau der Nazis residiert. Das Ergebnis dieser Vergangenheits-Bereinigung läßt sich an fast allen Bundesbauten wiederfinden: Aus unliebsamen Mahnmalen, an denen man sich reiben mußte, wurden Bauwerke, deren Ursprung mit dem Heute in keiner direkten Beziehung mehr steht: Aus Schicksal wurde Historie. Deutschland ist erwachsen genug, um sich in seiner Vergangenheit einzurichten, ohne sie zu wiederholen. Derartige Kontinuität war hierzulande bis dato undenkbar. Beide aus dem Zweiten Weltkrieg hervorgegangenen Staatswesen zogen ihre Legitimation aus der Abgrenzung gegenüber der Vergangenheit. Wenn Ererbtes nicht ersetzt wurde, suchte man Kontrast. Für den Neuanfang der DDR mußte das Berliner Stadtschlosses als Bastion überkommener Obrigkeiten geschleift werden. In Westdeutschland wurde der Bruch thematisiert, die gläserne Fuge zum gängigen architektonischen Kunstgriff, um auf Distanz zur eigenen Geschichte zu gehen.

Gleichwohl läßt sich nicht behaupten, daß sich das neueste Deutschland sich nun restlos zu seinem Vorleben bekennt. Wie die Väter des Grundgesetzes straften auch die Kinder der 89er-Revolution das Werk ihrer Eltern mit Nichtachtung. Keine einzige Bundesorganisation kommt in einem Gebäude der West-Berliner Nachkriegszeit unter. Noch härter traf es jene Bauten, die ihre Hauptstadttauglichkeit längst unter Beweis gestellt hatten: die der DDR. Man entsorgte das Außenministerium durch Abriß komplett, andere wurden, wie der Palast der Republik, einfach außer Dienst gestellt. Die wenigen anderen glaubte man nur nutzen zu können, wenn man sie bis zur Unkenntlichkeit überformte. Mit einer Lochstatt einer Skelettfassade gibt sich das ehemalige Bildungsministerium Unter den Linden heute als Nach-Wende-Produkt. Baulich wurde in keinem Fall ein Beitrag zur Inneren Einheit geleistet.

Noch weniger Verwendung als das materielle Werk der Nachkriegszeit findet der gedankliche Überbau, unter dem es einst errichtet wurde. Da man in der DDR von der totalen Identität von Volk und Staat ausging, brauch-

that a democratic Minister of Finance now resides in the main government building of the Nazis. The result of this purification of the past can be seen in almost all government buildings. Unloved memorials which were a source of friction have become buildings with an origin which is in no direct relationship with the present: destiny has become past history. Germany is adult enough to set itself up in buildings of the past without repeating the past. Previously, such continuity was unthinkable. Both states which arose after the Second World War drew their legitimisation from their clean break with the past. Where the heritage was not replaced, a contrast was sought. For the new beginnings in the GDR the Berlin city palace, which was a stronghold of traditional hierarchy, had to be removed. In West Germany the focus was on the break itself, and a glass seam became a standard architectural device to express distance to the nation's own past.

Nevertheless, it cannot be said that the New Germany has fully accepted its former life. Like the fathers of the constitution, the children of the revolution of 1989 also simply ignored the work of their parents. Not a single national organisation has moved into a building of the post-war era in West Berlin. And buildings that had long shown their suitability for use in a capital city – in the GDR – were even more harshly treated. The GDR Foreign Ministry has been completely demolished and others, like the Palast der Republik, have simply been taken out of service. For the few remaining buildings it was believed that they could only be used if they were changed beyond recognition. The former Ministry of Education on Unter den Linden now has a perforated facade instead of a skeleton facade, making it appear a product of the period after the fall of the Wall. In no case has the architecture contributed to inner national unification.

The intellectual superstructure under which the buildings were built has been taken into account even less than the buildings themselves. The GDR was based on a total identity between the people and the state, so its representatives did not need separate premises – and the People's Chamber in the Palast der Republik was far smaller than the more popular hall for public events. After 1989 it was even the only parliament in the world to allow a striptease establishment to use part of the same building. The Federal Republic also aimed to be close to the people, but not so much by conformity as by including different interests. Although the parliament had an address of its own, the Bonn parliament building by Günter Behnisch which was only completed

ten seine Vertreter keinen eigenständigen Dienstsitz, folglich nahm die Volkskammer im Palast der Republik einen ungleich kleineren Teil ein als der populäre Veranstaltungssaal. Als einziges Parlament der Welt duldete es nach 1989 sogar ein Striptease-Lokal im Haus. Auch die Bundesrepublik strebte nach Volksverbundenheit, freilich weniger durch Konformität als durch Einbeziehung unterschiedlichster Interessen. Hier hatte das Parlament zwar eine eigene Adresse, doch der von Günter Behnisch erst 1992 vollendete Bonner Bundestag verbot sich jedes Eigenleben. Es war ein Pavillon und bestand eigentlich nur aus einem Dach. Im Streben nach Transparenz waren alle Wände aus Glas. Schwellenlos gingen Straße und Plenarbereich ineinander über. Chaotisch anmutende Materialvielfalt stand für gesellschaftlichen Pluralismus. Die Architektur war, wie die Organisation, die sie in Auftrag gegeben hatte, kein Selbstzweck, sondern lebte erst durch die Bürger und folgte damit dem zu ihrer Entstehungszeit viel propagierten Ideal der Basisdemokratie.

Nimmt man das Versprechen der Bonner Bürgerinitiativ-Baukunst ernst, muß der Reichstag befremden. Zwar ist er wie alle Bundesinstitutionen zugänglicher denn je. Doch von der begehbaren Kuppel, die gleich nach ihrer Fertigstellung zum omnipräsenten Wahrzeichen der neuen Hauptstadt wie des neuen Berlins avancierte, kann das Volk sowohl seinen Vertretern auf die Finger schauen als den Blick auf Berlins Skyline genießen. Zugleich thront das Parlament auf einem massiven Sockel. Die reich verzierte Steinfassade des Reichstags wurde auch mit dem Umbau durch Norman Foster, dem alle Veränderungen der Nachkriegszeit zum Opfer fielen und der das verwinkelte Innere durch einen einzigen Großraum ersetzte, nicht offener. Nach wie vor gibt sich der 1894 von Paul Wallot fertiggestellte Bau unverhohlen repräsentativ. Damit kommt er der Verfassungswirklichkeit freilich näher als sein Vorgänger: Heute wie damals ist Deutschland nach dem Grundgesetz eine repräsentative Demokratie und keine direkte.

„Dem deutschen Volke Staat zeigen": Dieser Maxime, mit der Axel Schultes 1992 seinen Spreebogenentwurf erläuterte, folgen alle Bundesbauten. Wie die zuvor beschriebene „Wiederinbetriebnahme" der Geschichte, die sich in dem Bekenntnis zu Berlin wie zu seinen Altbauten ausdrückt, stellt sie eine Besinnung auf Traditionen dar, die in den Zentralen der gestandener Demokratien seit jeher gepflegt, in Deutschland aber vom Nationalsozialismus unterbrochen wurden. Bis hierher ist also alles lediglich eine Heilung von Brüchen. Die neu-alte Kapitale

in 1992 did not have a life of its own. It was a pavilion and actually consisted of just a roof. In its striving for transparency, it had walls of glass. There was a smooth transition from the street to the plenary chamber. The multiple materials appeared chaotic, but they stood for social pluralism. The architecture, like its client, was not an end in itself but drew its identity from its citizens – thus following the ideal of direct democracy which was much propagated at the time when the building was designed.

If we take the promise of the citizen's action architecture in Bonn seriously, the Reichstag appears incongruous. It is true that it is more accessible than ever, like all national institutions. But the dome which is open to visitors, which became an omnipresent symbol of the new capital and the new Berlin immediately after it opened, allows the people to see what politicians are doing and provides a fine view of the skyline of Berlin. And the parliament is set on a massive pedestal. The richly adorned stone facade of the Reichstag did not become any more open even with the alterations by Norman Foster, who cleared away all post-war alterations and changed the maze of interior walls into a wide open space. The building completed by Paul Wallot in 1894 still has an unashamed air of grandeur. But this very fact makes it closer to constitutional reality than its predecessor: according to the constitution, Germany is still a democracy of representatives, not a direct democracy.

"Showing the state to the German people". This slogan which Axel Schultes used in 1992 to explain his design for the meander of the Spree underlies all national government buildings. Like the reinstatement of history outlined above, which finds expression in the affirmation of Berlin and its old buildings, it represents a return to traditions which have always been maintained in the centres of established democracies, but which were interrupted by National Socialism in Germany. Up to this point, therefore, all that has been done is to heal old discontinuities. The new and old capital city expresses a normalisation of the German state. The capital city project reflects the fact that Germany is fully sovereign again for the first time since 1945.

Berlin merely adds two new elements in its role as a capital city. The first is the systematic involvement of the public in the capital city project, although it is not certain that this will continue after it has been completed. But more significant is the consistent orientation of the Berlin Republic to the laws of the media age. Here, it is no longer important that the people and their represen-

drückt die Normalisierung deutscher Staatlichkeit aus. Das Hauptstadtprojekt trägt der Tatsache Rechnung, daß Deutschland als Land erstmals seit 1945 wieder vollständig souverän ist.

Ins Konzert der Kapitalen bringt Berlin lediglich zwei neue Spielarten ein: zum einen die konsequente Beteiligung der Öffentlichkeit am Hauptstadtprojekt, von der freilich keineswegs sicher ist, ob sie über seine Vollendung Bestand haben wird. Bedeutsamer ist die nachhaltige Ausrichtung der Berliner Republik auf die Gesetze des Medienzeitalters. In ihm ist es nicht mehr wichtig, daß das Volk und seine Vertreter wirklich zusammenkommen, wie es Günter Behnisch in Bonn versuchte. Gefragt ist vielmehr die Telegenität der Politik. Beim Berliner Kanzleramt wurde sie sogar zum entscheidenden Gestaltungskriterium: Mehrmals mußte Axel Schultes seinen Entwurf umarbeiten, bis die Forderung nach sekundenschneller Erkennbarkeit im Fernsehen erfüllt war.

Noch deutlicher wird der Wandel von der Bürgerinitiativ- zur Mediendemokratie beim neuen Bundespresseamt. Daß sein Besucherzentrum als erster Baustein der Berliner Republik lange vor dem Umzugstermin eingeweiht wurde, offenbart den Bedeutungszuwachs, den die Regierung der Öffentlichkeitsarbeit zugesteht, genauso wie die städtebauliche Komposition: Dem Architekturbüro KSP Engel und Zimmermann wurde das Privileg zuteil, sich nicht an Bauflucht und Traufe orientieren zu müssen, was die PR-Zentrale der Bundesregierung inmitten der Friedrichstadt zur absoluten Ausnahmeerscheinung macht. Die schwarz bedruckten Scheiben, die vor der kompletten Brandwand hinter dem Pressepavillon zum Einsatz kamen, wollen nicht Transparenz herstellen, sondern monumentaler Bühnenhintergrund sein. Überflüssig zu erwähnen, daß die Regierung in Bonn über einen Bau, der ihr einen vergleichbaren Auftritt verschafft hätte, gar nicht verfügte.

Tatsächlich treffen sich hier die Sichtweisen von Bund und Berlin. Die Politik bekam eine erstklassige Bühne der Selbstdarstellung, die Stadt – wie es der Politikwissenschaftler Max Welch Guerra formulierte – ein Festival von Dauerhaftigkeit. Daß es dieses Fest der Demokratie zu feiern gilt, versteht sich von selbst.

tatives really come together as Günter Behnisch aimed to achieve in Bonn. Instead, politics must now be suitable for television. In the Chancellery in Berlin this even became a decisive design criterion: Axel Schultes had to revise his design several times before the demand for instant recognition on television was met.

The transition from the democracy of action groups to a media democracy is even clearer in the new Federal Press Office. The fact that its visitor centre was completed as the first element of the Berlin Republic long before the date for relocation shows the greater importance placed by the government on public relations in addition to the urban composition: the architectural office of KSP Engel and Zimmermann was privileged with exemption from the need to keep to the normal ground alignment line and eaves height, which makes the government's PR centre in the middle of Friedrichstadt an absolute exception. The black printed panels used in front of the fire wall behind the press pavilion are not intended to create transparency; instead, they are a monumental stage background. It goes without saying that the government did not even have a building in Bonn which enabled it to present itself in a comparable way.

In fact, the views of Berlin and the national government meet here. Politics now has a top rate stage for self presentation, and the city – as the political scientist Max Welch Guerra phrased it – has a permanent festival. And this festival of democracy must, of course, be celebrated.

Ulf Meyer
Das Band des Bundes / The Ribbon of Government Buildings

Mit der Einrichtung von Bundestag und Kanzleramt im Spreebogen, der größten zusammenhängenden Neuplanung für die Hauptstadt Berlin, kehren Regierung und Parlament an einen der Urprungsorte der deutschen Demokratie zurück.

Der Spreebogen hat eine bewegte Geschichte. Nach Plänen von Peter Joseph Lenné wurde der ehemalige Exerzierplatz im 19. Jahrhundert zum „freien, öffentlichen Tummelplatz" im Parlamentsviertel umgebaut. In den zwanziger Jahren gab es Konzepte, gegenüber vom Reichstag die Reichskanzlei zu errichten. Der Berliner Architekt Hugo Häring entwarf zur selben Zeit ein „Forum der Republik" in Ost-West-Richtung. Nach 1933 sollte im Spreebogen Albert Speers „Große Halle des Volkes" gebaut werden. Als die Bauplanung kriegsbedingt gestoppt wurde, war schon ein Großteil des Alsenviertels abgerissen. 1958 war im Rahmen des „Hauptstadt Berlin"-Wettbewerbs der Spreebogen abermals Zentrum der Hauptstadtpläne. Der Mauerbau 1961 machte das Viertel zum Grenzgebiet. Dennoch wurde auch in den achtziger Jahren im Spreebogen fleißig geplant. Aber erst mit der Entscheidung für Berlin als Regierungssitz wurde das Gelände tatsächlich bebaut. Die Standortentscheidung des Bundestags 1991 war eine Entscheidung für die Stadt, aber gegen das historische Zentrum Berlins, den Schloßplatz, von dessen einstiger Bedeutung heute leider nichts mehr zu sehen ist. Der Umzug steht für einen Paradigmenwechsel in der Politarchitektur: weg vom Legeren, Provinziellen, Unaufgeregten, Banalen hin zur Stadt, zur Auseinandersetzung mit der Geschichte, auch zu neuer Größe und Symbolik ohne Angst vor architektonischer Präsenz. Die transparente Fassade, als Symbol demokratischen Bauens gebraucht, wurde aufgegeben.

The establishment of the German parliament and Federal Chancellery in the meander of the Spree is the largest single newly planned area for the new capital city, and it means that the government and parliament are returning to one of the original locations of German democracy.

The meander of the Spree has been through a dramatic history. In the 19th century, the parade ground was converted to a "free public space" in parliament district to plans by Peter Joseph Lenée. In the 1920s there were plans to build the Reich Chancellery opposite the Reichstag. At the same time, the Berlin architect Hugo Häring designed a "Forum of the Republic" in an east-to-west direction. After 1933, Albert Speer's "Great Hall of the People" was designated for the meander of the Spree. When planning was discontinued because of the war, much of the Alsen district had already been pulled down. In 1958 the meander of the Spree was again the centre of plans in the "capital city of Berlin" competition. But the building of the Wall in 1961 made the district a border zone. Plans were nevertheless made for the meander of the Spree in the 1980s. But it was only actually developed further after the decision in favour of Berlin as the seat of government. The German parliament's decision in 1990 was a vote for the city, but against the historical centre of Berlin, Schlossplatz, where nothing can now be seen of its former significance. The move is a paradigm shift in political architecture, a change from informality, provincialism, indifference and banality to the big city, to a confrontation with history and to a new greatness and symbolism without any fear of an architectural presence. The transparent facade which was once a symbol of democratic building has been relinquished.

Der Berliner Architekt Axel Schultes gewann 1992 verdient den städtebaulichen Wettbewerb. Mit über 800 eingereichten Arbeiten hatte die Konkurrenz alle vorherigen Wettbewerbe in den Schatten gestellt. Schultes gelang mit der „Spur des Bundes" ein Entwurf, der Politiker, Öffentlichkeit und Planer gleichermaßen überzeugte. Das Ost-West-Band ist in doppelter Hinsicht symbolisch: Es vereint nicht nur die getrennten Hälften Berlins, sondern stellt sich auch quer zu der von den Nationalsozialisten geplanten monumentalen Nord-Süd-Achse. Durch seine klare Struktur und seinen Farb- und Formenreichtum dazu angetan, war das Band eine populäre Ikone der nationalen Identifikation und Symbol der deutschen Einheit zu werden. Die bauliche, aber nicht historische Leere ließ Raum für eine neue städtebauliche Figur. Der Entwurf sah die zweifache Querung der Spree vor. Auch das Kanzleramt wurde in das Band des Bundes eingebettet. Im Westen thront es als Kubus über dem Viertel. Jenseits des geplanten Bürgerforums steht der lange Verwaltungsriegel des Bundestags, das Löbe- und das Lüders-Haus.

Bei der Ausschreibung handelte es sich nur um einen Ideenwettbewerb. Schultes' Vorschläge wurden als Richtlinie für die folgenden Bauwettbewerbe genutzt. Mit Stephan Braunfels fand sich ein Architekt, der den undankbareren Teil von Schultes' Plan – das Löbe und das Lüders-Haus – kongenial, wenn auch weniger brillant auszufüllen vermochte.

Probleme bei der Realisierung von Schultes' Konzept traten erst auf, als es darum ging, die aus der Vogelperspektive gedachte und nachvollziehbare Figur in der Stadt umzusetzen. Die Ost-West-Verbindung drohte in der Ausarbeitung verlorenzugehen. Auf der Ostseite, wo das Band ursprünglich erst am Bahnhof Friedrichstraße enden sollte, kollidierte der Plan mit dem Bestand. Die Pläne für Gebäude östlich der Luisenstraße wurden daher aufgegeben. Um so deutlicher wurde, daß die Bundesbauten fast alle im ehemaligen Westteil liegen. Hinzu kam, daß das zentrale Bürgerforum nicht weiter verfolgt wurde und Schultes' Entwurf damit im wahrsten Sinne des Wortes seines Zentrums beraubt wurde. Auch die Sicherheitsmaßnahmen konterkarierten die ursprüngliche Intention eines offenen, demokratischen Stadtteils. Die Inbesitznahme durch die neuen Nutzer und Bürger steht noch aus. Ob sich Regierung und Stadt gegenseitig bereichern oder stören, wird sich erst zeigen. Ohne Bürgerforum ist das Regierungsviertel jedoch nicht komplett.

The Berlin architect Axel Schultes deservedly won the urban design competition in 1992. With over 800 entries, the competition dwarfed all previous architectural competitions. Schultes' "ribbon of government buildings" was a design that convinced politicians, planners and public alike. The east-west "ribbon" is doubly symbolic: it not only unites the two former halves of Berlin, it is also at right angles to the monumental north-south axis planned by the National Socialists. In its variety of colours and shapes, the ribbon was also suitable as a popular icon of national identification and a symbol of German unity. The land was empty of buildings but full of historical significance, and it left scope for new urban design structures. The design involved crossing the Spree at two points. The Chancellery was integrated into the ribbon structure. It is a cube to the west which towers over the district. And the other side of the planned citizens' forum is the long administrative block for the parliament, consisting of the Löbe and Lüders buildings.

The competition was only a contest of concepts. Schultes' proposals were used as a guideline for the subsequent architectural competitions. In Stephan Braunfels, an architect was found who was able to fill in the least promising part of Schultes' plan – the Löbe and Lüders buildings – in a congenial but less brilliant way.

Problems in the implementation of Schultes' concept only arose when the structure conceived from a bird's eye view had to be transferred to the city itself. The east-west link was in danger of being lost in the detailed planning. On the eastern side, where the ribbon was originally meant to end at Friedrichstrasse station, the plan collided with the existing development. The plans for buildings east of Luisenstrasse were therefore given up. It now became all the clearer that almost all government buildings were in the former western part of Berlin. Furthermore, the central citizens' forum was not developed further and Schultes' design was therefore literally robbed of its central element. And the paranoid security measures also spoiled the original intention of an open and democratic district. The development remains to be occupied by its new users and citizens. We will see whether the government and the city enrich or obstruct each other. But without the citizens' forum, the government district is not complete.

Deutscher Bundestag, Reichstagsgebäude /
German Federal Parliament, Reichstag

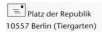 Platz der Republik
10557 Berlin (Tiergarten)

Paul Wallot, Paul Baum-
garten (Umbau/alterations);
Sir Norman Foster, London
(Umbau/alterations)

1884-1894, 1961-72,
1995-1999

Hauptportal/Main entrance

Als Ort der Volksvertretung war der Reichstag wichtigstes Projekt der Hauptstadtplanungen. Er bündelte alle Befürchtungen auf eine Restauration der Kapitale, die Berlin vor 1945 gewesen war, denn in den Wunden seines Mauerwerks war vieles präsent, was der Nation im Laufe ihrer Geschichte widerfahren war. Hier applaudierten die Parlamentarier des Kaiserreichs der Kriegserklärung Wilhelms II., hier wehte die Rote Fahne zum Zeichen des Triumphes über Hitler-Deutschland. Seither funktionslos, blieb der Reichstag ein Symbol der deutschen Teilung: Eher ohnmächtig trafen sich hier Bundesdelegationen, um den Anspruch auf deren Überwindung zu deklamieren. Entsprechend lieblos ging die Nachkriegszeit mit dem Gebäude um: Noch in den fünfziger Jahren ließen die Bonner Hausherren seine Kuppel sprengen. In den Sechzigern brach dann der Architekt Paul Baumgarten fast die Hälfte der Bausubstanz aus seinem Inneren.

Als sich der Ältestenrat des Bundestages am 30. Oktober 1991 darauf festlegte, den Reichstag wieder als Dienstsitz der Volksvertretung in Betrieb zu nehmen, drückte die Entscheidung ebensowenig einen breiten Konsens aus wie der kurz zuvor gefaßte Umzugsbeschluß. Günter Behnisch, der mit dem transparenten und unprätentiösen Bonner Plenarsaal der rheinischen Republik erst Anfang der neunziger Jahre ihre Heimstatt gegeben hatte, befand den Reichstag als „unangenehm, überheblich" und allenfalls für „schlechte Träume" geeignet. Selbst Norman Foster, der 1993 den Umbauwettbewerb gewann, wollte mit seinem damaligen Entwurf das Bauwerk vom Sockel holen, eingraben und mit einem gewaltigen Glasdach unter Quarantäne stellen.

Um sich mit dem Gebäude anzufreunden, brauchte die Fachöffentlichkeit drei Kolloquien, auf denen Bauge-

As the setting for the representatives of the people, the Reichstag was the most important project in the plans for the capital city. There were fears that Berlin may resume the role it had before 1945 because the scars in the building showed much of what the nation had experience in the course of its history. It was here that the parliamentarians of the Empire applauded the declaration of war by Wilhelm II., it was here that the red flag was hoisted to celebrate victory over Hitler's Germany. For many years it then had no function and was a symbol of the division of Germany. Federal German delegations met here and rather helplessly demanded an end to the division. The post-war period was correspondingly insensitive in its treatment of the Reichstag. In the 1950s the Bonn government had the old dome detonated, and in the 1960s the architect Paul Baumgarten ripped out almost half of the interior of the building.

When the Council of Elders of the German parliament decided on 30th October 1991 to reactivate the Reichstag as the parliamentary building, this decision was no more a broad consensus than the relocation vote shortly beforehand. Günter Behnisch, who created the transparent and unpretentious plenary chamber in Bonn as a home for the Rhine Republic, which was only completed in the early 1990s, considered the Reichstag to be "unpleasantly arrogant" and only suitable for "bad dreams". And Sir Norman Foster, in his winning alteration design of 1993, wanted to bring the building off its pedestal, dig it into the ground and place it in quarantine with an enormous glass roof.

To become reconciled with the building, the specialist public needed three colloquiums at which architectural historians and political scientists showed that German

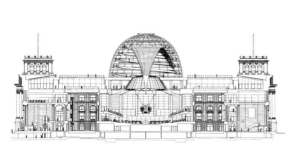 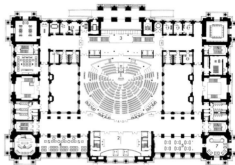

schichtler und Politikwissenschaftler klarstellten, daß sich der deutsche Parlamentarismus erst im Reichstag gegenüber der Krone emanzipiert hatte, daß sein Zierrat und seine Ingenieurkuppel damals durchaus fortschrittlich waren. Dem Rest der Gesellschaft genügte Christos Verpackungsaktion vom Sommer 1995, die fünf Millionen Menschen als ein Volksfest erlebten, das alle Skeptiker verstummen ließ.

Fortan verzichtete Norman Foster auf baukünstlerische Kraftakte. Er säuberte das Urgestein des Reichstags – wobei als Zeitzeugen nur die Einschußlöcher der Fassade und die sogenannten Russen-Graffiti, mit denen sich die Soldaten der Roten Armee 1945 in das Gebäude eingeschrieben hatten, erhalten blieben – und ergänzte es mit zeitgemäßen Materialien: Stahl und Glas sind einerseits so schlicht detailliert, wie man von dem Architekten gewohnt ist, dessen Leidenschaft Flughafenentwürfe darstellen, vor allem aber großzügig. Mit der gleichen Intention lichtete Foster das Innenleben des Reichstags: Der Haupteingang wurde auf die Schauseite gen Westen verlegt, das Geschoß über dem Sockel so entrümpelt, daß der einst nur 640 Quadratmeter große Plenarsaal nun 1.600 mißt und damit zum größten aller westlichen Demokratien aufstieg. Er erinnert nur noch durch den kaum modifizierten Bundesadler an das aus Bonn vertraute Erscheinungsbild. Leicht verändert wurde die dortige Sitzordnung: der Kreis ist nun so zu einer Ellipse gestaucht, daß sich Regierung und Parlament um sechs Meter näherkommen. Eine Zwischendecke wurde für Besucher eingezogen, die von ihren tief hängenden Tribünen nun sogar die Akten der Abgeordneten studieren können, zumindest die der Hinterbänkler. Für den Ältestenrat und das Präsidium ist die Etage darüber re-

parliamentary democracy had in fact emancipated itself from the crown in the Reichstag, that its ornamentation and engineered dome were progressive at the time. For the rest of society, Christo's "Wrapped Reichstag" in the summer of 1995 was sufficient; five million people experienced it as a festival of the people which silenced the sceptics.

Norman Foster then omitted excessive architectural efforts. He cleaned the original stone of the Reichstag, leaving as witnesses to history only the shell holes on the facade and the so-called Russian graffiti which soldiers of the Red Army had inscribed in the building in 1945. He added modern materials: steel and glass, which are simple in their detail like other works by this architect with a passion for airport design, but at the same time generous in their proportions. With the same intention, Foster brightened the interior of the Reichstag. The main entrance was moved to the western show facade, the storey above the pedestal was cleared to such an extent that the plenary chamber, which once measured only 640 square metres, was now 1,600 square metres and thus the largest in any western democracy. The only element which recalls the familiar appearance in Bonn is the Federal eagle, which has hardly been modified. The seating arrangement has been slightly changed, so that the circle has now become an ellipse and the government and parliament are six metres closer to each other. An intermediate floor has been inserted as a suspended gallery for visitors who can now even study the documents on the desks of the members of parliament, at least on the back benches. The next higher storey is reserved for the Council of Elders and the Presiding Committee, and the storey under the roof contains the press

serviert, um die Presselobby unterm Dach gruppieren sich die Fraktionssäle, die, sofern sie in den Ecktürmen liegen, beeindruckende Raumhöhe aufweisen.

Kann man den Prozeß bis hierher als bloße Aufräumen und Renovieren beschreiben, manifestiert sich die Gegenwart in zwei Bereichen als eigenständig. Was man dem Bauwerk nicht ohne weiteres ansieht: Es ist mit allem ausgestattet, was die zeitgenössische Ingenieurtechnologie an Insignien ökologischer Korrektheit zu bieten hat – rapsölbetriebenem Blockheizkraftwerk, Erdwärmespeicher und Solarzellen. Im Dienste der Nachhaltigkeit steht auch das einzig sichtbare neue Element: die Kuppel. Erst nach langem Streit zwischen den meist sozialdemokratischen Flachdachverfechtern und den häufig konservativen Anhängern einer Rekonstruktion der Orginal-Version, in dem der Architekt fast zwei Dutzend Planungsvarianten vorlegte, beschloß man den Wiederaufbau einer Kuppel in freilich moderner Form.

Seit dieser Entscheidung überzieht der spanisch-schweizer Architekt Santiago Calatrava, der mit genau diesem Vorschlag im Wettbewerb zwar prämiert worden, dann aber bei der Auftragsvergabe unterlegen war, Foster mit Plagiatsvorwürfen. Doch dessen eiförmiges Gebilde, das 23 Meter mißt und damit kaum halb so hoch ist wie sein historischer Vorläufer, unterscheidet sich nicht nur formal von beiden. Wichtiger ist: Seine Kuppel fungiert nicht nur als ausgebeulter Dachabschluß. Sie entlüftet einerseits den Reichstag, was den Verzicht auf eine Klimaanlage ermöglicht, und erhellt zudem den Plenarsaal, in den sie mit Hilfe eines Spiegeltrichters genau jenes Streulicht lenkt, das die Fernsehanstalten für ihre Übertragungen brauchen. Der größte Unterschied aber ist: Die neue Kuppel ist begehbar. Den Abgeordneten auf die Finger zu sehen, scheitert zwar an den vielen für technischen Funktionen nötigen Installationen, doch wer eine der beiden gegenläufigen, und je 240 Meter langen Spiralrampen hinaufschreitet, wird mit einem Blick auf die Stadt entschädigt. Er verdeutlicht, wofür auch das Projekt insgesamt steht: Daß der Reichstag nun nicht mehr das solitäre Mahnmal ist, als das man ihn zu Mauerzeiten kannte, sondern integraler Bestandteil der deutschen Gesellschaft und ihrer Hauptstadt. Im Ergebnis ist eine Repräsentanz entstanden, die im besten Sinne repräsentativ ist. Weder dominiert die Geschichte die Gegenwart, noch umgekehrt. Als das Haus am 14. April 1999 eingeweiht wurde, war der Auftraggeber denn auch voll des Lobes. Daß die Volksvertretung bereits in der Woche danach 180.000 Besucher anzog, wurde Gütesiegel für das gesamte Hauptstadtprojekt.   (hwh)

lobby and the meeting rooms of the parliamentary parties with impressively high ceilings in the corner towers. The process up to this point can be described as mere tidying and renovating, but the present has left its mark in two areas. It is not immediately apparent that the building is fitted with everything that contemporary engineering technology can offer in terms of ecological correctness – a block-type thermal power station operated with rapeseed oil, underground heat storage and solar panels. The only obviously visible new element also serves to enhance ecological sustainability: the dome. It was only after long arguments between the mainly Social Democrat proponents of a flat roof and the mainly conservative adherents of a reconstruction in the original form, in which the architect submitted almost two dozen planning variants, that the construction of a dome in a modern form was decided on.

Since this decision was made, the Spanish-Swiss architect Santiago Calatrava, who was awarded a prize with this proposal in the competition but not given the commission, has constantly accused Foster of plagiarism. But Foster's egg-shaped structure which measures 23 metres, and is thus hardly half the height of its historic predecessor, differs from the original and Calatrava's design in more than just form. More important is the fact that Foster's dome is not just a rounded form to complete the roof. It serves as an air extraction system for the Reichstag, thus eliminating the need for air conditioning, and it also brightens the plenary chamber by creating a funnel of mirrors to direct into the plenary chamber exactly the type of scattered light that the television companies need for their broadcasts. But the greatest difference is the fact that it is possible to walk in the new dome. Although visitors are not able to observe the members of parliament directly because the view is obstructed by the technical installations, the two spiral ramps with a length of 240 metres each provide an admirable view of the city. This underlines what the project as a whole stands for. The Reichstag is no longer the solitary commemorative memorial that it was in the period of the divided Germany, it is now an integral part of German society and the capital city. The result is a representation building which is really representative in character. History does not dominate the present, nor is the reverse true. When the building was officially opened on 14th April 1999, the client was full of praise. And the fact that 180,000 people visited the building during the following week was in itself a sign of the democratic quality of the new capital city.   (hwh)

Paul-Löbe-Haus / Paul Löbe Building

Paul-Löbe-Straße
10557 Berlin (Tiergarten)

Stephan Braunfels,
München/Berlin

1996-2000

Ansicht Höfe/
View of courtyards

Die Abgeordnetenbüros und die Verwaltung des Bundestags werden in einem langgestreckten Neubau auf beiden Ufern der Spree nördlich des Reichstags untergebracht. Eine schmale Fußgängerbrücke verbindet beide Flußseiten. Der Komplex vereint symbolisch die ehemals geteilte Stadt und ist an dem städtebaulichen Konzept des „Band des Bundes" orientiert. Den Wettbewerb gewann 1994 der Münchner Architekt Stephan Braunfels. Der Büroriegel ist 22 Meter hoch und nimmt über 500 Abgeordnetenbüros, mehr als ein Dutzend Sitzungssäle und weitere 400 Büros der Ausschußsekretariate auf. Hinzu kommen Räume des Besucherdienstes, für Öffentlichkeitsarbeit und Seminare, ein Restaurant mit Spreeblick und der große Sitzungssaal des Europaausschusses. Mit dem Reichstag ist das Gebäude durch einen Fußgängertunnel verbunden.

Paul-Löbe-Haus: Der 200 Meter lange und 100 Meter breite Block im östlichen Spreebogen hat die Form eines Doppelkamms mit acht dreiseitig umschlossenen Außenhöfen. Sie liegen ein Geschoß tiefer als die Straße, so daß von den acht Vollgeschossen nur sieben in Erscheinung treten. Die Höfe werden von geometrisch beschnittenen Eibenhecken und weißem Kies geprägt. Die über tausend Büros sind zweibündig organisiert.

Der Haupteingang liegt im Westen unter einem großen Vordach. Eine Treppe führt in die abgesenkte Halle, die in die Außenhöfe übergeht. Der große, glasbedeckte Raum mit offenen Galerien, gläsernen Aufzügen und transparenten Treppen liegt in der Mitte des Riegels. Er gibt den Blick bis zur Bibliothek frei und erleichtert die Orientierung. Die verglasten, zweigeschossigen Ausschußsitzungssäle mit Besuchergalerie liegen rechts und links der Achse in Rotunden. Sie enthalten je zwei große

The offices of members of parliament and the parliamentary administration are accommodated in an elongated new building on both banks of the Spree to the north of the Reichstag. A narrow pedestrian bridge links the two sides of the river. The complex symbolically unites the formerly divided city and is part of the urban planning concept of the "ribbon of government buildings". The 1994 competition was won by the Munich architect Stephan Braunfels. The long office block is 22 metres high and contains over 500 members' offices, over a dozen conference rooms and a further 400 committee secretarial offices. There are also rooms for the visitor service, seminar rooms, public relations, a restaurant overlooking the Spree and the large meeting room of the Europe committee. The building is linked to the Reichstag by a pedestrian tunnel.

Paul Löbe Building: The block in the eastern meander of the Spree is 200 metres long and 100 metres wide and has the form of a double comb with eight outer courtyards enclosed on three sides. They are one storey lower than the street so that only seven of the eight full storeys are visible. The courtyards have geometrically cut yew hedges and white gravel. The offices are arranged on both sides of the corridors.

The main entrance is in the west under a large porch. A flight of stairs provides access to the lower hall leading to the outer courtyards. A large, glass-roofed hall with open galleries, glass-enclosed lifts and transparent staircases is in the middle of the block. It gives a view as far as the library and makes it easier to find one's way in the complex. The glazed, two-storey committee rooms with visitors' galleries are situated to the right and left of the axis in rotunds. Each rotund contains two large rooms

Marie-Elisabeth-Lüders-Haus /
Marie Elisabeth Lüders Building

 Spreebogen, Schiff-
bauerdamm
10117 Berlin (Mitte)

Stephan Braunfels,
München/Berlin

1996-2000

Der sogenannte „Spreesprung"
von Süden, (rechts: Lüders,
links: Löbe-Haus)/The so-called
"Leap across the Spree" from
the south (right: Lüders, left
Löbe building)

und einen kleineren Saal. Um Belichtung sowie Aus- und Einblicke zu schaffen, hat das Haus große Außenflächen. Zwei doppelstöckige Restaurants und der dreistöckige Europasaal formen einen siebenstöckigen Rundbau am Fluß. Offenheit und Transparenz sind dem Architekten ein Symbol der Demokratie. Das Haus ist nach dem letzten demokratischen Reichstagspräsidenten Paul Löbe benannt.

Marie-Elisabeth-Lüders-Haus: Weil die benötigten Räume im Löbe-Haus allein kaum unterzubringen waren, wurde der „Spreesprung" ersonnen. In dem nach der Reichstagsabgeordneten Marie-Elisabeth Lüders benannten Haus auf der östlichen Seite der Spree liegt die Bundestagsbibliothek. Flugdächer stellen eine symbolische Verbindung zum anderen Ufer dar. Durch einen Fußgängersteg über den Fluß sind die Blöcke miteinander verbunden. Die offene untere Ebene ist für die Öffentlichkeit und die überdachte obere nur für Abgeordnete. Neben der Bibliothek dient das Haus dem Wissenschaftlichen Dienst, der Pressedokumentation und dem Archiv des Bundestages. Es ist die drittgrößte Parlamentsbibliothek der Welt. Der dreistöckige, runde Bibliotheksturm mit Foyer, Katalograum und Lesesaal liegt in der Mitte. Vor dem Haus liegt der Spreeplatz mit Freitreppe und Skulpturenterrasse am Ufer sowie Fragmenten der Berliner Mauer als Denkmal. Der quadratische Stadtraum wird dreiseitig gefaßt von der Ostfassade, der Bibliothek und der Spreebrücke.

Die Fassaden beider Häuser werden von großen, hellen Sichtbetonflächen mit großen Fenstern geprägt. Im Kontrast dazu stehen die gläsernen Höfe, die Stirnseiten und das gerasterte Glasdach. Die Bürofassaden sind sachlich und klar gehalten.

and one smaller room. To provide light and a view into and out of the rooms, the building has large external areas. Two two-storey restaurants and the three-storey Europe room form a seven-storey round building. The architect regards openness and transparency as a symbol of democracy. The building is named after the last democratic Reichstag speaker, Paul Löbe.

Marie Elisabeth Lüders Building: Because it was hardly possible to fit the necessary rooms into the Löbe building alone, the "leap over the Spree" was conceived. The building on the east of the Spree is named after the Reichstag member Marie Elisabeth Lüders and contains the parliamentary library. Overhanging roofs create a symbolic link to the other bank. The blocks are connected via a footbridge across the river. The open lower level is accessible to the public, and the covered lower level is only for members of parliament. Apart from the library, the building is also used for the scientific service, for press documentation and the parliamentary archive. It is the third largest parliamentary library in the world. The three-storey round library tower with the foyer, catalogue room and reading room is in the middle. In front of the building is the Spreeplatz with outdoor stairs and a sculpture terrace on the river bank and with fragments of the Berlin Wall as a monument. The square urban space is enclosed on three sides by the eastern facade, the library and the Spree bridge.

The facades of both buildings are characterised by large, light-coloured exposed concrete surfaces with large windows. They contrast with the glass courtyards, the end facades and the grid-type glass roof. The office facades are rational and clear in style.

Jakob-Kaiser-Haus / Jakob Kaiser Building

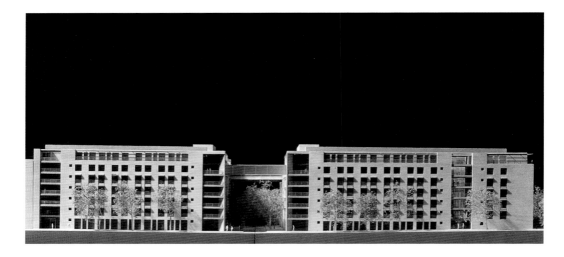

Das Jakob-Kaiser-Haus im Nordosten der Dorotheen-stadt setzt deren Parzellenstruktur fort und nimmt zwei Drittel der Abgeordnetenbüros des Bundestages auf. Die Blocks haben sechs offene Innenhöfe zur Belichtung, die eine zweibündige Büroanordnung ermöglichen. Zur Spree liegen kleinere Blocks, deren dreiseitig umschlos-senen Höfe sich zum Spreeufer öffnen. Ihre aufgestän-derten Kopfbauten orientieren sich im Maßstab am früheren Reichstagspräsidentenpalais.

Die fünf beteiligten Architekturbüros haben sich in der „Planungsgesellschaft Dorotheenblöcke" verbunden und eine gemeinsame Konzeption mit individuellen Einzelgebäuden entwickelt. In den insgesamt 1800 Räu-men der Häuser sind Büros für 395 Abgeordnete, Frak-tionen und Mitarbeiter des Bundestages sowie Sitzungs-säle für die Ausschüsse, Pressezentrum, Bundestagsver-waltung und Parlamentsdienst untergebracht. Geglie-dert wird die Anlage durch ein orthogonales Erschlie-ßungsraster. Durch den nördlichen Block führt in der Achse des Reichstags eine haushohe, gläserne Passage. Der Wechsel von Glas und Stein soll den blockhaften Charakter mildern. Ein sechs Meter tiefer Tunnel mit 50 Meter langen Laufbändern und Oberlichtern führt zum Reichstag und Paul-Löbe-Haus. Zwei Skywalks verbin-den die Häuser über die Straße und verstellen den Blick auf den Reichstag. Trotz des Versuchs, die Bürohäuser als normale Stadtbausteine zu behandeln, geriet das Kaiser-Haus als „introvertierte Beamtenstadt" in die Kritik. Übertriebene Sicherheitsvorgaben und Angst vor langen Wegen machen das über die Straße hinweg vernetzte Quartier abgeschlossener als nötig.

Haus 1 und 2 / Schweger + Partner: Das Haus 1, gegen-über vom Reichstag, hat einen zweigeschossigen Sockel

The Jakob Kaiser building at the north-east of Doro-theenstadt continues the small plot structure of the dis-trict and contains two thirds of the offices of the mem-bers of parliament. The blocks have six open inner court-yards to provide light, enabling the offices to be placed on both sides of the corridors. Courtyards enclosed by smaller blocks open out to the bank of the Spree. The end buildings are supported on pillars and as high as the former Reichstag president's palace.

The five architectural offices combined to form the "Dorotheenblock planning cooperative" and developed a joint concept with individual buildings. The total of 1800 rooms in the buildings contain offices for 395 members of parliament, parliamentary groups and em-ployees of the parliament, meeting rooms for commit-tees, a press centre. the parliamentary administration and parliamentary service. The complex is sub-divided by an orthogonal access grid. Through the northern block there is a glass-covered passage as high as the building which is aligned with the Reichstag. The alter-nation of glass and stone aims to alleviate the block char-acter. A tunnel at a depth of six metres with skylights and 50 metre long moving walkways leads to the Reichstag and the Paul Löbe building. Two skywalks link the build-ing above street level and obstruct the view of the Reichs-tag. In spite of the efforts taken to treat the office com-plex as normal city buildings, the Kaiser building came in for criticism as an "introverted civil service city". Exces-sive security requirements and the fear of walking great distances made the complex, which is linked across the road, more hermetically sealed than was necessary.

Buildings 1 and 2 / Schweger + Partner: Building 1 op-posite the Reichstag has a two-storey pedestal with

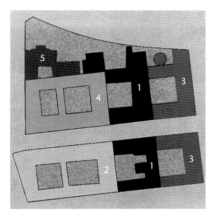

Dorotheenstraße
10117 Berlin (Mitte)

Paul Wallot u.a. (Altbau/
old building); Busmann und Haberer, Köln; De Architekten Cie,
Amsterdam; v. Gerkan, Marg &
Partner, Hamburg; Schweger
und Partner, Hamburg; Thomas
van den Valentyn, Köln
1857, 1904, 1914,
1997-2000

1 Busmann & Haberer, Köln

2 De Architekten Cie, Amsterdam

3 von Gerkan, Marg und Partner, Hamburg

4 Architekten Schweger + Partner, Hamburg

5 Thomas van den Valentyn, Köln

S.26: Blick von der Wilhelm-
straße/View from Wilhelmstrasse
S.27: Lageplan/Site plan

mit kleineren Fenstern. Als Ausdruck der „steinernen Berliner Architektur" ist die ruhige, glatte Fassade mit grau-grünem Werkstein verkleidet, in die hohe Kastenfenster eingeschnitten sind. Die Hoffassaden mit Holzfenstern und -paneelen als Wandbekleidung beleben die Fassade. Der Hof ist mit Naturstein ausgekleidet, den ein Wasserfilm überzieht. Im Untergeschoß liegt ein quadratischer Lichthof mit Birkenhain. Glas, Sichtbeton und Stahl prägen das Innere.

Kopfbau Haus 2, Haus 3 und 7/Busmann + Haberer: In den transparenten Kopfbauten an der Spree sind die Büros der Fraktionsvorstände untergebracht, in den Häusern 3 und 7 liegen die Abgeordnetenbüros, ein Restaurant und ein Lesesaal. Dem ehemaligen Reichstagspräsidentenpalais in der Dorotheenstraße 105 wird ein Kopfhaus zur Seite gestellt. Im Haus 2 liegt der Saal für Untersuchungsausschüsse, im Haus 3 jener für Enquetekommissionen, der aus der Fassade hervorspringt. Die Innenwände sind holzverkleidet, das zusammen mit Sichtbeton und Metalldecken das Innere prägt. Zwischen den Kopfbauten liegt eine transparente Halle. Die Sicherheit an der Spreepromenade wird durch eine Glaswand gewährleistet. Unter den aufgeständerten Gebäuderiegeln liegen Flachbauten. Die Fassaden haben französische Fenster aus Holz, das Stahldach trägt Photovoltaikmodule.

Haus 4 und 8 / von Gerkan, Marg + Partner: Das Gebäude bildet als östlicher Abschluß ein Tor zur Dorotheenstadt. An der Spree schließt es die Reihe der Kopfbauten. Die Häuser 4 und 8 haben an der Wilhelmstraße ihren Eingang. Die Erschließung erfolgt über eine große Treppe in einem sechsgeschossigen Foyer, die zu einer der Brücken führt. Die bepflanzten Höfe enthalten Wasserflächen. Im Inneren dominieren Holz, Stuccoflächen

small windows. As an expression of "Berlin stone architecture" the calm, smooth facade is faced with greyish green ashlar stone with tall recessed box-type windows. The courtyard facades with their wooden windows and panels as wall cladding make the facade more lively. The courtyard is faced with natural stone covered with a film of water. In the basement is a square light courtyard with a grove of birch trees. The interior is dominated by glass, fair-faced concrete and steel.

End block of Buildings 2, 3 and 7/Busmann + Haberer
The end blocks facing the Spree contain the offices of the leaders of the parliamentary parties; buildings 3 and 7 contain the offices of the members, a restaurant and a reading room. The former Reichstag president's palace at Dorotheenstrasse 105 is provided with an end building. Building 2 contains the meeting room for committees of investigation, and the room for the commission of enquiry projects out of the facade of building 3. The interior walls are faced with wood; the predominant materials in the interior are wood and fair-faced concrete with metal ceilings. Between the end buildings is a transparent hall. There is a glass wall along Spreepromenade for security purposes. Below the structures on pillars there are low buildings. The smooth facades have wooden French windows, and photovoltaic panels are mounted on the steel roof.

Building 4 and 8 / von Gerkan, Marg + Partner
The building stands at the eastern end forming a gateway into Dorotheenstadt. On the Spree it is the last of the end buildings. The entrance to building 4 and 8 is on Wilhelmstrasse, where a large flight of stairs provides access to a six-storey foyer leading to a bridge. The courtyards contain vegetation and areas of water. The interior

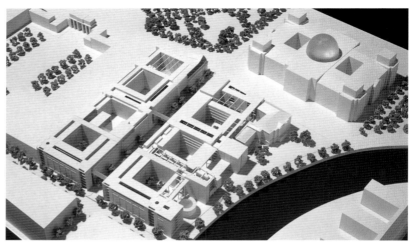

Gesamtansicht von Nordosten/
General view from the north-east

und Naturstein. Die Natursteinfassade hat französische Fenster.

Haus 5 und 6 und Kammer der Technik / De Architekten Cie: Der Hof von Haus 5 im Südwesten ist überdacht und mit Holz verkleidet. Eine Treppe führt von der Unterführung in das Obergeschoß. Mittendrin liegt ein nierenförmiger Sitzungssaal. Der Hof von Haus 6 ist offen. Beide Höfe trennt nur eine Glasfassade. Das städtebauliche Raster wurde zugunsten von „Transparenz und Verspieltheit" aufgelöst. Ab dem Obergeschoß hat das Haus eine Sandsteinfassade und raumhohe Fenster. Das Unter- und Erdgeschoß und die Kerne sind mit dunklem Naturstein abgesetzt. An der Dorotheenstraße wurde eine Glasfassade vorgehängt. Straßenseitig ist der Neubau durch eine Zäsur von der Kammer der Technik (1914) getrennt, auf die ein neues Geschoß aus Stahl, Aluminium und Glas gelegt wurde.

Reichstagspräsidentenpalais / van den Valentyn: Das Palais wurde 1904 nach Plänen von Paul Wallot im Stil der Neorenaissance erbaut. Die im Erdgeschoß liegenden Club- und Speiseräume werden durch die große Marmortreppenhalle mit der Beletage verbunden; im zweiten Stock lagen die Wohnräume. Eine Freitreppe führt vom Festsaal in den Garten. Die prachtvolle Hauptfassade liegt an die Spreeseite, der schmucklose Haupteingang an der Ebertstraße. Nach 1933 wurde der Bau als Außenstelle der Reichstagsbibliothek zweckentfremdet.

Der ehemalige Kaisersaal wird heute von der Parlamentarischen Gesellschaft als Club genutzt, denn dem Bundestagspräsidenten genügen seine repräsentativen Räume im Reichstag. Das Dach wird in seiner alten Höhe wiederaufgebaut, das Gebäude restauriert und um notwendige Einbauten ergänzt.

is dominated by wood, plaster surfaces and natural stone. The natural stone facade has French windows.

Building 5 and 6 and Chamber of Technology / De Architekten Cie: The covered courtyard of building 5 in the south-west is clad with wood. Stairs lead from the passageway to the upper storey. In the middle is a kidney-shaped room for meetings. The courtyard of building 6 is open, and the two courtyards are separated only by a glass facade. The urban development grid is broken up to create "transparency and buoyancy". From the upper storey upwards the building has a sandstone facade and windows from floor to ceiling. The basement, ground floor and access cores are faced with dark natural stone. There is a suspended glass facade on Dorotheenstrasse. On the street side, the building is visually separated from the Chamber of Technology (1914) which has a new top storey of steel, aluminium and glass.

Reichstag president's palace / van den Valentyn: The palace was built in the neo-Renaissance style in 1904 to plans by Paul Wallot. The ground floor club and dining rooms are linked with the upper ground floor by a large marble stair hall; the residential rooms were on the second floor. Outdoor steps lead into the garden from the festival hall. The splendid main facade faces the Spree, and the main entrance on Ebertstrasse is austere. After 1933, the building was used as the auxiliary premises of the Reichstag library.

The former Emperor's hall is now used as a club by the parliamentary society because the speaker of the parliament has sufficient rooms for representation in the Reichstag. The roof is being restored at its old height, the building restored and necessary new fittings added.

Deutscher Bundesrat / Federal Council

 Leipziger Straße 3-4,
Niederkirchnerstraße 5,
10117 Berlin (Mitte)

✎ Friedrich Schulze-Colditz
(Altbau/old building); Schweger
und Partner, Hamburg/Berlin
(Umbau/alterations)

🛠 1904, 1997-2000

Zustand dreißiger Jahre/The
building in the 1930s

Erst spät entschied sich der Bundesrat, nach Berlin umzuziehen. Für einen geplanten Neubau gegenüber vom Reichstag fehlten jedoch die Mittel, so daß 1996 das ehemalige Preußische Herrenhaus (Architekt: Friedrich Schulze-Colditz) gewählt wurde. Dieses Haus wurde 1904 als Sitz des Oberhauses des Preußischen Parlaments bezogen. Die Architektur zeigt das Rollenverständnis: Während das Herrenhaus wie ein dreiflügliges Adelspalais betont monumental wirkt, zitiert das benachbarte „bürgerliche" Preußische Abgeordnetenhaus die italienische Renaissance. In der Weimarer Republik tagte im Herrenhaus der Staatsrat. Nach Auflösung des Parlaments durch die Nazis 1934 wurde das Gebäude dem benachbarten Reichsluftfahrtministerium zugeordnet. Nach schweren Kriegszerstörungen fand nach Wiederaufbau die Akademie der Wissenschaften der DDR hier ihren Sitz. Der abgeteilte Ostflügel wurde vom benachbarten „Haus der Ministerien" genutzt. Nach ersten Plänen von 1992 sollten hier die Außenstellen mehrerer Bundesministerien untergebracht werden.

Das denkmalgeschützte Haus wurde nach Plänen des Hamburger Architekten Peter Schweger aufwendig saniert. Auf Grund von Kriegsschäden und späterer Einbauten konnte es nicht voll rekonstruiert werden. Durch das Herausreißen zwischenzeitlich eingefügter Decken erhielt das Haus seine alten Raumhöhen von bis zu 4,90 Metern wieder. Zwei neue Lichthöfe bilden eine „Wandelzone". Einzelne Bereiche, wie die Eingangshalle mit der steinernen Treppe, wurden restauriert. Historische Konturen sollten wieder erkennbar gemacht und Veränderungen nur „als Zeitdokumente erhalten werden, wenn sie mit der jetzigen Nutzung in Einklang gebracht werden können". Ziel der Architekten war die „Wieder-

The Federal Council decided late to move to Berlin. But there were no funds for a planned new building opposite the Reichstag, so finally in 1996 the former Prussian Lords House (architect: Friedrich Schulze-Colditz) was chosen. This building was first used in 1904 as the seat of the Upper Chamber of the Prussian parliament. The architecture shows the hierarchical thinking of the time. Whereas the Lords' House appears monumental like a three-wing palace of the nobility, the adjacent "bourgeois" Prussian House of Representatives reflects the Italian Renaissance. During the Weimar Republic, the State Council met in the Lords' House. After parliament was dissolved by the Nazis in 1934, the building was allocated to the neighbouring Reich Air Force Ministry. After heavy damage during the war, the building was reconstructed and used by the Academy of Science of the GDR. The east wing was separated from the rest of the building and used by the adjacent "House of Ministries". The first plans in 1992 envisaged using this building as auxiliary offices for several Federal Ministries. The listed building was extensively renovated to plans by the Hamburg architect Peter Schweger. Due to war damage and later alterations, full reconstruction was not possible. Intermediate floors that had been inserted were removed again, restoring the old room heights of up to 4.90 metres. Two new light courtyards create space to "stroll". Some areas such as the entrance hall with the stone staircase have been restored. Historical contours are to be made visible again, and alterations only "preserved as documents of their time if they can be brought into harmony with the present use". The aim of the architects was the "restoration of the characteristic sequence of rooms and the clear routing of pedestrians

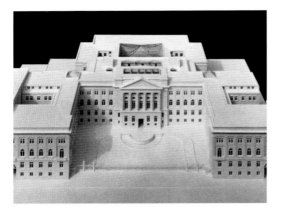

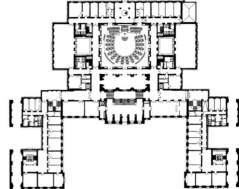

herstellung der charakteristischen Raumfolgen und die klare, vom Tageslicht bestimmte Wegeführung". Im 18 Meter hohen, holzverkleideten Plenarsaal finden 180 Personen Platz sowie weitere 120 auf den Besuchertribünen. Das Oberlicht wurde rekonstruiert, doch statt der alten Eisenkonstruktion der Kuppel erhielt der Saal ein pyramidenförmiges Glasdach. Die Sitzreihen fallen zur Saalmitte hin in zwei Stufen ab. In der Mitte sitzt der Bundesratspräsident, rechts davon Vertreter der Bundesregierung und links Mitarbeiter der Ausschußbüros. Die Ministerpräsidenten sitzen im Halbkreis davor, in alphabetischer Reihenfolge ihrer Länder.

Die Wege sind für Besucher und Abgeordnete streng getrennt: Gäste gelangen über die Eingangshalle ins zweite Obergeschoß, wo eine Galerie zu den dreiseitigen Besuchertribünen führt, während die Mitglieder des Bundesrates den Plenarsaal im ersten Obergeschoß über umlaufende Gänge betreten. In den Seitenflügeln liegen die Länderzimmer für die Ministerpräsidenten, im Westflügel der Länderbereich, im Osten der Empfangssaal des Bundesratspräsidenten. Zusätzlich wurden sechzehn moderne Konferenzräume geplant. Die Ausschußsekretariate werden in den Obergeschossen und im angrenzenden Rohwedder-Haus untergebracht. Dort sind auch Bibliothek, Rechenzentrum und Hausverwaltung angeordnet. Für die 160 Mitarbeiter wurden Büros, Tagungs- und Repräsentationsräume geschaffen, die doppelt so groß sind wie in Bonn. Der Ehrenhof mit Springbrunnen wird mit Buchsbaumhecken in quadratischen Mustern modern gestaltet.

guided by daylight". The plenary chamber, which is 18 metres high and lined with wood, accommodates 180 persons, with a further 120 on the visitor's galleries. The skylight has been reconstructed, but instead of the old iron structure of the dome, the chamber now has a pyramid-shaped glass roof. The rows of seats slope down in two steps to the centre of the room. In the middle is the seat for the President of the Federal Council, to the right are the representatives of the Federal Government and to the left the staff of the committee offices. The Minister Presidents of the federal states sit in a semi-circle in front of them in the alphabetical order of the federal states.

The access routing for visitors and representatives is strictly separate. Visitors are led from the entrance hall to the second storey where a gallery leads them to the three-sided visitors' galleries, whereas the members of the Federal Council enter the plenary chamber on the first floor from corridors around the chamber. The side wings contain the federal state rooms for the Minister Presidents, the west wing contains the section for the federal states, and the east wing contains the reception hall of the President of the Federal Council. In addition, sixteen modern conference rooms have been planned. The committee secretaries will be accommodated in the upper storeys and the adjacent Rohwedder building, which also contains the library, the computer centre and the administration for the building. The offices, conference and representation rooms for the staff of 160 are twice as large as they were in Bonn. The court of honour with the fountain is being designed on modern lines with boxwood hedges in square patterns.

Ulf Meyer
Die Bundesbauten / The Federal Government Buildings

Der Umzug der Bundesinstitutionen nach Berlin mußte sich von Anfang an gegen Widerstände behaupten. Fest stand von vornherein nur, daß die Bundesgebäude in Berlin nicht wie in Bonn wie „die Kühe auf der Weide" in der Landschaft stehen könnten, sondern sich in die existierende Stadt einfügen und behaupten müssen.

Oft wird übersehen, daß Berlin auch vor 1989 schon Hauptstadt war und deshalb eine funktionierende, wenn auch ungeliebte, Regierungsinfrastruktur zur Verfügung stand. Ausgerechnet in dem Moment, wo in Bonn endlich einige ansehnliche Gebäude entstanden waren, wurde der geordnete Rückzug von dort angetreten.

Erst 1994 kam die Wende zu einem behutsameren Umgang mit der Stadt und ihrem baulichen Erbe. Nur gut ein Fünftel der benötigten Büroflächen wird in Neubauten untergebracht. Lediglich die prestigeträchtigen Behörden wie das Bundeskanzleramt und das Bundespräsidialamt bekamen Neubauten zugesprochen. Der ursprüngliche Plan für einen Neubau des Bundesrats gegenüber vom Reichstag wurde wieder fallengelassen. Die Ministerien mußten sich alle mit Altbauten begnügen, was ihnen architektonisch mitunter durchaus zum Vorteil gereichte.

Der Bund als Bauherr hatte sich als Konsequenz aus dieser Entscheidung mit dem baulichen Erbe aus zwei wesentlichen Epochen der jüngeren deutschen Geschichte auseinanderzusetzen: dem „Dritten Reich" und der DDR, die die Nazigebäude meist ohne große bauliche Veränderungen weitergenutzt hatten. Der Umgang mit der Nazi-Vergangenheit bei der Herrichtung für die Bundesbehörden schien bisweilen weniger problematisch zu sein als der mit dem DDR-Erbe, obwohl sowohl die ehemalige Reichsbank, das Luftfahrtministerium als auch das

The relocation of the national institutions to Berlin had to overcome resistance from the outset. The only thing that was clear in advance was that the federal buildings in Berlin could not stand in the landscape "like cows in a field" as they did in Bonn, but would have to fit into the existing city and establish their own identity. It is often overlooked that Berlin was already a capital city before 1989 and therefore had a working government infrastructure, even though it was unpopular. And just when a number of attractive buildings had been built in Bonn, an orderly retreat from Bonn began.

It was only in 1994 that the reunified Germany began to treat the city of Berlin and its architectural heritage with greater care. Just over a fifth of the necessary office space is accommodated in new buildings. Only the prestige institutions such as the Federal Chancellery and the Federal President's office were assigned new buildings. The original plan for a new building for the Federal Council opposite the Reichstag was abandoned. All ministries had to make do with old buildings – and in some cases this is a considerable architectural advantage.

As a result of this decision, the national government as a client for construction work had to come to terms with the architectural heritage of two major epochs in recent German history: the "Third Reich" and the GDR, which had mainly continued to use the Nazi buildings without any significant structural changes. Dealing with the National Socialist past often seemed less of a problem in adapting buildings for federal institutions than dealing with the heritage of the GDR, although demolition was rashly and prematurely approved for the former Reichsbank, the Air Travel Ministry and the State Council build-

Staatsratsgebäude vorschnell zum Abriß freigegeben worden waren. Ein „kapitales Dilemma" (Michael Wise) war der Bezug der „historisch kontaminierten" Gebäude in keinem Fall.

Ein seltsamer Kompromiß sah vor, von einer Handvoll Ministerien nur jeweils einen zweiten Dienstsitz nach Berlin zu verlegen, um dem bundesweiten Proporz zu genügen und die Bonner Berlingegner zu beruhigen. Ob diese „Arbeitsteilung" auf Dauer sinnvoll ist, oder ob auch diese Ministerien ganz nachziehen würden, wird sich erst erweisen.

Für die zentralen Bundesbauten wurden Architekturwettbewerbe mit außergewöhnlich großer Beteiligung durchgeführt: Für den Reichstag, den Spreebogen und die Spreeinsel haben insgesamt mehrere tausend Architekten vergeblich Pläne gezeichnet, selbst zwei der siegreichen Vorschläge blieben unberücksichtigt: Weder wurden die Pläne für die Spreeinsel weiter verfolgt, noch der Reichstag nach den ursprünglichen Vorstellungen der Wettbewerbsgewinner umgebaut. Die in der Summe ebenfalls umfangreichen Aufträge für die Um- und Anbauten der Zweitsitze der Ministerien wurden jedoch durchgehend ohne Wettbewerb direkt vergeben.

In den frühen neunziger Jahren entbrannte der „Berliner Architekturstreit" zwischen antimonumentaler Glasarchitektur und steinerner Blockmentalität, zu dem die „Demokratie als Bauherr" Position beziehen mußte. Zwischen den Fronten konnte sich der Architekt des Kanzleramtes behaupten. Axel Schultes fand einen „dritter Weg". Obwohl die Mehrheit der Bundesinstitutionen in angestammte Staatsbauten einzog, kam nur das Bundesparlament in den Reichstag und damit an seinen einstigen Standort zurück.

Durch die Verteilung der Ministerien auf verschiedene Altbauten entstand zwar kein neues Berliner Regierungsviertel, wie ehemals in der Wilhelmstraße, aber ein kleines Parlamentsviertel hat sich am Spreebogen durchaus entwickelt. Mit der historischen Mitte Berlins am ehemaligen Schloßplatz konnte der Bund hingegen weniger anfangen. Er dämmert zusammen mit dem verwaisten Palast der Republik vor sich hin. Die Bauten, die ihm wieder seine Bedeutung als Machtzentrum hätten verleihen können, entstanden anderswo.

ing. The decision to move into the "historically contaminated" buildings was certainly not a "capital dilemma" (Michael Wise).

In a strange compromise, it was decided that a handful of ministries would only move auxiliary offices to Berlin in order to comply with ideas of proportional federalism and to assuage the anti-Berlin feelings in Bonn. It remains to be seen whether this "division of labour" is rational in the long term, or whether these ministries will also eventually move to Berlin.

For the central federal buildings, architectural competitions were held and attracted an unusually large number of participants: a total of several thousand architects vainly drew plans for the Reichstag, the meander of the Spree and the island of the Spree, and even two of the winning entries were laid aside: the plans for the island of the Spree were abandoned and the Reichstag was not altered on the basis of the original proposals of the prizewinners. And the considerable commissions for alterations and extensions to the auxiliary offices of the ministries were all awarded directly without a competition.

In the early 1990s, there arose a "Berlin architectural dispute" between anti-monumental glass architecture and the block-type stone and brick mentality, and the "client democracy" had to adopt a position. The architect of the Federal Chancellery was able to assert himself between the two extremes: Axel Schultes found a "third way".

Although the majority of federal institutions moved into existing state buildings, the only institution to return to its former location was the national parliament in the Reichstag.

The distribution of ministries among various old buildings meant that there was not a new government district like the former district around Wilhelmstrasse, but a small parliamentary district has nevertheless developed around the meander of the Spree. But the national government could not integrate the historical centre of Berlin on the former Schlossplatz. It is languishing with the vacant Palast der Republik. The buildings that could have restored its importance as a centre of power were created elsewhere.

oben/above: Reichstag, Hauptportal/Reichstag, main entrance
unten/below: Jakob-Kaiser-Haus, nördlicher Innenhof/Jakob Kaiser building, northern courtyard

oben/above: Bundesrat, Plenarsaal/Federal Council, plenary chamber
unten/below: PBZ, Vorplatz des Konferenzgebäudes von Norden/Government press and visitor centre,
square of the conference building from the north
S. 35: Bundespräsidialamt/P.35: Federal President's Office

oben/above: Auswärtiges Amt/Foreign Office
unten/below: BM für Verteidigung, Blick vom Landwehrkanal/Federal Ministry of Defence,
view from Landwehrkanal

S. 37 oben/above: BM für Verkehr, Alt- und Erweiterungsbau/Ministry of Transport, old building and extension
Mitte/in the middle: BM für Wirtschaft, Blick vom Kanal auf den Neubauteil/ Ministry of Economic Affairs, view of the new building from the canal
unten/below: BM des Innern, Blick von der Spree/Ministry of the Interior, view from the Spree

oben/above: SPD-Bundeszentrale, Atrium/National SPD headquarters, atrium
unten/below: Friedrich-Ebert-Stiftung/Friedrich Ebert
Foundation
rechts/right: CDU - Bundeszentrale, Blick von Südost/National
CDU headquarters, view from the south-east

oben/above: LV Nordrhein-Westfalen, Eingangsseite/North Rhine-Westfalia state office, entrance side
rechts/right: BM für Ernährung, Landwirtschaft und Forsten, Blick von der Wilhelmstraße/Ministry of Food, Agriculture and Forestry, view from Wilhelmstrasse; LV Brandenburg und Mecklenburg-Vorpommern/Brandenburg and Mecklenburg-Lower Pomerania state offices
unten/below: LV Berlin, Blick von der Wilhelmstraße/
view from Wilhelmstrasse Berlin state office

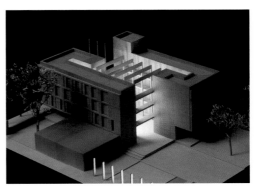

links/left: LV Thüringen, Blick von der Mohrenstraße/
Thuringia state office, view from Mohrenstrasse
1. unten/below: LV Niedersachsen und Schleswig-
Holstein, Eingangsseite/Lower Saxony and Schleswig-
Holstein state offices
2. unten/below: LV Bremen/Bremen state office

Bundespressekonferenz / Federal Press Conference

Reinhardtstraße 53-59
10117 Berlin (Mitte)

Nalbach + Nalbach, Berlin

1998-2000

links/left: Blick von Westen/
View from the west
rechts/right: Grundriß 1. OG /
Ground plan, first floor

Der lichtdurchflutete Saal der Bundespressekonferenz, der heiter über einem Meer von Blumen schwebte, bestimmte gut drei Jahrzehnte lang das Image der Bonner Republik. Auf blauen Sesseln und vor einer Wand aus grob gerastertem Eichenholz präsentierten Regierungs- wie Oppositionspolitiker ihre Sicht der Dinge. Niemals hatten sie ein Heimspiel: In einer weltweit einmaligen Konstellation waren sie nur Gäste der Bundespressekonferenz.

In Berlin wird der Verein nicht mehr das alleinige Hausrecht besitzen, denn wie die Regierung mit dem Bundespresseamt haben viele Nachrichtenproduzenten hier eigene „Marktplätze" errichtet. Mit einer Deutlichkeit, die angesichts der von den elektronischen Informationstechnologien produzierten Ortslosigkeit geradezu nostalgisch wirkt, unterstreicht das neue, von der Allianz-Versicherung errichtete Domizil dennoch den Anspruch der Nachrichtenhändler, die vierte Macht im Staate zu sein: Erstens durch die Lage am Schiffbauerdamm – niemand hat Bundeskanzler und Parlamentarier direkter im Visier. Zweitens durch die Baugestalt: Das österreichische Architektenduo Johanne und Gernot Nalbach zog die Grundstücksgrenzen geradewegs bis zur Traufe. Die Fassade des Klotzes, hinter der 600 Korrespondenten in gleichförmigen Boxen tätig sind, ist im Stakkatotakt von 1,20 Metern streng gerastert und mit Vulkanbasalt gräulich verkleidet. Die kaum zu überbietende Neutralität dient nur der Inszenierung des Herzstücks des Hauses: Als einziges exponiertes Element reckt der große und über fünf Meter hohe Saal der Bundespressekonferenz im Piano Nobile seine vollkommen verglaste und von schwarzem Marmor gerahmte Front dem Machtzentrum deutscher Poltik entgegen. (hwh)

The light-flooded room of the Federal Press Conference in Bonn poised above a sea of flowers determined the image of the Bonn Republic for a good three decades. On blue armchairs before a wall of panelled oak, government and opposition politicians presented their view of things. They never had a "home" appearance: in a constellation that was unique in the whole world, they were only the guests of the Federal Press Conference.

In Berlin, the association will no longer be the only hosts. Not only has the government established its Federal Press Office, but many media have also set up their own market place. However, with a clarity that seems nostalgic in view of the abstraction created by electronic information technology, the new domicile of the newsmongers built by the Allianz insurance company nevertheless underlines its claim to be a fourth power in the state. First of all with its location on Schiffbauerdamm – no-one has a more direct view of the Chancellor and members of parliament. Secondly with the form of the building: the Austrian architectural duo of Johanne and Gernot Nalbach extended the boundaries of the plot vertically up to the eaves. The facade of the geometrical block, behind which 600 correspondents work in identical boxes, has an austere staccato grid with 1.20 metres between the elements and a greyish volcano basalt facing. The almost unparalleled neutrality highlights the main element of the building: the only outstanding element is the main room of the Federal Press Conference in the "piano nobile" with an area of 300 square metres and a height of over five metres which extends its fully glazed front, framed in black marble, towards the power centre of German politics. (hwh)

Presse- und Informationsamt der Bundesregierung /
The Press and Information Centre of the Federal Government

Eine besonders kuriose Situation zeichnet den Ort des Bundespresseamtes aus. Es kam auf insgesamt acht Parzellen unter und bildet den östlichsten Teil des „Band des Bundes". Zwei Altbauten, das ehemalige Postscheckamt und ein Plattenbau, wurden umgebaut und zwei Neubauten hinzugefügt. Die Berliner Filiale des Büros KSP konnte sich in einem internationalen Bewerbungsverfahren 1995 mit ihrem Konzept durchsetzen, das vorsah, an der Konstellation festzuhalten, „keine Harmonie zu suchen", dennoch aber dem Amt einen selbstbewußten Auftritt, der seinem Bedeutungszuwachs entspricht, zu verschaffen.

Das Konglomerat wirkt heterogen, denn die Gebäude könnten kaum unterschiedlicher sein: Das Postscheckamt erstreckt sich durch die Tiefe eines ganzen Blocks. Es wurde 1917 von Alfred Lemp errichtet und jetzt umgebaut. Das Gros der über 500 Berliner Mitarbeiter des Amtes hat hier sein Büro. Nur für Sonderräume wurde in die Substanz eingegriffen, obwohl das Haus unter Denkmalschutz steht. Vor dessen Brandwand war 1965 ein Pavillon (Architekten: Mehlan und Reichert) mit großem Vorplatz entstanden, der zu DDR-Zeiten als Kantine für Mitarbeiter der umliegenden Ministerien diente und bis auf den Keller abgerissen wurde. Auf dem Untergeschoß des „Freßwürfels" entstand das Presse- und Besucherzentrum der Bundesregierung (PBZ) als öffentlicher Teil des Ensembles. Der Parkplatz entlang der Neustädtischen Kirchstraße wird vielleicht später bebaut. Bis dahin markieren Bäume die Bauflucht, der Blick auf den Bahnhof Friedrichstraße bleibt frei. Wegen der möglichen Bebauung ist die Seitenfassade des Würfels mit grauem Muschelkalk fensterlos. Der Kubus entspricht in seiner Dimension dem Vorgänger, in seinem Innern be-

The site of the Federal Press Office is in a particularly curious situation. It is located on a total of eight plots and forms the eastern end of the "ribbon of government buildings". Two old buildings, the former postal cheque office and a concrete slab building, have been adapted and two new buildings added. The Berlin branch of the KSP office won an international competition in 1995 with its concept which envisaged maintaining this constellation and "not seeking harmony", but nevertheless giving the press office a self-confident character which would correspond to its increasing importance.

The complex has a heterogeneous appearance because the buildings could hardly be more different in character. The postal cheque office spans the entire depth of the block. It was built in 1917 by Alfred Lemp and has now been converted. Most of the 500 Berlin staff of the press office have an office here. Structural alterations were made for special purpose rooms, although the building is a listed monument. In front of its fire wall a pavilion with a large forecourt was built in 1965 (architects: Mehlan and Reichert). This pavilion was used in the GDR period as a canteen for the staff of the surrounding ministries and has been demolished down to the basement. On top of the basement of the "eating cube", the press and visitor centre of the Federal Government – the public part of the complex – has been built. The car park along Neustädtische Kirchstrasse will perhaps be built on later. Until then, trees mark the alignment line and the view of Friedrichstrasse station remains free. Because of the possibility of further building work, the sidefacade of the cube is faced with grey shell limestone and has no windows. The cube is the same size as its predecessor and contains a black box, a sort of "building within a build-

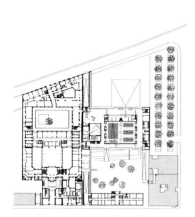

 Neustädtische Kirchstraße
4-15, Dorotheenstraße 74, 80-84
10117 Berlin (Mitte)

Alfred Lemp (Altbau/old
building); Heinz Mehlan, Harry
Reichert (Nachkriegsbau/post-
war building); KSP Engel Zimmermann, Berlin (Umbau/altera-
tions)

1917, 1965, 1995-2000

S.42: Konferenzsaal mit Vorplatz/
Conference hall with square
S.43 links/left: Grundriß EG/
Ground plan, ground floor

findet sich wie ein „Haus im Haus" eine Black Box, in der die Pressekonferenzen stattfinden. Es ist auf allen Seiten mit Foyers umgeben. Die Fläche ist je nach Bedarf in unterschiedlich große Säle zu unterteilen. Werden alle Räume zusammengelegt, finden über 300 Gäste darin Platz.

Besucher betreten den Würfel über eine breite, flache Rampe, Politiker dagegen die „Schublade" von hinten, denn die Zufahrt erfolgt über den Hof. Dort wurden die spärlichen Reste des Landhauses Kamecke von Andreas Schlüter ausgestellt, das hier bis 1950 stand.

Der Bau in der Dorotheenstraße wurde erst 1989 fertiggestellt. Die „ungeliebte Platte" hat roten Putz, ein gläsernes Staffelgeschoß und quadratische Fenster mit vorstehenden Laibungen erhalten. Ein kleiner Teil wurde abgerissen. Dort sieht man heute die Schmalseite des zweiten Neubaus. Sie erscheint als Turm in der Straßenfassade: Der Brandwand wurde eine gläserne Büroscheibe vorgesetzt, die öffentliche von internen Bereichen trennt. Die Verteilung der Baumassen entspricht den Aufgaben im Amt: Viel „unsichtbarer" Schreibtischarbeit im Altbau steht weniger Repräsentationsfläche im Würfel gegenüber.

Die 120 Meter lange „Bürospange" liegt direkt am Altbau. Sie übernimmt seine großzügigen Geschoßhöhen und verbindet alle Teile des Presseamtes miteinander. Die äußere Schicht seiner doppelten Glasfassade ist mit einem schwarzen Punktraster bedruckt und zeigt sich je nach Lichtverhältnissen variabel. Sie erscheint morgens schwarz und „öffnet" sich im Laufe des Tages. Eine Natursteinkante über der modischen Lamellenfassade verbindet die Bauteile miteinander. An der Schmalseite am Reichstagsufer konnten sich die Architekten in den Besprechungsräumen herausgedrehte „Erker für den Blick aufs Parlament" nicht verkneifen.

ing", which is used for press conferences. It is surrounded with foyers on all sides. The area can be sub-divided into different sized rooms as required. If all the rooms are combined, over 300 visitors can be accommodated.

Visitors enter the cube via a wide, gently sloping ramp, but politicians enter the "drawer" from the rear because vehicle access is via the courtyard. There, the meagre remains of the Kamecke country house by Andreas Schlüter, which stood here until 1950, can be seen.

The building on Dorotheenstrasse was only completed in 1989. The "unloved slab building" has been finished with red rendering, a glass staggered storey and square windows with protruding surrounds. A small part has been pulled down, and now the narrow side of the second new building can be seen there. It appears as a tower in the street facade. In front of the fire wall, a glass office slab has been set which separates the public areas from the internal departments. The distribution of the building mass reflects the tasks in the office, with a great deal of "invisible" desk work in the old building and a small amount of representation space in the cube.

The 120 metre long "office bracelet" is directly next to the old building. It takes up the generous ceiling heights of the old building and acts as a link between all parts of the press office. The outer layer of its double glass facade is printed with a black dot pattern and appears variable depending on the light conditions. It looks black in the morning and "opens" during the day. A natural stone ledge above the fashionable louvered facade acts as a visual link between the buildings. On the narrow side facing Reichstagsufer, the architects were unable to resist the temptation of creating a "parliament view bay window" which twists out of the conference rooms.

Das Bundespräsidialamt / The Federal President's Office

Das Amt des Bundespräsidenten kehrte als eine der ersten oberen Bundesbehörden vollständig nach Berlin zurück. Der Sitz des Bundespräsidenten im Schloß Bellevue war für das Amt jedoch zu klein. Nachdem verschiedene andere Gebäude erwogen worden waren, entschied man sich für einen Erweiterungsbau am Schloß, mitten im Tiergarten. Als modernes Verwaltungsgebäude sollte es niedriger als das Schloß und der Baumbestand sein. Bei einem Wettbewerb 1994 entschied man sich für den Entwurf der jungen Architekten Gruber+Kleine-Kraneburg. „Wir wollten den Eindruck des Schlosses schonen – das geht am besten mit einem Gebäude, das keine Ecken hat", so die Architekten. Die 80 Meter lange Ellipse hat vier Ober- und drei Untergeschosse. Ihre Ausrichtung ergibt sich aus der Lage zur Siegessäule und den Lichtungen des Englischen Gartens. Das Haus steht nah am Schloß, dennoch stört es die Beziehungen im Schloßpark nicht, sondern fügt sich ein. Eine überdachte Verbindung zwischen Präsidialamt und Schloß fehlt. Gäste des Hauses können zwar in die neue Tiefgarage fahren, müssen aber unter freiem Himmel zum Schloß zurücklaufen. Der Neubau für 150 Mitarbeiter liegt in einem Abstand von etwa 300 Metern zum Schloß.

Für das auch bei Bauten der öffentlichen Hand längst nicht mehr selbstverständliche Engagement als Bauherr wurde das Präsidialamt mit guter Architektur belohnt.

Die poliert-schwarze Granitfassade wirkt blank und schwer, aber unaufdringlich. Die Spiegelungen verstärken ihren geschlossenen Charakter. Die fast raumhohen Kastenfenster liegen bündig in der Fassade, lassen sich öffnen und machen eine Klimatisierung der Arbeitsräume überflüssig. Die Büroräume liegen in einem äußeren Ring und die Nebenräume in einem rechteckigen

The office of the Federal President was one of the first national bodies which completely returned to Berlin. But the residence of the Federal President in Bellevue Palace was too small for the office premises. After a number of other buildings had been considered, it was decided to build an extension by the palace in the middle of Tiergarten. As a modern administrative building, it was to be less high than the palace and the existing tree growth. In a competition in 1994, the decision was made in favour of the design by the young architects Gruber + Kleine-Kraneburg. "We wanted to conserve the impression of the palace – and that is best done with a building that has no corners", as the architects stated. The 80 metre long elipse has four storeys above and three below ground level. Its alignment results from its position in relation to the victory column and the clearings in the park. Although the building is close to the palace, it fits in discretely without disturbing the lines of vision in the palace park. There is no covered link between the president's office building and the palace. Visitors can drive into the new underground car park, but they then have to walk back to the palace without a roof. The new building, which accommodates a staff of 150, is about 300 metres from the palace.

The unusual involvement of the government as the client for this project was rewarded with a fine design for the Federal President's office.

The polished black granite facade appears bare and heavy, but unobtrusive. The reflections reinforce its closed character. The high box-type windows fit flush into the facade, can be opened and thus do away with the necessity of air conditioning in the rooms. The office rooms are in an outer ring, and the auxiliary rooms in a

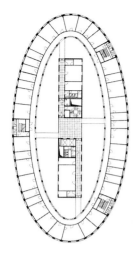

Spreeweg 1
10557 Berlin (Tiergarten)

Gruber + Kleine-Krane-
burg, Frankfurt a. Main/Berlin

1996-1999

S.45: links/left: Grundriß Büro-
geschoß/Ground plan, office
floor
rechts/right: Blick in die
Halle/View into the hall

Kern. Beide Teile sind durch Brücken miteinander verbunden. Das glasgedeckte, introvertierte Atrium ist strahlend weiß. In der Mitte steht ein massiver Riegel, der die Erschließungs- und Nebenräume und die Bibliothek aufnimmt. Die Büros werden über eine umlaufende, zum Lichthof offene Galerie erschlossen und haben alle Ausblick ins Grüne. Das Glasdach über der Halle kann mit Sonnensegeln vor Überhitzung im Sommer geschützt werden. Auf dem Dach wurde eine Photovoltaikanlage installiert. Die strenge, kühle Eleganz konnten die Architekten in fast allen Details durchhalten. Während das Schloß sich mit den Flügeln zur Stadt ausbreitet, tritt das neue Amtsgebäude zurück. Der Bau verschließt sich nach außen und öffnet sich nach innen.

Das Haus ist ein gutes Beispiel für die „neue architektonische Ernsthaftigkeit" der Berliner Bundesbauten. Gegenüber der bescheidenen „weichen" Architektur in Bonn fehlt ihr die Angst vor großen Gesten. Erst nach einiger Kritik an dem „reaktionären" Entwurf hatten die Architekten ihren Entwurf für das „Oval Office" verändert und die Größe der Fenster verdoppelt. Der Bauherr wollte eine „Architektur, die Staat macht", die der „Bedeutung für das Erscheinungsbild des Staates" mit makelloser Schönheit Rechnung trägt und den „Vorrang des Schlosses als Amtssitz des Bundespräsidenten respektiert".

Trotz anfänglicher Bedenken gegen das dunkle Gebäude, sind die Besucher mehrheitlich beeindruckt von dem Haus. Damals hatte das Preisgericht den „geometrisch eindeutigen Körper als glatt und abweisend" interpretiert, aber gleichzeitig die „spannungsreichen, klaren Räume" gelobt. Diese Einschätzung trifft auch auf das fertige Werk zu. Das Präsidenten-Ei ist eine wahre „Black Beauty".

rectangular central block. The two parts are linked together by bridges. The glass-roofed, introverted atrium is in bright white. In the middle is a solid block-type structure containing the access facilities, auxiliary rooms and library. The offices are reached via an open gallery around the inner courtyard which is open to daylight. The glass roof above the atrium can be protected against overheating in summer by sun sails. A photovoltaic system has been installed on the roof. The architects were able to maintain their strict, cool elegance in almost all the details. Whereas the palace with its wings opens up to the city, the new office building recedes. The building appears closed to the outside and open on the inside.

The building is a good example of the "new architectural solemnity" of the government buildings in Berlin. Compared with the modest "soft" architecture in Bonn, it has lost its fear of great gestures. It was only after the "reactionary" design had been criticised that the architects altered their design for the "Oval office" and doubled the size of the windows. The client wanted an "architecture of state" which would do justice to the "importance for the image of the state" in flawless beauty and would "respect the priority of the palace as the official headquarters of the Federal President".

In spite of initial misgivings about the dark building, the majority of visitors are impressed. Initially, the prize jury interpreted the "geometrically unambiguous structure as smooth and inhospitable", but at the same time they praised the "dynamic clear use of space". This evaluation also applies to the finished work. The egg-shaped presidential building is a real "Black Beauty".

Das Bundeskanzleramt / The Federal Chancellery

Nachdem Axel Schultes mit dem „Band des Bundes" bereits die städtebauliche Vorgabe für das Kanzleramt geschaffen hatte, konnte sich sein Architekturentwurf beim Wettbewerb 1994 nur knapp durchsetzen. Die Entscheidung war damals in der Fachöffentlichkeit weitgehend mit Erleichterung aufgenommen worden. Ein weiterer erster Preis war an das Berliner Architekturbüro Krüger/Schuberth/Vandreike (KSV) vergeben worden, und erst nach einer Überarbeitung und Kanzlervotum entschied man sich 1995 für Schultes' Vorschlag, der mühsam einen poetischen Zugang zu der schwierigen Bauaufgabe gesucht hat. Sein Entwurf durchlief verschiedene Phasen und wurde mehrfach grundlegend überarbeitet.

Das Kanzleramt besteht aus zwei langen Büroriegeln an der Nord- und Südallee und dem Leitungsgebäude. Es steht in der Mitte der Anlage als heller, 36 Meter hoher, gedrungener Kubus. Darin sind die Büros des Kanzlers, des Chefs des Kanzleramtes, der Kabinetts- und Pressesaal, Empfangsräume und im neunten Obergeschoß die Privaträume des Kanzlers untergebracht. Der Kubus bildet mit dem Reichstag und dem geplanten Bundesforum eine Dreiheit. Als Solitär steht er dennoch in Einklang mit dem städtebaulichen Band.

Während die Nord- und Südfassaden flach wirken, entwickeln sich im Osten und Westen über dem Hof und Garten große Loggien. Der Kanzlerwürfel wird flankiert durch fünfgeschossige, kammartige Flügel mit über 300 Büros, die sich U-förmig zu je einem der 13 Wintergärten öffnen, die die homogenen Fassaden auflockern. Sie sind betont repetitiv gereiht. Vom Foyer im Kubus aus führen große Freitreppen zum „internationalen Konferenzsaal". Das Zeremoniell für Staatsgäste findet im Ehrenhof an der Ostseite statt. Ursprünglich waren dort zwölf Meter

After Axel Schultes had created the urban planning framework for the Chancellery with the "ribbon of government buildings", his design was only successful in 1994 after much uncertainty. The decision was mainly received with relief by the specialist public. A further first prize had been awarded to the Berlin architectural office of Krüger/Schuberth/Vandreike (KSV), and it was only after revision of the design and a casting vote by the Chancellor that the decision was made in 1995 in favour of Schultes' proposal which strove to find an aesthetic approach to the difficult building task. His design went through various phases and was thoroughly revised several times.

The Chancellery consists of two long office blocks on Nordallee and Südallee and the main building in the middle of the complex, a light-coloured, 36 metre high compact cube. It contains the offices of the Chancellor, the Chancellery head, the cabinet room and press room, reception rooms and, on the ninth floor, the Chancellor's private quarters. The cube forms a triangle with the Reichstag and the planned federal forum, but as a solitary building it is also in harmony with the ribbon of government buildings.

Whereas the northern and southern facades appear flat, there are large loggias to the east and west above the court and garden. The Chancellery cube is flanked by five-storey comb-type office wings with over 300 offices which each open in a U shape to one of the 13 winter gardens which break up the plainness of the facades. They are lined up in repetitive rows. Large outdoor staircases lead from the foyer of the cube to the "international conference room".

State visitors are ceremonially received in the court of

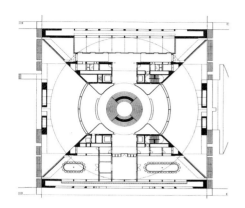

Willy-Brandt-Straße 1,
10557 Berlin (Tiergarten)

Axel Schultes und Char-
lotte Frank, Berlin

1997-2000

S.46: Leitungsbereich Kanzleramt vom Ehrenhof/Main section
of the Federal Chancellery, view
from the court of honour
S.47: Grundriß Leitungsbereich/
Ground plan, main section

hohe „Türen" aus gewellten Sichtbetonwänden vorgesehen. Schließlich entstanden Stelen in weichen Formen
mit einer Glaswand dahinter. Sie wirken wie ein steinerner Vorhang am Cours d'honneur zwischen Foyer und
Stadt. Die „wohlbeleibten Stelen tragen Bäume hinauf
auf die Bankettebene" (Schultes); der Blick schweift von
den Terrassen über den Garten zur Stadt. Die Bäume sollen „die Isolation des Hauses mildern".

Der Kubus darüber hat paarweise einander gegenüberlie-
gende, verspielte Fassaden. Hinter einer plastischen Wand
mit Einschnitten liegt eine Glasfassade mit Lamellen.
Schultes war bemüht, eine populäre Fassade zu finden,
die dem Gebäude trotz der aus Sicherheitsgründen nötigen Abgeschlossenheit ein identitätsstiftendes und me-
dienwirksames Bild gibt. Die Einschnitte in den flächi-
gen, figurativen Fassaden wandelten sich vom Kreis (als
„Sonne, Globus oder Augen") über den Baum (als Bild
von globaler Verantwortung) zu großen Kreissegmenten.
Die bogenförmigen Fassadenausschnitte im Norden und
Süden geben den schweren Wänden Gesicht. Westlich des
Leitungsgebäudes erstreckt sich ein hügeliger Garten. Ein
Steg führt über die Spree in den Kanzlerpark.

Der nicht öffentlich zugängliche Bau will ein Symbol
sein, das intuitiv verstanden wird. Er will „gelassenes
Selbstbewußtsein ausstrahlen, Bescheidenheit, Würde
und Eleganz vereinen".

Mit Ernst, aber ohne hohles Pathos oder falsche Bescheidenheit geht er gegen das Bonner Understatement vor.
Der Bau soll „Aufforderung sein, dem Geist der Schwere
Widerstand zu leisten". Die geheimnisvolle Schönheit des
Bonner Kunstmuseums (1992), die durch Schultes sub-
straktives Entwerfen entstanden ist, läßt für das Kanzleramt Bestes hoffen.

honour to the east. Originally, twelve metre high "doors"
of corrugated exposed concrete walls were planned
there. But in the end, pillars in softer forms were created
with a glass wall behind them. They appear like a stone
curtain for the court of honour between the foyer and the
city. The "sturdy pillars bear trees up to the banqueting
level" (Schultes). The view roams from the terraces over
the garden to the city. The trees are intended to "alleviate
the isolation of the building".

The cube above them has whimsical pairs of opposite facades. Behind a textured wall with recesses is a glass facade with louver structures. Schultes strove to find a
popular facade which would give the building a visual
identity and an effective media image in spite of the
aloofness that was necessary for security reasons. The recesses cut into the large, figurative facades changed
from a circle ("the sun, the globe or eyes") through a
tree (as an image of global responsibility) to large circle
segments. The arched recesses cut into the north and
south facade give form to the heavy walls. To the west of
the main building is a hilly garden. A bridge leads across
the Spree into the Chancellery park.

The building, which is not accessible to the public, aims
to create a symbol which is intuitively understood. It
aims "to radiate a relaxed self-confidence, to combine
moderation, dignity and elegance".

It responds to the understatement in Bonn with solemnity, but without empty pathos or false humility. The
building aims to be "a call to resist the spirit of heavi-
ness". The enigmatic beauty of the art museum in Bonn
(1992), which was created by Schultes' subtractive design process, bodes well for the Chancellery.

Bundesministerium des Innern / Federal Ministry of the Interior

Auf den ersten Blick scheint das Bundesinnenministerium als einziges Ressort in Berlin in einem reinen Neubau zu residieren. Sein Dienstsitz ist ein modernes, mit rotbraunem Granit verkleidetes Gebäude. Der 120 Meter lange und in seinen beiden spiegelgläsernen Zylindertürmen 49 Meter hohe, U-förmige Bau, der von einer runden Eingangshalle von 20 Metern Durchmesser erschlossen wird, dominiert mit unverhohlener Monumentalität die Moabiter Spree, nicht zuletzt weil die Uferbebauung entgegen sonstiger Berliner Gepflogenheiten keine klare Wasserkante ausbildet, sondern die Qualitäten des Flusses in die Tiefe des Grundstückes zu holen versucht. Mit dem Fluß ist das Haus auch funktional verbunden: als einziger Berliner Bundesbau verfügt es von Anfang an über eine Bootsanlegestelle, von der Spreetaxen die Beamten zum Amtssitz des Bundespräsidenten, zu Kanzleramt, Alsenblock, Reichstag und Auswärtigem Amt chauffieren.

Das Gebäude ist allerdings keineswegs für die Bundesregierung errichtet worden, sondern ein typisches Beispiel für die Revitalisierung vormals industriell genutzter Uferbrachen. Seit dem 19. Jahrhundert befand sich dort die Meierei Bolle. Nachdem die Milchverarbeitung in der Nachkriegszeit schrittweise eingestellt wurde, nutzte der stadtbekannte Berliner Lebensmittelhandel das Areal als Lager. Seit den siebziger Jahren vermietete er Teile an andere Unternehmen. Einer der Mieter war Ernst Freiberger, dessen kleiner Lieferbetrieb zur größten Pizzabäckerei Europas aufstieg. Nachdem Bolle 1988 in ein neues Logistikzentrum umgezogen war, hatte Freiberger das Glück, das Grundstück unmittelbar vor dem Mauerfall günstig kaufen zu können. Er finanzierte daraufhin die Umnutzung zu hundert Wohnungen, zwanzig Läden,

At first sight, the Federal Ministry of the Interior seems to be the only ministry in Berlin that occupies a purely new building – a modern structure faced with reddish brown granite. The 120 metre long U-shaped building, with two 49 metre high mirror glass cylindrical towers and a round entrance hall with a diameter of 20 metres providing access to the storeys, dominates the Spree in Moabit with its unashamed monumentalism – not least because it does not form a clear line along the water like most riverside buildings in Berlin, but attempts to reflect the quality of the river in the depth of the land property. The building also has a functional link with the river – it is the only government building in Berlin with its own boating jetty from which river taxis are intended to ferry officials to the offices of the Federal President, the Federal Chancellery, the Alsenblock parliamentary offices, the Reichstag and the Foreign Office.

But the building was not built for the German government at all – it was a typical example of the revitalisation of formerly industrial wasteland next to the waterways. From the 19th century it was used by the Bolle dairy. Milk processing was gradually discontinued after the war, and the traditional Berlin grocery chain Bolle used it for storage. From the 1970s it let parts of the complex to other companies. One of the tenants was Ernst Freiberger, whose small delivery service grew to become the largest pizza bakery in Europe. After Bolle had moved to a new logistics centre in 1988, Freiberger was fortunate enough to buy the land for a moderate price shortly before the fall of the Wall. He then financed the development of 100 apartments, 20 shops, a theatre, a kindergarten, a hotel and almost 100,000 square metres of office space. The implemented design is by the office

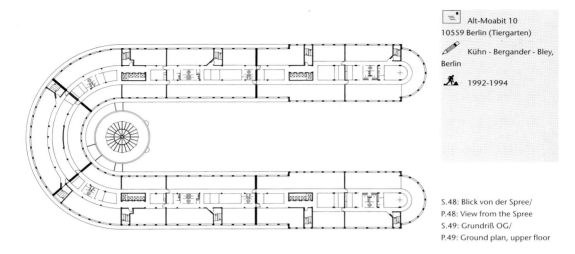

Alt-Moabit 10
10559 Berlin (Tiergarten)

Kühn - Bergander - Bley, Berlin

1992-1994

S.48: Blick von der Spree/
P.48: View from the Spree
S.49: Grundriß OG/
P.49: Ground plan, upper floor

einem Theater, einer Kita, einem Hotel und riesiger Bürofläche. Mit dem realisierten Entwurf setzte sich das Büro Kühn-Bergander-Bley, das zuvor an der Erweiterung der Berliner Messe mitgearbeitet hatte, in einem 1990 ausgeschriebenen Wettbewerb gegen den renommierten kalifornischen Architekten Charles Moore durch. Hierfür wurde ein eigens aufgestellter Bebauungsplan legitimiert.

Das Projekt, das damals das größte Bauvorhaben eines Privatinvestors in Berlin darstellte, war trotz der Wendeeuphorie ein enormes Risiko – war doch die Berliner Justizverwaltung, die einen Teil der Bebauung entlang der Kirchstraße bezog, lange Zeit der einzige bedeutende Mieter. Es gelang Freiberger, die Bundesregierung als Nutzer zu gewinnen. Sie beschloß 1996, gut zwei Drittel des Baus für dreißig Jahre zu mieten. Die Entscheidung gegen das ehemalige Innenministerium der DDR in der Mauerstraße, das sich seit der Wende in Bundesbesitz befand, wurde mit Kostenvorteilen begründet, die vom Bundesrechnungshof in Zweifel gezogen wurden. Das Ressort ist der einzige Hauptsitz, der an der Spree in gemieteten Räumen Platz findet. Sie sind damit – jenseits aller Geschmacksfragen – für eine Behörde, die im wesentlichen die Verwaltung der ganzen Bundesregierung steuert, höchst angemessen. (hwh)

of Kühn-Bergander-Bley, who previously worked on the extension of the Berlin Fair Centre and who came first in the competition declared in 1990 ahead of the famous Californian architect Charles Moore. A special zoning plan was legitimized for the purpose.

The project with its budget of 470 million DM, which was then the largest building project of a private investor in Berlin, was an enormous risk in spite of the general euphoria after the fall of the Wall because the Berlin justice department, which occupied part of the development on Kirchstrasse, was the only significant tenant for a long time. When construction began, only one tenant was committed to the project: the Berlin justice department which moved into part of the complex along Kirchstrasse. But Freiberger succeeded in gaining the national government as a tenant. In 1996, the government decided to rent a good two thirds of the building for thirty years. The decision against the former Ministry of the Interior of the GDR in Mauerstrasse, which was government property after the fall of the Wall, was justified by cost benefits, although this argument was doubted by the federal audit office. The ministry is the only main government department which occupies rented rooms by the Spree. Apart from any questions of taste, the premises are highly appropriate for a public authority which basically controls the administration of the entire German government. (hwh)

Bundesministerium der Justiz / Federal Ministry of Justice

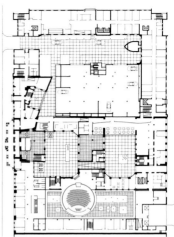

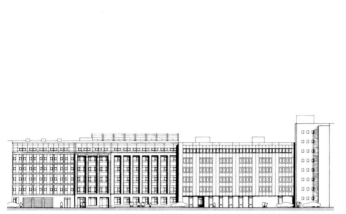

In Berlin hat das Justizministerium unter den Ministerien den unscheinbarsten Sitz, denn es wurden lediglich mehrere bundeseigene Altbauten durch einen Neubau ergänzt. Gleich einem Amalgam jüngerer Berliner Baugeschichte besitzen die nicht sonderlich repräsentativen Häuser an der Jerusalemer Straße kein einheitliches Gesicht. Das Architekturbüro Eller+ Eller (EMW) aus Düsseldorf, das sich in einem Auswahlverfahren 1994 als Generalplaner durchsetzte, wollte die Altbauten dennoch zu einer „starken Gebäudeeinheit zusammenfassen". Unübersichtlichkeit war der Preis für den Erhalt der Altbauten. Das „Ministerium der Höfe" hat viel Berliner Atmosphäre und wirkt nicht wie mancher Neubau als Fremdkörper. Die Vielfalt des Bestandes wurde von den Architekten als Chance begriffen; es unterblieb der Versuch, ein Ministerium „aus einem Guß" zu schaffen, was der Gegend zwischen Hausvogteiplatz und Gendarmenmarkt gut tut.

Die Blockrandbebauung des Ministeriums besteht aus vier Teilen: einem Plattenbau, der ursprünglich als Erweiterung des Patentamts der DDR dienen sollte, aber erst 1993 fertiggestellt wurde, und drei Altbauten, die von der Geschichte des Quartiers als Standort von Textilmanufakturen zeugen: Das Haus Stern (Architekt: Carl Bauer, 1896), das ehemalige Kaufhaus Nagel, das Hermann Muthesius 1898 schuf, und der Prausenhof von Ludwig Otto. Man betritt das Ministerium durch den ältesten Teil des Ensembles, eine der beiden Mohrenkolonaden, die von Carl Gotthard Langhans, dem Architekten des Brandenburger Tores, 1787 errichtet worden sind. Nur die Besucher des Informationszentrums nutzen den Eingang an der Jerusalemer Straße. Die Altbauten bilden vier Höfe. Mit dem Neubau kam noch ein

The new home of the Ministry of Justice is the most modest complex of the ministries in Berlin because it merely combines a number of government-owned old buildings and adds a new building. Like a haphazard collection of recent architectural history in Berlin, the rather unspectacular buildings on Jerusalemer Strasse do not present a uniform appearance. The architectural office of Eller, Maier, Walter und Partner (EMW) from Düsseldorf, which was selected as the general planner in a 1994 competition, wanted to combine the old buildings to create a "strong cohesion of buildings". Impenetrability results from the preservation of the old buildings. The "ministry of courtyards" has a great deal of Berlin atmosphere and does not appear out of place like some new buildings do. The architects saw the variety of the existing buildings as a bonus; they did not try to create a uniform ministry, and this is an advantage for the area between Hausvogteiplatz and Gendarmenmarkt.

The buildings of the ministry around the edge of the block consist of four parts: a concrete slab building which was originally designed as an extension for the patents office of the GDR but was only completed in 1993, and three old buildings which bear witness to the history of the site as a location of textile factories: the Haus Stern (1896 by Carl Bauer), the former Nagel shop building which Hermann Muthesius created in 1898 and the Prausenhof by Ludwig Otto. Access to the ministry is through the oldest part of the ensemble, one of the two colonnades on Mohrenstrasse which were built in 1787 by Carl Gotthard Langhans, the architect who built the Brandenburg Gate. Only visitors to the information centre use the entrance in Jerusalemer Strasse. The old buildings form four inner courtyards. The new building cre-

Jerusalemer 24-28, Moh-
renstraße 36-37 b, Kronenstraße
38-41
10117 Berlin (Mitte)

Carl Bauer; Ludwig Otto,
Hermann Muthesius; Carl Gotthard Langhans (Altbau/old
building); Eller+Eller, Düsseldorf
(Um- und Neubau/alterations)

1993-2000

S.50: links/left: Ansicht Kronen-
straße/View from Kronenstrasse
rechts/right: Grundriß EG/
Ground plan, ground floor
S.51: Ansicht Höfe/View of
courtyards

fünfter hinzu. Die Architekten wollten den bruchstück-
haften Block behutsam ergänzen und die Innenhöfe ver-
binden. Jeder Hof erhielt eine andere Funktion. Die beiden Höfe im Prausenhof von 1914 wurden mit Glas-
dächern versehen. Sie fungieren als „Repräsentations-"
und „Casinohof". Um die geringe Gebäudetiefe der Seitenflügel besser zu nutzen und ein rechtwinkliges Wege-
system einzuführen, wurden entlang der kriegsbeschädigten Kachelfassaden Brücken gebaut. Durch die Ton-
nendächer wurden die Höfe zu Innenräumen, deren Fassaden deswegen nicht aufwendig wärmegedämmt werden mußten. Die anderen Höfe sind offen.

Ein dreigeschossiger Bibliothekswürfel ist das Herz des
Ministeriums. Er sitzt auf einem bestehenden Bau und
hat Zugang zum neuen Dachgarten. Ein weiterer Hof
wurde zum Garten, in den nur ein pavillonartiger Sitzungssaal eingefügt wurde. Von außen verrät der introvertierte Block wenig vom Leben in den Höfen. Für den
Sitz des Ministers in der fünften Etage wurden die Obergeschosse vergrößert, um repräsentative Flächen zu schaffen. Um die unterschiedlichen Niveaus der Altbauten
auszugleichen, mußten vielerorts Treppen und Rampen
eingebaut werden. Der Neubau orientiert sich in seiner
Geschoßhöhe am Prausenhof, um einen zusätzlichen
Höhensprung zu vermeiden. Lediglich zur Kronenstraße
ist die Fassade mit den überhöhten Fenstern von außen
sichtbar; zu den anschließenden Parzellen hat der Neubau nur eine Brandwand. Das Haus Stern wurde weitgehend abgerissen. Die denkmalgeschützte Jugendstilfas-
sade von Otto Rieth wurde grundlegend renoviert. Im
Haus Stern residierte ehemals das Presseamt der DDR.
Hier verkündete Günther Schabowski am 9. November
1989 den Fall der Mauer.

ated a fifth courtyard. The architects wanted to supple-
ment the fragmented block carefully and to link the
courtyards. Each courtyard was given a different function. The two courtyards in the Prausenhof dating from
1914 were given glass roofs. They are used as the "reception courtyard" and the "canteen courtyard". To make
better use of the modest depth of the side wings and in-
troduce a right-angled system of access ways, bridges
were built along the war-damaged tile facades. The barrel
roofs made the courtyards into interior rooms, and the facades therefore did not need to have extensive insulation
layers added. The other courtyards are open to the sky.

A three-storey library cube is at the heart of the ministry. It
is situated on a previously existing building and leads to
the new roof garden. A further courtyard was made into a
garden into which a pavilion-type meeting room has been
inserted. From the outside, the inward-looking block
structure reveals little of the life inside the courtyards.

For the offices of the Minister of Justice on the fifth floor
the upper floors were enlarged to create impressive
space. Many ramps and flights of stairs had to be inserted
to compensate for the different floor levels in the old
buildings. The ceiling heights of the new building follow
the Prausenhof to avoid yet another difference in floor
heights. The facade with its tall windows can only be seen
from the outside on Kronenstrasse; on the sides facing
the other plots the new building only has a fire wall. The
"Haus Stern" has been largely pulled down. The listed Art
Nouveau facade by Otto Rieth has been renovated and
freed from the layers added in the 1950s. The "Haus
Stern" formerly accommodated the press office of the
GDR. It was here that Günther Schabowski announced
the fall of the Berlin Wall on 9th November 1989.

Bundesministerium für Arbeit und Sozialordnung /
Federal Ministry of Employment and Social Order

Das Ministerium für Arbeit und Soziales ist neben dem Auswärtigen Amt und dem Finanzministerium eine der drei Bundesbehörden, die sich mit dem Problem konfrontiert sahen, ihren Sitz in ehemaligen Nazibauten zu errichten. Das Arbeitsministerium bezog Teile des ehemaligen „Reichsministerium für Volksaufklärung und Propaganda", das zu DDR-Zeiten auch als „Presseamt beim Vorsitzenden des Ministerrates der DDR" genutzt wurde und ist somit der erste demokratisch legitimierte Hausherr im „Goebbelsbau". Das Gebäude völlig umzubauen schied ebenso aus wie die Idee, die Nazibauten zu konservieren. Die Frage des Umgangs mit dem schwierigen baulichen Erbe verursachte auch hier allgemeine Ratlosigkeit. Das Propagandaministerium hatte sich ursprünglich in dem barocken Ordenspalais am Wilhelmplatz eingerichtet. Angesichts der Bedeutung, die die Nazis der Propaganda beimaßen, stellte sich das Haus für das neu gegründete Ministerium schnell als zu klein und unrepräsentativ heraus. Schon 1933 wurden Pläne für eine Erweiterung erstellt: Das Palais, von Karl Friedrich Schinkel 1828 umgebaut und deshalb denkmalgeschützt, wurde erhalten und durch einen Anbau ergänzt. Ironischerweise diffamierte der Architekt des Umbaus, Karl Reichle, den „trostlosen Kasernenstil" der Architektur der Anbauten nur, um später Fassaden zu entwerfen, auf die diese Bezeichnung viel besser paßt. Vier Jahre später expandierte das Propagandaministerium erneut: Das benachbarte ehemalige Kolonialministerium mußte einem weiteren Neubau weichen. Das Ensemble erstreckte sich nun bis zur Mauerstraße. Als Architekt wurde abermals Reichle bestimmt.

Der Neubau von 1940 bildete einen zweiten Hof aus. Im Riegel dazwischen befindet sich heute wie ehemals das

The Ministry of Employment and Social Affairs, the Foreign Office and the Ministry of Finance are the three government bodies which were confronted with the problem of moving into former Nazi buildings. The Ministry of Employment moved into parts of the former "Reich Ministry of Propaganda", which was used in the GDR period as the "Press Office of the Chairman of the Council of Ministers of the GDR" – so the present ministry is the first democratically legitimated occupant of the "Goebbels building". A complete alteration of the structure was out of the question, but conserving the Nazi buildings was equally unacceptable. Here, too, the question of how to deal with a difficult architectural heritage led to general bewilderment.

The propaganda ministry had originally occupied the baroque "Ordenspalais" on Wilhelmplatz. But in view of the importance which the Nazis gave to propaganda, the newly founded ministry was soon found to be too small and not impressive enough. Plans for an extension were made as early as 1933. The palace, which had been altered by Karl-Friedrich Schinkel in 1828 and was therefore a listed monument, was preserved and supplemented by an extension. Ironically, the architect of the alteration work, Karl Reichle, criticised the "barren barracks style" of the architecture of the extension, but later he himself designed facades for which this description is even more fitting. Four years later, the propaganda ministry expanded again – the adjacent colonial ministry had to make way for a further new building. The ensemble now extended as far as Mauerstrasse. Reichle was again chosen as the architect.

The new building of 1940 formed a second courtyard. The block between the courtyards now contains the can-

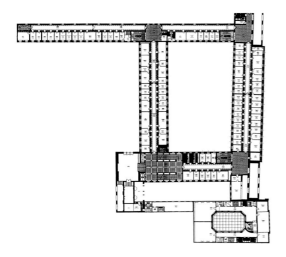

📄 Mauerstraße 45-53, Wilhelmstraße, 10117 Berlin (Mitte)

✏️ Karl Reichle (Altbau/old building); Bodo Ebhardt (Kleisthaus); Josef Paul Kleihues, Berlin (Umbau und Neubau/alterations)

🏗️ 1937, 1940, 1996-99

S.52: Ansicht Mauerstraße, im Vordergrund das Kleisthaus/P.52: View from Mauerstrasse, in the foreground: the Kleist building
S.53: Grundriß Normalgeschoß/P.53: Ground plan, main floor

Kasino. In den oberen Geschossen dieses Gebäudeteils ist der Leitungsbereich des Ministeriums untergebracht. Der Arbeitsminister blickt vom Büro auf den tristen steinernen Hof, dessen Bepflanzung unmöglich ist, weil sich darunter eine Tiefgarage befindet.

Blickfang der über 100 Meter langen, monumentalen Natursteinfront sind zwei Eckpfeiler, früher mit Reichsadler und Hakenkreuz versehen. Das Gebäude steht zurückgesetzt, um einer geplanten Verbreiterung der Straße nicht im Weg zu sein. Mit Ausnahme eines Studios, in dem Goebbels seine Reden hielt, waren die Innenräume nüchtern gestaltet, die endlosen Flure spröde und streng. Die Ruine des kriegsbeschädigten Palais wurde 1947 gesprengt; nur die Nazi-Anbauten blieben teilweise erhalten. Diese Vorgeschichte erklärt, warum die einstige Rückheute Hauptfassade ist und das Ministerium vom verbliebenen „Zwickel" aus erschlossen wird. An dieser kuriosen städtebaulichen Situation wird sich vermutlich nichts ändern, denn eine Grundschule, die sich heute auf dem Grundstück des Palais befindet, wird bleiben.

Das Ministerium, dessen historische Architektur nahezu unverändert blieb, wurde nach Plänen von Josef Paul Kleihues umgebaut, der sich 1994 in einem Wettbewerb durchsetzte. Sein Entwurf sah die Einbeziehung des benachbarten „Kleisthauses" von 1912 (Architekt: Bodo Ebhardt) und dessen Umbau zum „Infocenter" vor. Der Hof wurde überdacht. Ein kleiner Neubau, über zwei Brücken mit dem ehemaligen Propagandaministerium verbunden, schließt den Hof ab. Auch er erhielt ein Glasdach. Der Raum zwischen den Gebäuden wurde zum zentralen Innenraum des Hauses.

teen – as it did then. The upper storeys of this part of the building accommodate the senior ministry personnel. The Minister of Employment looks out of his office onto a drab stone courtyard in which it is not possible to plant vegetation because it is above an underground car park. On the monumental natural stone frontage which is over a hundred metres long, the main features are two corner pillars which also bear the Reich eagle emblem and swastika. The building is set back from the road to leave room for possible widening work. With the exception of a studio where Goebbels made his speeches, the interior rooms were plain in style, and the endless corridors were rigorous and austere. The palace was damaged in the war and the ruins were detonated in 1947; only the Nazi extensions were partly preserved.

This history explains why the former rear facade is now the main facade and the entrance to the ministry is now from the remaining "patch". And there is not likely to be any change in this strange urban setting because a primary school which is now on the land of the former palace will remain.

The ministry, which has remained almost unchanged in its architecture, has been altered to plans by Josef Paul Kleihues who gained the commission in a competition in 1994. His design envisaged integrating the adjacent "Kleisthaus" of 1912 (architect: Bodo Ebhardt) and converting it for use as an "Infocenter". A roof was erected over the courtyard. A small new building which is linked with the former propaganda ministry by two bridges completes the courtyard. It, too, has a glass roof. The space between the buildings became the central interior space in the building.

Bundesministerium für Verkehr, Bau- und Wohnungswesen / Federal Ministry of Transport, Construction and Residential Development

Zum Dienstsitz des Bundesverkehrsministerium wurde das Gebäude der ehemaligen Geologischen Landesanstalt und Bergakademie bestimmt, als dieses Dezernat noch eigenständig war. Bei der Herrichtung, die das Büro Gerber und Partner betreute, ging es zunächst darum, die ursprünglich repräsentative Wirkung des 1878 von August Tiede fertiggestellten Neorenaissancebaus wiederzugewinnen. Dafür wurden Einbauten der DDR-Zeit, in der das Haus als Ministerium für Geologie genutzt wurde, entfernt, Zwischendecken und Wände, die weite Säle in Einzelzimmer unterteilten, herausgerissen und die zugemauerten Arkaden des Lichthofes geöffnet, der zuletzt nur als Lager gedient hatte. Freilich war das Haus damit für das Verkehrsressort definitiv zu klein. Die Mehrheit der 527 Mitarbeiter kommt daher in einem Erweiterungsbau am Schwarzen Weg unter, dessen Entwurf von dem deutsch-schweizer Architekten Max Dudler stammt, der sich 1996 gegen neun Konkurrenten durchsetzte und hier – anders als beim Kopfbau des Auswärtigen Amtes, wo er fast zeitgleich den entsprechenden Wettbewerb gewann – den Auftrag auch bekam. Dudler setzte die bestehende Komposition des Ensembles aus Ministerium, Naturkundlichem Museum und Landwirtschaftlicher Hochschule fort und übernahm für den Erweiterungsbau auch die Proportionen des Haupthauses. Seine gerasterte, mit grün-grauem Naturstein verkleidete Lochfassade und seltsam verspiegelt erscheinenden Fenstern, erreicht nicht deren gestalterischen Reichtum. Wo der Altbau aus abwechslungsreichen Raumfolgen besteht, reiht Dudler immer gleiche, 15 Quadratmeter große Büromodule aneinander. Auch in der dritten Dimension kommt sein Erweiterungsbau nicht an den Altbau heran: Wo letzterer nur drei Geschosse unter-

The building of the former Geological State Institute and Mining Academy was designated as the set of the Ministry of Transport when this ministry was still independent. The alterations which were supervised by Gerber and partner initially aimed to restore the original impressive effect of the neo-Renaissance building completed in 1878 by August Tiede. To this end, fittings added in the GDR period when the building was used as the Ministry of Geology were removed, intermediate floors and walls which divided large rooms into small rooms were pulled out and the bricked-in arcades of the light courtyard, which had been used for storage, were opened again. However, the building was then definitely too small for the Ministry of Transport. Most of the staff of 527 are therefore moving into an extension building on Schwarzer Weg which was designed by the German-Swiss architect Max Dudler, who won a competition in 1996 against nine competitors and was then – by contrast with the end building of the Foreign Office, where he also won a competition at almost the same time – actually given the commission. Dudler continued the existing composition of the ensemble consisting of the ministry, the Natural History Museum and the College of Agriculture, and for the extension he also used the same proportions as the main building. His grid-type perforated facade faced with greenish grey natural stone, with windows with a strange reflection, does not achieve the same variety of design. Where the old building consists of varying sequences of rooms, Dudler simply creates rows of identical office modules measuring 15 square metres. In the third dimension, his extension also falls short of the old building: where the latter only contains three storeys, Dudler crams in four. The new

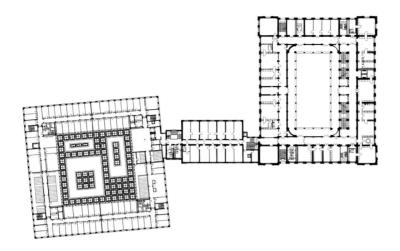

✉ Invalidenstraße 44/
Schwarzer Weg
10115 Berlin (Mitte)

✏ August Tiede (Altbau/old
building); Gerber + Partner
(Umbau/alterations); Max Dudler, Zürich/Berlin (Erweiterung/
extension)

🚧 1878, 1996-1999

S.54: Blick von der Invalidenstra-
ße/View from Invalidenstrasse
S.55: Grundriß, links: Neubau,
rechts: Altbau/Ground plan,
left: new building /right:
old building

bringt, zwängt ersterer vier zusammen. An Großzügig-
keit schließlich unterbietet auch der neue Innenhof den
alten: er ist nicht erst auf Traufhöhe, sondern schon über
dem Erdgeschoß überglast. Zudem zerteilen den flachen
Raum drei Besprechungssäle. Funktional begründen
sich diese Reduktionen aus der Tatsache, daß Dudlers
Gebäude ein reiner Verwaltungsbau ist, während im
Tiede-Trakt die repräsentativen Räume der Leitungs-
ebene unterkommen.

Doch die Erweiterung stellt nicht nur die Arbeitsfähigkeit des Ministeriums sicher, sie bietet auch der Öffentlichkeit stadträumlichen Gewinn: Am Schwarzen Weg
wurde das Flußbett der Panke, die das Grundstück lange
nur unterirdisch querte, wieder geöffnet. Durch diesen
Kunstgriff wurden zugleich die sicherheitsrelevanten Bereiche des Ministeriums vom öffentlichen Invalidenpark
getrennt.

Als mit der Planung des Projekts begonnen wurde, ahnte
niemand, daß das Verkehrsministeriium dereinst mit
dem Bauressort verschmolzen würde. Gleichwohl hatte
Max Dudler schon im Wettbewerb eine zweite Extension
vorgesehen. Sie zu realisieren, wurde beschlossen; die Invalidenstraße wird der Standort des neuen „Infrastruk-
turministeriums"sein. (hwh)

inner courtyard is also less generous than the old one – it
is glazed not just from the eaves height but from above
the ground floor. And the low space is broken up by
three conference halls. These reductions are functional,
resulting from the fact that Dudler's building is a purely
administrative building, whereas the Tiede building
accommodates the representation rooms of the man-
agerial level.

But the extension not only ensures that the ministry is
able to function, it also offers a gain in urban quality for
the public: on Schwarzer Weg the river bed of the Panke,
which only crossed the land below ground level for
many years, has been opened up again. And this strata-
gem also enabled the security-sensitive areas of the ministry to be separated from the public "Invalidenpark".

When the planning of the project began, nobody sus-
pected that the Ministry of Transport would later be mer-
ged with the Ministry of Building. Nevertheless, Max
Dudler envisaged a second extension even at the competition stage. It has now been decided that this extension will be built. Invalidenstrasse will be the location of
the new "Ministry of Infrastructure". (hwh)

Auswärtiges Amt / The Foreign Office

 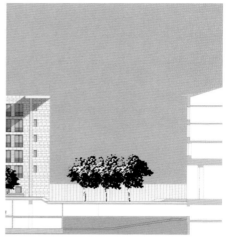

Der Erweiterungsbau der ehemaligen Reichsbank war das erste große Gebäude, das unter nationalsozialistischer Herrschaft in Berlin gebaut wurde. Das Haus am Friedrichswerder im ehemaligen Bankenviertel ist baulicher Nachfolger des Münzgebäudes von 1871. Zwar hat es 1933 einen Wettbewerb gegeben, an dem auch „Meister der Moderne" teilnahmen, Hitler entschied sich jedoch für eine Direktvergabe an den Reichsbankbaudirektor Heinrich Wolff, der seinen Entwurf außer Konkurrenz eingereicht hatte. Erst 1939 wurde das Gebäude bezogen. Es markiert den Umbruch der 30er Jahre, denn sein enormes Volumen vereint moderne Architekturelemente, wie die horizontale Fensterteilung, einen relativ hohen Glasanteil in den Fassaden sowie die Stahlskelettbauweise, mit einer innovativen Konstruktion für die Oberlichter der Kassenhallen. Andererseits trägt es schon Elemente der „Nazi-Architektur", wie die Anordnung der Räume um eine Zentralachse und den verschwenderischen Gebrauch von Naturstein. Die „modernen" gekrümmten, dem Straßenverlauf folgenden Seitenfassaden, stehen in Kontrast zur neoklassizistischen Schaufassade und einem geplanten Säulenwandelgang zu beiden Seiten.

Das Gebäude wurde seit 1959 vom ZK der SED genutzt. Beim Innenausbau wurden Möbel der Werkstätten Hellerau verwendet. Glasflächen wurden zugemauert, die Lichtdecken der Hallen verschlossen und dem Bau damit fast alle Qualitäten genommen: War die Reichsbank mit ihrer großen Ehrenhalle für repräsentative Funktionen konzipiert worden, nutzte die Machtzentrale der DDR das Haus unter umgekehrten Vorzeichen. Das Gebäude schloß sich vollständig von seiner Umgebung ab. Pomp wurde in den spießig-plüschigen Innenräumen nicht ausgebreitet.

The extension of the former Reichsbank was the first large building that was built under National Socialist rule in Berlin. The building on Friedrichswerder in the former banking district is the architectural successor to the "Münze" (1871). Although there was a competition in 1933 in which several "masters of Modernism" participated, Hitler decided to award the commission directly to the Reichsbank director of building, Heinrich Wolff, who had submitted his design outside the competition. The building was not occupied until 1939. It marked the changes of the 1930s because its enormous volume combined modern architectural elements such as horizontal separation of the windows, a relatively high proportion of glass in the facades and the steel skeleton structure with an innovative design for the skylights in the cashier halls. On the other hand, it already bore elements of Nazi architecture such as the arrangement of the rooms around a central axis and the lavish use of natural stone. The "modern" side facades, which are curved to follow the road, contrast with the neo-classical front facade and a planned column ambulatory on both sides.

From 1959 the building was used by the Central Committee of the ruling SED Communist party. Furniture from the Hellerau workshops was used in the interior. Glass surfaces were bricked over, the skylights of the halls were closed, and thus the building was robbed of almost all its architectural features. Whereas the Reichsbank, with its large hall of honour, was designed for impressive functions, the power centre of the GDR used the building in the opposite way. The building closed itself off completely from the surrounding area, and there was no pomp in the drab plush interior.

Werderscher Markt, 10117 Berlin (Mitte)

Heinrich Wolff (Altbau/old building); Hans Koll- hoff, Berlin (Umbau/alterations); Müller Reimann Architekten, Berlin (Neubau/new building)

1939, 1997-1999

S. 56 links/left: Erweiterungsbau Reichsbank, dreißiger Jahre/Ex- tension of Reichsbank, 1930s S. 56 rechts/right: Schnitt/Cross section; S.57: Ansicht Neubau/ View of the new building

Das Auswärtige Amt bezog nicht nur die ehemalige Reichsbank-Erweiterung, sondern auch einen benach- barten Neubau. Beide Bauten sind unterirdisch mitein- ander verbunden. Der Wettbewerb für den Neubau wurde 1996 ausgeschrieben. Erst nach allgemeiner Empörung über die Strenge des Entwurfs von Max Dudler, der mit dem 1. Preis ausgezeichnet worden war, wurde das junge, mit dem zweiten Preis bedachte Berliner Architektenduo Müller/Reimann mit der weiteren Bearbeitung beauf- tragt. Ihr Entwurf arbeitet mit drei unterschiedlichen Lichthöfen, die aus der Baumasse mit steinernen Fassa- den ausgeschnitten sind. Für die Renovierung des Altbaus hat man sich für den Berliner Architekten Hans Kollhoff entschieden. Sein Konzept sieht eine „dritte Schicht" mit sparsamen Mitteln vor, die den Bestand akzeptiert. Mo- derne Elemente der Reichsbank kommen wieder zum Vorschein. Nur die ursprüngliche Keramikfassade zu den Innenhöfen ließ sich aus Kostengründen nicht wieder- herstellen. Dachgärten auf niedrigeren Gebäudeteilen ermöglichen Mitarbeitern, deren Büros zum Hof hin orientiert sind, einen freundlicheren Ausblick. Als einzi- ges neues Element führt Kollhoff an exponierten Stellen im Haus Farbflächen ein, die er zusammen mit Gerhard Merz entwickelt hat. Kritiker bemängelten, daß mit dem Umbau eine Verharmlosung des Gebäudes einhergehe. Kunsthistoriker schätzen den Wert der Reichsbank hoch ein, weil moderne Elemente noch deutlich zu erkennen sind. Der Neubau verstellt den Blick von der Französi- schen Straße auf die historische Hauptfassade. Leider wird auch die Straße zwischen den beiden Gebäuden für die Öffentlichkeit gesperrt. Auch die Wegeverbindung über die Jungfernbrücke am Spreekanal bleibt vom Aus- wärtigen Amt dauerhaft versperrt.

The Foreign Office did not only move into the former Reichsbank extension, it also occupies an adjacent new building. The two buildings are linked below ground level. The competition for the new building was declar- ed in 1996. It was only after the general criticism of the austerity of the design by Max Dudler, who won the first prize, that the second-placed young Berlin architects Müller/Reimann were commissioned with the further development of the project. Their design works with three different light courtyards which are cut out of the solid building volume with stone facades. The commis- sion for the renovation of the old building was awarded to Hans Kollhoff. His concept envisaged a "third layer" with modest resources which accepts the existing build- ings. Modern elements of the Reichsbank were to be brought to the surface again. But the original ceramic facade facing the inner courtyards could not be restored for reasons of cost. Roof gardens on lower parts of the building gave a more friendly view to staff whose offices face the courtyard. The only new element in Kollhoff's design is the use of colour surfaces in exposed positions in the building, which he developed together with Ger- hard Merz. Critics complain that the alterations made the building harmless. But art historians have a high re- gard for the value of the Reichsbank because the mod- ern elements are still apparent. The new building blocks the view of the historical main facade from Französische Strasse. Unfortunately, the road between the two build- ings will also be closed to the public. And the Foreign Office is also permanently closing the path across the Jungfernbrücke bridge over the Spree canal.

Bundesministerium der Finanzen / Federal Ministry of Finance

Noch 1992 wollte die damalige Bauministerin Adam-Schwaetzer das ehemalige Reichsluftfahrtministerium, das Ernst Sagebiel 1934-1936 errichtet hatte, abreißen und neu bauen: Groß war der Widerstand des Finanzministeriums, in den ersten vollendeten Regierungsneubau der Nazis zu ziehen. Das Bauwerk, dessen gestalterische Härte an keiner Stelle gebrochen und dessen Fassade in über fünfzig Jahren enorm düster geworden war, symbolisierte mehr als nur den Stellenwert, den militärische Luftfahrt im „Dritten Reich" genoß, es schien so finster und übermächtig wie die ganze Nazi-Vergangenheit.

Gleichzeitig war das von der Zimmerzahl damals größte Bürohaus Berlins ob der soliden Bauweise in gutem Zustand, seine 2400 Arbeitsräume entsprachen in etwa dem, was die Behörde benötigte. Ein Gutachten des Architekturbüros Hentrich, Petschnigg & Partner kam zu dem Schluß: „Mit gewissen Einschränkungen ein anpassungsfähiges Gebäude." Aus Pragmatismus beschloß man 1994, es für 250 Millionen herzurichten. Die Denkmalpflege legte fest, daß für Nazi-Bauten keine anderen Grundsätze zu gelten hatten als für Gebäude anderer Epochen. Nicht zeitabhängige Wirkungen wurden konserviert, sondern ursprüngliche Gestalt, wo sie noch vorhanden ist, auch oder gerade, wenn sie steingewordene Ideologie darstellt. So blieb die suggestiv-dunkle Raumfolge Ehrenhof-Säulenhalle-Haupttreppe-Großer Festsaal Kernstück der Anlage. Da sich der Bauherr gleichwohl mehr Licht wünschte, die Denkmalpflege Deckenleuchten aber untersagte, werden nun die Wände indirekt angestrahlt. An Boden und Fassade wurden gesprungene Platten möglichst originalgetreu ersetzt, der Rest gereinigt, wodurch sich das Erscheinungsbild entsprechend aufhellte.

As recently as 1992, the former Minister of Building wanted to pull down and rebuild the former Reich Air Travel Ministry which was built by Ernst Sagebiel in 1934-1936. The Ministry of Finance hotly resisted moving into the first government building completed under Nazi rule. The building, which is unbroken in its austerity of design and had acquired a grimy facade in its over fifty years, symbolised more than just the importance that military air travel had in the "Third Reich" – it seemed to be as sombre and overpowering as the whole of Nazi history.

But the building was also the office building with the greatest number of rooms in Berlin at the time, was solidly built and in good condition, and its 2,400 working rooms were approximately what the ministry needed. An appraisal by the architectural office of Hentrich, Petschnigg & Partner came to the conclusion "with certain restrictions, it is an adaptable building". For pragmatic reasons, it was decided in 1994 to refurbish it for 250 million DM. The monument conservation authority stipulated that the principles for Nazi buildings should be no different than for buildings from other eras. It is not temporary effects that are conserved, but the original form where it is still present, even (and especially) where it represents ideology cast in stone. Thus, the suggestive and dark sequence of the court of honour, portico, main stairs and festival hall remained the heart of the complex. The client wished for more light, but the conservation authority prohibited ceiling lights, so the walls are now indirectly illuminated. Fractured floor and facade slabs are replaced as faithfully to the original as possible and the rest are cleaned, which makes the general appearance brighter.

Leipziger Straße 5-7/
Wilhelmstraße 96
10100 Berlin (Mitte)

Ernst Sagebiel (Altbau/
old building); Hentrich-Petsch-
nigg & Partner (HPP), Berlin
(Umbau/alterations)

1936, 1994-1999

S.58: Sicht von Osten, Modell
1937/View from the east, model
1937
S.59: Fassade Wilhelmstraße/
Facade on Wilhelmstrasse

Der Herrichtung fielen alle Spuren des konfrontativen Umgangs zum Opfer, mit dem die Weiternutzung des Gebäudes in der Teilungszeit legitimiert wurde, als darin neun Ministerien unterkamen und unter anderem die Zentrale Planungskommission die gesamte ostdeutsche Wirtschaft steuerte: Schon unmittelbar nach der Einheit, als das Haus Sitz der Treuhandanstalt war, wurde das Innere der Cafeteria, die Kurt Tausendschön 1960 als provokativen Glaskasten gegen den alten Muschelkalk gestellt hatte, weitgehend überformt. Im Zuge des neuerlichen Umbaus wurden alle Türen, die die DDR zunächst mit Klinken versehen hatte, die sich nicht an den alten Rahmen anpaßten, durch bruchlose Exemplare ersetzt. Der in den siebziger Jahren butterfarben überstrichene Große Festsaal wurde wieder in den Zustand zurückgeführt, den er 1949 hatte, als hier die Verfassung der DDR beschlossen wurde.

Auf eigene baukünstlerische Kraftakte verzichtete die Gegenwart, ging es doch nicht darum, die vorhandene Wirkung den neuen Herren dienstbar zu machen. Im kleinen Festsaal zum Beispiel, der für Konferenzen hergerichtet wurde, legt sich ein Velours-Teppich über den Natursteinboden, auf dem man sich bisher nicht rühren konnte, ohne Lärm zu verursachen und unangenehm aufzufallen. Statt der beiden langen Tafeln, denen das Präsidium einst die Stirn zeigte, gibt es nun einen runden Tisch. Das Heldenepos in ihrem Rücken ersetzt eine Medienwand. Die Botschaft ist eindeutig: Arbeitsfähigkeit ist der Demokratie wichtiger als Repräsentation. (hwh)

The refurbishment removed all traces of the confrontation treatment with which the continued use of the building was legitimised in the GDR period when nine ministries used the building, including the central planning commission which controlled the entire East German economy. Directly after reunification, the building became the headquarters of the government privatisation agency and the interior of the cafeteria, which Kurt Tausendschön had in 1960 provocatively added as a glass box to contrast with the old shell limestone, was already largely disfigured. In the course of the recent alterations, all doors were replaced by uniform models with new handles which did not go with the old frames. The great festival hall, which had been painted in a butter colour in the 1970s, was restored to the condition it had in 1949 when the constitution of the GDR was passed here.

Major feats of architectural aesthetics were omitted in the latest alterations, after all, the concern was to place the existing effect in the service of the new clients. The small festival hall, for example, was refurbished for conferences and now has a velvet carpet on the natural stone floor – previously it was not possible to move on the floor without creating an embarrassing noise. And instead of the two long tables which were end on to the presiding committee, there is now a round table. The heroic epic behind them has been replaced by a media display wall. The message is clear: functionality is more important in a democracy than representation. (hwh)

Bundesministerium für Wirtschaft und Technologie / Federal Ministry of Economic Affairs and Technology

Für das Bundeswirtschaftsministerium wurden im Bezirk Mitte Altbauten aus drei Jahrhunderten hergerichtet und um einen Neubau erweitert.1910 wurde im Garten des Invalidenhauses von 1748 – von dem nur der kleine Invalidenpark erhalten blieb – die kaiserliche „Akademie für das militär-ärztliche Bildungswesen" errichtet. Der Prachtbau an der Invalidenstraße hat zwei Lichthöfe und bot einst Platz für Hörsäle, Labors, Festräume, eine Bibliothek, Dienstwohnungen, Büros, eine Aula, einen großen Speisesaal und ein Internat für 300 Studenten. Er wurde später in „Kaiser-Wilhelm-Akademie" umbenannt. Die Architekten Cremer & Wolffenstein gestalteten die Sandsteinfassade des Hauses im Stil des „friderizianischen Neobarocks" mit einem Mansardendach. Nach dem Ersten Weltkrieg zogen Teile des Reichsarbeitsministeriums in das Gebäude ein. Das Invalidenhaus wurde im Zweiten Weltkrieg so schwer beschädigt, daß von der ehemals dreiflügeligen Anlage nur die beiden Seitenflügel erhalten blieben. Nach Kriegsende unterhielt die Rote Armee bis 1949 ein Lazarett auf dem Gelände. In der ehemaligen Akademie im Vorderhaus tagte zunächst das Oberste Gericht der DDR, während im ehemaligen Internat ein Arbeitsamt unterkam. Die Umnutzung zum Regierungskrankenhaus machte in den sechziger Jahren erhebliche Umbaumaßnahmen notwendig. Mit dem Bau der Berliner Mauer 1961 geriet das Haus in eine städtische Randlage.

Mit der Umzugsentscheidung wählte man das Gelände für den Sitz des Wirtschaftsministeriums, das ursprünglich in das Preußische Herrenhaus und später in die Reichsbank ziehen sollte. Die denkmalgeschützten Gebäude hätten ohnehin saniert werden müssen. Weil der Platz in der alten Akademie nicht reichte, wurde das ehe-

For the Ministry of Economic Affairs, old buildings from three different centuries in the district of Mitte have been restored and a new building added. In 1910, the Imperial "Academy for Military and Medical Education" was set up in the garden of the invalid house dating from 1748 – of which only the small invalids' park has survived. The splendid building on Invalidenstrasse has two light courtyards and provided space for lecture rooms, laboratories, rooms for festive events, a library, apartments, offices, an assembly hall, a large dining room and residential accommodation for 300 students. It was later called the "Emperor Wilhelm Academy". The architects Cremer & Wolffenstein designed the sandstone facade in the style of "Friedrich age neo-baroque" with a mansard roof. After the First World War, parts of the Reich Ministry of Labour moved into the building. The invalids' building was so heavily damaged in the Second World War that only the two side wings of the former three-wing complex survived. After the end of the war, the Red Army maintained a military hospital on the premises until 1949. The former academy in the front building was then used by the Supreme Court of the GDR, whereas an employment exchange occupied the former dormitory accommodation. The conversion to the government hospital in the 1960s made extensive alterations necessary. When the Berlin Wall was built in 1961, the building was situated at the edge of the city.

When the national government decided to move to Berlin, the complex was chosen for the Ministry of Economic Affairs, which was originally designated to move to the Prussian House of Lords and later to the Reichsbank. The buildings in the complex are listed monu-

✉ Invalidenstr. 48/49
Scharnhorststr. 34-37
10115 Berlin (Mitte)

✎ Cremer & Wolffenstein
(Altbau/old building); Thomas
Baumann und Dieter Schnittger,
Berlin (Um- und Neubau/altera-
tions)

🏗 1748, 1910, 1996-2000

S.60: Blick vom Schiffahrtskanal
auf den Neubauteil/View of the
new building from the
Schiffahrtskanal
S.61: Altbau/Old building

malige Invalidenhaus an der Scharnhorststraße mitein-
bezogen, und es entstand zusätzlich ein Neubau. Ziel des
Umbaus war es, möglichst viel vom ursprünglichen Bau-
zustand wiederherzustellen. Die historische Ausstattung
der Repräsentationsräume wurde restauriert und ergänzt, erhaltenswerte Umbauten wurden sichtbar belas-
sen. Das ehemalige Internat eignete sich besonders für
die Büronutzung. Es wurde als erster Bauabschnitt bereits 1994 fertiggestellt.

Im Neubau nach Plänen der Architekten Thomas Baumann und Dieter Schnittger entstanden 400 Büroar-
beitsplätze, sowie eine Kantine auch für die Beschäftigten
des benachbarten Verkehrsministeriums. Er liegt am Ber-
lin-Spandauer Schiffahrtskanal gegenüber dem Hamburger Bahnhof und ergänzt als Mittelteil das historische
städtebauliche Arrangement. In Größe, Form und Fassade ist er am historischen Vorgänger orientiert. Das Sat-
teldach hat auf einer Seite Ziegel und auf der anderen
eine große Photovoltaik-Anlage. Mit der Wiederherstellung der Dreiflügelanlage wurde auch der alte Hof neu
gefaßt. Die Seitenflügel des Invalidenhauses mit ihrer
kleinteiligen Struktur wurden restauriert. Der Mittel-
trakt erhielt innen eine neue Struktur. Im wiederentstan-
denen Ehrenhof an der Scharnhorststraße liegt der
Haupteingang. Am Kanalufer entstand eine öffentliche
Promenade. Das Angebot an repräsentativen Sälen über-
stieg jedoch den Bedarf des Ministeriums, einige Räume
sollen deshalb vermietet werden.

ments and needed refurbishment in any case. As the old
academy did not provide enough space, the former invalids' building in Scharnhorststrasse was included and
a new building was added. The aim of the alteration
work was to restore as much as possible of the original
state. The historical interior of the representation rooms
was restored and supplemented, and alterations worth
preservation were left visible. The former dormitory accommodation was especially suited for use as offices. It
was completed in 1994 after the first phase of the construction work.

The new building to plans by the architects Thomas
Baumann and Dieter Schnittger contains 400 office
workplaces and a canteen and kitchen which also serves
the staff of the adjoining Ministry of Transport. It is on
the Berlin-Spandau shipping canal opposite Hamburger
Bahnhof and is a central element to complete the historical urban development complex. In its size, form and
facade it is based on its historical predecessor. The ridge
roof has tiles on one side and a large photovoltaic instal-
lation on the other. As part of the reconstruction of the
three-wing complex, the old courtyard has also been re-
created. The side wing of the invalids' building with its
small structures has been restored. The central section
has been given a new interior structure. The main entrance is in the reconstructed courtyard of honour in
Scharnhorststrasse. However, there are more splendid
large rooms than the ministry can use, so some rooms
will be let.

Bundesministerium für Familie, Senioren, Frauen und Jugend / Federal Ministry for Family and Youth Affairs

📧 Jägerstraße 9 und Taubenstraße 42-43
10117 Berlin (Mitte)

✏️ Moritz Ernst Lesser und Leopold Stelten; Kayser & Großheim (Altbau/old building); Gibbins, Bultmann und Partner, Berlin (Umbau/alterations)

🏗️ 1896, 1928, 1951, 1999

Altbau Jägerstraße/
Old building Jägerstrasse

Nur die Spitze des Familienministeriums zieht nach Berlin, während der Großteil der 400 Mitarbeiter in Bonn bleibt. Es bezieht zwei Häuser in Mitte.

Der siebengeschossige Verwaltungsblock in der Taubenstraße von Moritz Ernst Lesser und Leopold Stelten ersetzte 1928 zwei niedrigere Häuser. Im Zweiten Weltkrieg schwer beschädigt, wurde er 1951 von Erich Kuhnert als Verkehrsministerium der DDR wieder aufgebaut. Es liegt neben den Häusern der KPMG und dem ehemaligen Haus der deutsch-sowjetischen Freundschaft.

1991 hat der Bund das Haus herrichten lassen. Das Büro Gibbins, Bultmann und Partner erhielt den Auftrag für eine grundlegende Instandsetzung. Die ehemalige Kantine im Souterrain wird zur Bibliothek umgebaut. In der Taubenstraße arbeiten der Minister und die Hälfte der Berliner Mitarbeiter.

Die strenge Lochfassade im Süden zur Straße hin erinnert an die Architektur von Adolf Loos. Die sechsgeschossige Steinfassade hat eine identische Gliederung vom zweiten bis zum sechsten Geschoß. Nur im obersten Geschoß haben die Fenster Rundbögen. Im zweiten Obergeschoß sind die drei Mittelfenster wie ein Erker herausgehoben.

40 weitere Mitarbeiter beziehen ein Haus in der nahegelegenen Jägerstraße. Es wurde 1896 von Kayser & Großheim für einen Bankier errichtet. Nach der Wende wurde es zunächst für das Bundesarbeitsministerium hergerichtet und dabei mit schußsicherem Glas versehen. Zwischen beiden Häusern wird eine ständige Richtfunkverbindung geschaltet. Mit seiner gegliederten Sandsteinfassade mit zwei Erkern und einem Balkon wirkt das Gebäude wie eine Wohnburg.

Only the leadership of the Family Ministry is moving to Berlin, whereas most of the staff of 400 are staying in Bonn. The ministry is moving into two buildings in Mitte. The seven-storey administration block in Taubenstrasse by Moritz Ernst Lesser and Leopold Stelten replaced two lower buildings in 1928. The building was heavily damaged in the Second World War and reconstructed by Erich Kuhnert in 1951 as the Ministry of Transport of the GDR. It is next to the buildings of the KPMG and the former house of German-Soviet friendship.

The German government had the building renovated in 1991. The office of Gibbins, Bultmann and partner was commissioned to carry out thorough repairs. The former canteen in the basement is being converted to a library. The minister and half of the Berlin staff will be based in Taubenstrasse.

The austere perforated facade on the south facing the road is reminiscent of the architecture of Adolf Loos. The six-storey stone facade is identical from the second to the sixth floor. The windows only have round forms on the top floor. On the second floor, the three central windows project like a bay.

40 additional staff members will move into a building in nearby Jägerstrasse. It was built for a banker in 1896 by Kayser & Grossheim. After the fall of the Wall it was initially prepared for the Ministry of Employment and fitted with bullet-proof glass. There will be a permanent direct radio transmission link between the two buildings. With its structured sandstone facade with two bays and a balcony, the building looks like a fortress.

Bundesministerium für Gesundheit / Federal Ministry of Health

Mohrenstraße 62
10117 Berlin (Mitte)

Georg Rathenau (Altbau/old building); Gibbins, Bultmann und Partner, Berlin (Umbau/alterations)

1906, 1999

Blick von der Mohrenstraße/
View from Mohrenstrasse

Der zweite Dienstsitz des Bundesministeriums für Gesundheit wurde mit 50 Mitarbeitern in einem Altbau an der Mohrenstraße / Ecke Glinkastraße in der westlichen Friedrichstadt Mitte eingerichtet. Der Hauptsitz des Ministeriums bleibt in Bonn.

Das viergeschossige Haus diente ehemals als Sitz einer Versicherungsgesellschaft. Im Norden liegt der kleine Garten des spätbarocken Nachbarhauses. Der Kopfbau mit seiner Steinfassade wirkt unauffällig in der Reihe der Geschäftshäuser in der Nachbarschaft. Das Berliner Architekturbüro Gibbins, Bultmann und Partner erhielt den Auftrag zum Umbau.

Ursprünglich stand auf dem Grundstück ein gründerzeitliches Wohnhaus. Es wurde an eine Versicherung veräußert, die es 1906 durch ein großes Verwaltungsgebäude mit Souterrain und vier Vollgeschossen nach einem Entwurf von Georg Rathenau ersetzte. Die Sandsteinfassade war reich geschmückt und hatte Rundbogenfenster. Im zweiten Obergeschoß befand sich eine große herrschaftliche Wohnung, die 1923 zu Büros umfunktioniert wurde. In den dreißiger Jahren wurde das Haus von der Allianz-Versicherung erheblich umgebaut. Nach Brandschäden aus dem Zweiten Weltkrieg wurde das Dachgeschoß abgerissen und neu aufgebaut, darauf entstand ein Holzdach. Die zusätzliche Büroetage verfügt nur über kleine Fassadenfenster und zusätzliche Dachfenster. Die Fassade der Aufstockung wurde ebenfalls in Sandstein ausgeführt. Die Kriegsspuren an den vereinfachten Fassaden wurden beseitigt. Auf der Hofseite wurde die Aufstockung lediglich geputzt und nicht wie die unteren Geschosse gefliest. Zu DDR-Zeiten wurde das Gebäude vom Robotron-Kombinat genutzt.

The auxiliary offices of the Ministry of Health have been set up with a staff of fifty in an old building on the corner of Mohrenstrasse and Glinkastrasse in the western part of Friedrichstadt in Mitte. The main headquarters of the ministry will remain in Bonn.

The four-storey building was formerly used by an insurance company. To the north is a small garden belonging to the low baroque building next door. The end building with its stone facade is unobtrusive in the row of commercial buildings. The Berlin architectural office of Gibbins Bultmann and partner was commissioned with the alteration work.

A building with a four-storey residential section and a two-storey commercial wing dating from the industrial expansion period at the end of the 19th century was sold to an insurance company which, in 1906, built a large administrative building with a basement and four full storeys to a design by Georg Rathenau. The sandstone facade was richly decorated and had round arch windows. On the second floor was a large and splendid apartment which was converted to office space in 1923. The building was drastically altered in the 1930s by the Allianz insurance company. After fire damage in the Second World War, the attic was pulled down and built up again and a wooden roof was added. The extra office storey has small facade windows and additional roof windows. The facade of the raised section was also faced with sandstone. The war damage to the simplified facades was repaired. On the side facing the courtyard, the raised section was only rendered and not tiled like the lower storeys. The building was used by the Robotron collective combine during the GDR period.

Bundesministerium der Verteidigung /
Federal Ministry of Defence

Das Verteidigungsministerium richtet nur seinen zweiten Dienstsitz in Berlin ein. Der vordere Teil des sogenannten Bendlerblocks mit acht Höfen im Bezirk Tiergarten wurde dafür saniert. Die Wahl des Standorts hat symbolische Bedeutung. Denn das Gebäude spielte eine wichtige Rolle in der deutschen Militärgeschichte und gilt auch als Symbol des Widerstands gegen den Nazi-Terror. Es wurde gewählt, weil „die Offiziere um Stauffenberg, die Widerstand gegen Hitler leisteten, Deutschland seine Würde wiedergegeben haben". Es steht also für gute und schlechte Traditionen.

Das fünfgeschossige Gebäude am Landwehrkanal war 1914 als Reichsmarineamt von den Architekten Reinhardt und Süssenguth gebaut worden. Die repräsentative Hauptfassade ist aus Muschelkalk. Hinter dem neobarocken Haupteingang liegt eine große Säulenhalle. Nach dem Ersten Weltkrieg residierte das Reichswehrministerium und später auch das Oberkommando des Heeres und der Kriegsmarine darin. 1938 wurde der Komplex um den „Bendlerblock" am damaligen Tirpitzufer im Norden für den Admiralsstab, das Reichsmarineamt und das Marinekabinett erweitert. Er wurde nach dem Berliner Stadtbaumeister Johann Christoph Bendler benannt. Im Zweiten Weltkrieg war das Gebäude der Sitz von Hitlers Generälen, aber auch die Zentrale der Widerstandskämpfer des 20. Juli 1944, von denen vier im Hof des Gebäudes erschossen wurden. An sie erinnert seit 1954 eine Plastik von Richard Scheibe und die Dauerausstellung „Gedenkstätte deutscher Widerstand".

Der „Bendlerblock" wurde im Krieg schwer beschädigt; die Innenausstattung war fast vollständig verloren. Nach 1945 diente das wiederhergerichtete Haus verschiedenen gewerblichen Nutzern und Bundesbehörden wie der

The Federal Ministry of Defence is only setting up auxiliary offices in Berlin. The front part of the so-called Bendlerblock with eight courtyards in the district of Tiergarten has been renovated for the purpose. The selection of the location is symbolic because the building played a major role in German military history and is regarded as a symbol of resistance to the terror of the Nazis. It was selected because "the officers associated with Stauffenberg, who resisted Hitler, restored the honour of Germany". It stands for both good and bad traditions.

The five-storey building next to the Landwehrkanal was built in 1914 as the Reich Naval Authority by the architects Reinhardt and Süssenguth. The splendid main facade is made of shell limestone. Behind the neobaroque main entrance is a large portico. After the First World War the building was initially used by the Reich Army Ministry and then also by the high command of the army and navy. In 1938 the complex was extended by the addition of the "Bendlerblock" in the street then known as Tirpitzufer in the north for the admiralty, the Reich Naval Authority and the Naval Cabinet. It was named after the chief architect in Berlin, Johann Christoph Bendler. In the Second World War the building was the headquarters of Hitler's generals, but it was also the centre for the resistance fighters of 20th July 1994, four of whom were shot in the building's courtyard. They have been commemorated since 1954 by a memorial sculpture by Richard Scheibe and by the permanent exhibition "German Resistance Memorial Site". The "Bendlerblock" was severely damaged in the war and the interior was almost completely destroyed. After 1945, the restored building was used by various business

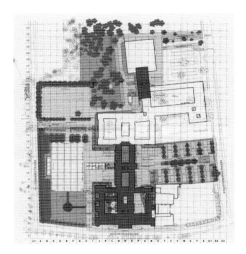

Reichpietschufer 74-76
10785 Berlin (Tiergarten)

Reinhardt und Süßen-
guth (Altbau/old building);
Burckhardt, Emch und Berger,
Berlin/Basel (Umbau/alterations)

1914, 1938, 1997-1999

S.64: Blick vom Landwehrkanal/
View from the Landwehrkanal
S.65: links/left: Lageplan/Site
plan, rechts/right: Eingangspor-
tal am Reichpietschufer/
Entrance from Reichpietschufer

Schuldenverwaltung, dem Aufsichtsamt für das Kredit- und Versicherungswesen und einem Bundesbauamt. Die Mieter mußten für den Umzug des Ministeriums ausziehen. Die Aufsichtsämter für das Kredit- und Versicherungswesen zogen nach Bonn. Bereits 1997 wurden die Freianlagen, ein Hubschrauberlande- und ein Paradeplatz geplant. Die Herrichtung des denkmalgeschützten Gebäudes wurde vom Schweizer Büro Burckhardt, Emch und Berger betreut. Zwei Höfe wurden mit Glas überdacht für das Gästekasino, protokollarische Zwecke und das Besucherzentrum, das von der Stauffenbergstraße aus zugänglich ist. Die Kantine liegt außerhalb des vom Ministerium genutzten Bauteils und wurde ebenfalls neu hergerichtet. Sie versorgt die Mitarbeiter sämtlicher Institutionen im Bendlerblock.

Es wurden neue Fenster in den ca. 400 Büroräumen eingesetzt, die Fassaden gereinigt und die Installationen modernisiert. Zwei Wachhäuser wurden neu errichtet.

Streit gab es um den Zaun. Ein zwei Meter hoher Gitterzaun reicht von der Einfahrt bis zum Hauptportal. Bei Staatsbesuchen wird die Straße durch einen transportablen Steckzaun gesichert. Der Plan, einen im Gehweg versenkbaren Zaun zu errichten, wurde verworfen.

Nur etwa jeder zehnte der rund 3000 Mitarbeiter des Ministeriums wird am zweiten Dienstsitz tätig sein, darunter aber die politische Leitung: Minister, Staatssekretäre, Pressestab und der Militärattaché. Das Ministerium benutzt nur zwei Drittel der Anlage, die übrige Fläche steht anderen Bundesinstitutionen zur Verfügung.

users and national authorities like the debts administration, the federal banking and insurance authority and a federal construction authority. The tenants had to move out to make way for the ministry. The supervisory authorities for banking and insurance moved to Bonn. The outdoor facilities, a helicopter landing site and a parade ground were planned in 1997.

The refurbishment of the listed building was supervised by the Swiss office of Burckhardt, Emch and Berger. Two courtyards were fitted with glass roofs for the visitors' canteen and protocol purposes and for the visitors' centre which is accessible from Stauffenbergstrasse. The canteen is outside the part of the building used by the ministry and has also been refurbished. It is used by the staff of all institutions in the Bendlerblock.

New windows have been fitted in the roughly 400 office rooms, the facades have been cleaned and the installations modernised. Two new guardhouses have been erected.

There were disputes about the fence. A two metre high trellis fence reaches from the vehicle entrance to the main portal. The street is secured by a transportable temporary fence for state visits. The plan to build a fence that could be anchored in the pavement was rejected.

Only about ten per cent of the approximately 3000 staff of the ministry will work in the auxiliary offices, but they include the political leadership: the minister, the state secretaries, the press staff and the military attaché. The ministry only uses two thirds of the complex, the rest is available for other government institutions.

Bundesministerium für Bildung und Forschung / Federal Ministry of Education and Science

Hannoversche Straße 30
10114 Berlin (Mitte)

Hans Scharoun (Umbau/
alterations 1949); Jourdan Müller, Frankfurt (Modernisierung
und Anbau/extension)

1999 - 2000

Altbau Hannoversche Straße/
Old building Hannoversche
Strasse

Ausgerechnet das „Zukunfts"-Ministerium muß in Berlin in dem ältesten aller Regierungsaltbauten residieren. An der Hannoverschen Straße ließ Friedrich der Große die „Caserne der reitenden Garde-Artillerie" errichten. Ihrem einzig überlebenden Bau verlieh Hans Scharoun unmittelbar nach dem Zweiten Weltkrieg die Gestalt einer modernistisch-unschuldig weißen Kiste. Das Dach des Hauses mit der Nummer 30 erweiterte er um Meisterateliers, in denen das „Institut für Bauwesen" 1951 die Stalinallee zeichnen ließ. In ganz anderer Formensprache entstand in den siebziger Jahren ein lichter Pavillon im Hof, nachdem die „Ständige Vertretung der Bundesrepublik Deutschland in der Deutschen Demokratischen Republik" das Gebäude übernommen hatte.

Um aus diesem Ensemble die unverwechselbare Adresse des Ministeriums für Bildung und Wissenschaft zu machen, blieb es nicht bei der schlichten Renovierung, die für alle anderen Berliner Zweitsitze genügen mußte. 1998 wurde das Frankfurter Büro Jourdan Müller beauftragt, die heterogenen Teile mit einem Anbau zusammenzubinden, der so „zukunftsweisend" sein sollte wie die Projekte der dort tätigen Beamten. Nach ihren Vorstellungen wird das Haupthaus als einziger Bundesbau im Nachkriegszustand erhalten. Ein neuer konstruktivistischer Riegel, der an seiner Westseite in die Tiefe des Grundstücks ragt und den zu entsiegelnden Hof faßt, gibt sich noch spektakulärer: Das oberste Geschoß seiner Stirnfassade kragt weit aus, der Rest ruht nur auf zwei schräg gestellten Stützen. Wie jeder Bundesbau ist er mit ökologischer Haustechnik ausgestattet, die aber nirgendwo so offen wie hier zur Schau gestellt wird.

(hwh)

Ironically, the "Ministry of the Future" occupies the oldest of all the old government buildings in Berlin. As early as 1800, Friedrich the Great had the "barracks of the riding artillery guards" built on Hannoversche Strasse. Directly after the Second World War, Hans Scharoun gave the sole surviving building the form of a modernistic and innocent white box. He extended the roof of building number 30 by adding crafts studios in which the "Institute for Building" drew the plans of Stalinallee in 1951. In a completely different formal language, a bright pavilion was erected in the courtyard after the "Permanent Delegation of the Federal Republic of Germany in the German Democratic Republic" had taken over the building.

The transformation of this ensemble into the unmistakable address of the Ministry of Education and Science involved more than the simple renovation which had to suffice for all other external ministry offices in Berlin. In 1998, the Frankfurt office of Jourdan Müller was commissioned to link the heterogeneous parts with an extension which was to be as "progressive" as the projects of the officials who work there. In their design, the main building is the only government building that is preserved in its post-war condition. A new structure to the west, which extends the depth of the plot and encloses the courtyard, in which the sealed floor is to be restored as soil, looks even more spectacular. The highest storey of its end facade projects dramatically, and the rest is supported only on two oblique pillars. Like every government building it has ecological utility services, although they are shown more openly here than anywhere else.

(hwh)

Bundesministerium für Ernährung, Landwirtschaft und Forsten /
Federal Ministry for Food, Agriculture and Forestry

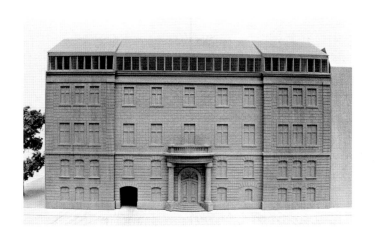

Wilhelmstraße 54
10117 Berlin (Mitte)

Carl Vohl (Altbau/old building); Elisabeth Rüthnick, Berlin (Umbau/alterations)

1898, 1999-2000

Front zur Wilhelmstraße/
View from Wilhelmstrasse

Nur ein Zehntel der etwa tausend Mitarbeiter des Landwirtschaftsministeriums zieht nach Berlin. Der zweite Dienstsitz liegt auf dem Grundstück des ehemaligen Palais Bleichröder in der Wilhelmstraße in Mitte. Es ist einer der wenigen erhaltenen Altbauten in der ehemaligen „Regierungsstraße". Das Haus wurde Ende des 19. Jahrhunderts vom preußischen Staat erworben und sukzessive dem benachbarten Justizministerium einverleibt. Das baufällige Gebäude wurde schließlich abgerissen und 1898 durch einen neobarocken Bau von Carl Vohl für das geheime Zivilkabinett des Kaisers ersetzt. Im Erdgeschoß befanden sich Büroräume, darüber Wohnungen und Archive. Zwei Seitenflügel und ein Quergebäude umschließen einen Innenhof. Im Zentrum liegt das Marmortreppenhaus. Die symmetrischen Natursteinfassaden werden durch zwei Eckrisalite mit drei Rundbogenfenstern akzentuiert. In der Mitte liegen das zweigeschossige Hauptportal und ein Balkon. Das Mansarddach hatte Rundgauben und Ziergiebel. 1920 bezog der preußische Ministerpräsident hier eine Dienstwohnung. Bis 1932 wohnte der Präsident des preußischen Staatsrates, Konrad Adenauer, in dem Haus. Nach 1933 wurde es von verschiedenen Mitgliedern der nationalsozialistischen Regierung, darunter auch Rudolf Heß, genutzt. Das Haus wurde im Zweiten Weltkrieg beschädigt und vereinfacht wiederaufgebaut. Die Seitengebäude sind freie Rekonstruktionen der Nachkriegszeit. Die unvollendet gebliebene Dachaufstockung aus den achziger Jahren wird durch ein neues Dachgeschoß ersetzt. Die Straßenfassade wird restauriert. Beim Umbau sollen alle Phasen des Baus dokumentiert werden. Die Architekten wollen die „Würde des Hauses erhalten und akzentuieren".

Only a tenth of the approximately one thousand employees of the Ministry of Agriculture are moving to Berlin. The auxiliary offices are on the land of the former Palais Bleichröder in Wilhelmstrasse in Mitte. It is one of the few surviving old buildings in the former "government street". The building was purchased by the Prussian state at the end of the 19th century and successively integrated into the adjoining Ministry of Justice. The derelict building was finally pulled down and replaced in 1898 by a neo-baroque building by Carl Vohl for the Emperor's secret civil cabinet. The ground floor contained offices, and the higher floors had apartments and archives. Two wings and a transverse building enclose a courtyard. At the centre is the marble staircase. The symmetrical natural stone facades are accentuated by two corner projections with three round arch windows. The two-storey main portal and a balcony are in the middle. The mansard roof had round gable widows and decorative gable ends. In 1920, the Prussian Minister President moved into an official apartment here. Until 1932 the President of the Prussian state council, Konrad Adenauer, lived in the building. After 1993 it was used by various figures of the National Socialist government, including Rudolf Hess. The building was damaged in the Second World War and rebuilt in simplified form. The side buildings are free post-war reconstructions. The incomplete raised roof from the 1980s is being replaced by a new attic. The street facade is being restored. All phases of the alteration work will be documented. The architects wish to "preserve and accentuate the dignity of the building".

Bundesministerium für Umwelt, Naturschutz und Reaktorsicherheit / Federal Ministry of the Environment, Nature Protection and Nuclear Safety

Alexanderplatz 6
10100 Berlin (Mitte)

Heinz Mehlan, Emil Leibold, Peter Skujin

1969

Eingang Alexanderplatz/
Entrance from Alexanderplatz

Kein Ministeriums findet seinen Berliner Amtssitz in einem so zentralen Baustein der DDR-Hauptstadtplanung wie das Umweltressort. Zur Miete residiert es im ehemaligen „Haus der Elektroindustrie", das den östlichen Abschluß des in der Nachkriegszeit geschaffenen Zentrumbandes bildet. Wie einst sein westliches Pendant besteht es aus einem riesigen Riegel. 220 Meter lang und 38 Meter hoch gibt er mit einer schlicht gehaltenen Fassade der freien Baukörperkomposition des Alexanderplatzes den nötigen Halt. Von der Horizontalstruktur des mit grünlichen Sicherheitglas ausgefachten Aluminiumrasters setzen sich lediglich die drei Erschließungskerne rot ab, die mit gefalzten Paneelen verkleidet sind, wie sie auch am Centrum-Warenhaus (*Kaufhof*) oder am inzwischen abgerissenen DDR-Außenministerium Verwendung fanden.

Im Zuge der allgemeinen Entwertung dieses städtebaulichen Erbes gewannen Hans Kollhoff und Helga Timmermann 1993 den Alexanderplatz-Wettbewerb mit dem Vorschlag, alle Nachkriegsbauten durch 13 Blöcke zu ersetzen, aus denen 150 Meter hohe Wolkenkratzer wachsen sollten. Während die meisten übrigen Eigentümer inzwischen die städtebaulichen Verträge unterzeichneten, um diese Idee umzusetzen, denkt die Treuhand-Liegenschafts-Gesellschaft, der das „Haus der Elektroindustrie" heute gehört, angesichts der guten Vermietungslage nicht an Veränderungen. Sie dürfte sich zukünftig noch verbessern, hat doch Ressortchef Trittin bereits angekündigt, mehr als die bisher 180 Mitarbeiter an den zweiten Dienstsitz Berlin zu holen. Mit dem Mietobjekt dürfte diese Abweichung vom Bonn-Berlin-Gesetz weitaus leichter durchsetzbar sein als mit dem ursprünglich ins Auge gefaßten Neubau am Schiffbauerdamm. (hwh)

No other ministry has its Berlin offices in such a central feature of the former GDR capital city as the Ministry of the Environment. It is in rented accommodation in the former "House of the Electrical Industry" which forms the eastern end of the central ribbon of buildings erected after the war. Like its former western counterpart, it consists of an enormous long block measuring 220 metres in length and 38 metres in height and has a plain facade which gives stability to the free composition of Alexanderplatz. The horizontal structure of the aluminium grid filled with greenish safety glass contrasts with the three red vertical access towers which are faced with folded panels such as those used for the "Centrum" department store *(Kaufhof)* and in the former DDR Foreign Ministry building which has now been demolished. In the course of the general debasement of this urban development heritage, Hans Kollhoff and Helga Timmermann won the 1993 Alexanderplatz competition with their suggestion that all post-war buildings should be replaced by 13 blocks out of which skyscrapers with a height of 150 metres should rise. Whereas most other property owners have now signed the urban development contracts to implement this idea, the trustee property management company which now owns the "House of the Electrical Industry" has no intention of making any changes because of the good tenancy position. The tenancy situation is likely to improve still further in future because minister Trittin has already announced that he proposes to move more than the present 180 staff members to Berlin. In rented accommodation, this deviation from the Bonn-Berlin Act should be far easier to implement than with the originally planned new building on Schiffbauerdamm. (hwh)

Bundesministerium für wirtschaftliche Zusammenarbeit und Entwicklung / Federal Ministry of Economic Cooperation and Development

Stresemannstr. 92-102
10163 Berlin (Kreuzberg)

Bielenberg & Moser, Hans Schmuckler, Otto Firle (Altbau/old building); Wolfgang Schäfer, Berlin (Umbau/alterations)

1927, 1931, 1935, 1999-2000

Blick vom Askanischen Platz/
View from Askanischer Platz

Das Europa-Haus in der Stresemannstraße ist der zweite Dienstsitz des Entwicklungshilfeministeriums. Das Ensemble besteht aus drei Teilen. Das viergeschossige „Deutschlandhaus" an der Ecke am Askanischen Platz und die zweigeschossige Ladenpassage wurden 1927 von Bielenberg & Moser entworfen. Hans Schmuckler hat 1935 beide Bauteile um ein bzw. zwei Stockwerke erhöht. Der Flachbau wurde jedoch bei der Wiederherstellung 1966 beseitigt. Das elfgeschossiges Hochhaus im Stil der Neuen Sachlichkeit wurde 1931 nach amerikanischem Vorbild in Stahlskelettbauweise errichtet. Otto Flirle hat es als eines der ersten Hochhäuser in Berlin entworfen. Es hat einen offenen Lichthof und Flachdach. Berühmt wurde es durch sein 35 Meter langes Reklameschild und den 15 Meter hohen Lichtturm auf dem Dach.

Die originale „gestreifte" Fenstergliederung wurde 1990 wiederhergestellt. Im Norden wurde im Zuge der Umbauten für das Ministerium eine neue Vorfahrt mit Windfang und Foyer eingerichtet. Im 8. und 9. Obergeschoß liegen die Büros für die ca. 70 Mitarbeiter des Ministeriums, im 10. der Leitungsbereich und im 11. Obergeschoß schließlich ein Konferenzsaal sowie eine Cafeteria. Die Fassade wurde dafür bündig nach außen verschoben. In den unteren Stockwerken ist genügend Platz für eine etwaige Expansion des Bundesministeriums in Berlin.

The Europe building in Stresemannstrasse is the auxiliary building of the ministry of development aid. The ensemble consists of three parts. The four-storey "Deutschlandhaus" on the corner of Askanischer Platz and the two-storey shopping arcade were designed by Bielenberg & Moser in 1927. In 1935 Hans Schmuckler increased the height of the two buildings by one and two storeys respectively. But the low building was demolished in the restoration in 1966. The eleven-storey tower building in the New Rationalist style was built in 1931 as a steel framework structure following the American model. Otto Flierle designed it as one of the first tower buildings in Berlin. It has an open light courtyard and a flat roof. It became famous because of its 35 metre long advertising sign and the 15 metre high light tower on the roof. The original "striped" window pattern was restored in 1990. In the course of alterations for the ministry, a new vehicle entrance was created in the north with a wind screen and foyer. The offices for the 70 ministry staff are on the 8th and 9th floor, and the leadership are on the 10th floor. The 11th floor contains a conference room and the cafeteria. To create space, the facade was moved flush outwards. The lower storeys have sufficient space for any expansion of the ministry in Berlin.

SPD-Bundeszentrale (Willy-Brandt-Haus) / SPD Headquarters (Willy Brandt Building)

Wilhelmstraße 141/
Stresemannstraße 28
10963 Berlin (Kreuzberg)

Helge Bofinger & Partner, Wiesbaden/Berlin

1993-1996

links/left: Blick von Süden/
View from the south
rechts/right: Grundriß EG/
Ground plan, ground floor

Die Bonner Zentrale der Sozialdemokraten stand für den Wandel der SPD von der Arbeiter- zur Volkspartei. Entsprechend war sie als eine offene Landschaft konzipiert, in der Vorstandssitzungen und Pressekonferenzen quasi auf der Straße, unter den Augen der Öffentlichkeit stattfanden. In Berlin läßt sich von diesem Geist nichts wiederfinden. Der Entwurf von Helge Bofinger ist ein kompakter Block. Blaugetönte Scheiben erschweren den Einblick. Der Parteivorsitzende thront im obersten Geschoß in der Spitze des dreieckigen Hauses. Auf verschlungenen Wegen erreicht man das Herzstück des Hauses erst, nachdem man einige Sperren passiert hat. Im glasgedeckten Atrium herrscht wie überall unterkühlt geschäftsmäßige Atmosphäre. Dieses für Bürobauten typische Bauteil ist durch seine Tortenstück-Kubatur eher als Repräsentationsraum denn als Veranstaltungssaal nutzbar. Alles in allem drückt die SPD mit ihrem hauptstädtischen Hauptquartier, das sie schon 1996 einweihte, als ihre Konkurrenten kaum die Standortfrage geklärt hatten, vor allem ihren Anspruch aus, in einem Zeitalter, da von Politikern vor allem Manager-Qualitäten verlangt werden, Regierungspartei zu sein.

Traditionell ist der Standort in der südlichen Friedrichstadt. Ganz in der Nähe, auf dem Stadtplan quasi an der Friedrichstraße gespiegelt, findet sich zudem immer noch das ehemalige „Haus des Deutschen Metallarbeiterverbandes", das Erich Mendelsohn 1931 fertigstellte und dessen dynamische Horizontalität und helle Steinverkleidung Helge Bofinger unübersehbar zitiert. (hwh)

The Bonn headquarters of the Social Democrats stood for the transition of the SPD from a workers' party to a people's party. It was therefore designed as an open party centre in which executive committee meetings and press conferences were held under the gaze of the public, almost on the street. Nothing of this spirit can be found in Berlin. The design by Helge Bofinger is a compact block. Blue tinted windows reduce the building's transparency. The party chairman resides on the top floor at the point of the triangular building. To reach the heart of the building, the visitor must pass through a labyrinth and several barriers. The atrium under a glass roof has the same cool business-like atmosphere as other buildings. This part of the building with its pie-segment shape is better suited for representation purposes than as a venue for official events. The national SPD headquarters, which was opened in 1996 when the other parties were still deciding on their location, expresses the party's claim to be a party of government in an age in which politicians need above all to show management qualities.

The location in the south of the Friedrichstadt district is traditional. Nearby, and almost as a mirror image on the other side of Friedrichstrasse on the map, stands the "metalworkers' trade union building" completed by Erich Mendelsohn in 1931 – which Helge Bofinger obviously refers to in its dynamic horizontal dimension and the light-coloured stone facade. (hwh)

CDU–Bundesgeschäftsstelle / National headquarters of the CDU

Klingelhöferstraße 8/
Ecke Corneliusstraße
10785 Berlin (Tiergarten)

Petzinka, Pink und Partner, Düsseldorf

1999-2000

Blick von der Kreuzung Klingelhöferstraße/View from the junction of Klingelhöferstrasse

Die CDU errichtete ihre Bundesgeschäftsstelle auf einer Ecke des Tiergarten-Dreiecks. Sie war die letzte Partei, die ihren Sitz nach Berlin verlegte. Die konservative Partei sah sich im „futuristischen" Entwurf der Architekten Petzinka, Pink und Partner am besten repräsentiert, der sich in einem Workshopverfahren durchsetzen konnte. Das sechsgeschossige, betont dynamische Gebäude ragt wie der Bug eines Dampfers über die spitze Straßenecke am Tiergartenrand. Das Gebäude hat eine über fünf Etagen reichende zweite Glasfassade, die wie ein Wintergarten energiesparend wirken soll. Das innere Haus liegt wie ein Oval in der unregelmäßigen Raute des Grundstücks und öffnet sich zu einem großen Atrium.

Die Traufhöhe war mit 18 Meter vorgegeben. Die Architekten gingen über die Vorgaben hinaus, in dem sie das stromlinienförmige „innere Haus" zwei Geschosse höher planten. Dort liegen die Räume des Parteivorstands. Von der verglasten Galerie fällt der Blick in die Räume darunter. Im steinernen Sockel der CDU-Zentrale sind die Verwaltung und die Sitzungssäle untergebracht. Im Erdgeschoß liegen Räume für Veranstaltungen und Pressekonferenzen, im vierten Stock tagt der Bundesvorstand und im sechsten das Parteipräsidium. In der „gläsernen Birne" der christdemokratischen Bundeszentrale haben 150 Mitarbeiter ihren Arbeitsplatz.

Eine Immobilienfirma hat das Gelände, auf dem sich in der unmittelbaren Nachbarschaft auch die Botschaften von Luxemburg und Malaysia befinden, entwickelt und das Haus an die CDU verkauft.

The CDU set up its national party headquarters on a corner of the Tiergarten Triangle. It was the last political party to move its headquarters to Berlin. Although the party is conservative, it saw itself best represented in the "futuristic" design by the architects Petzinka and Pink which was the winner in a workshop process. The dynamic six-storey building towers like the bow of a ship over the pointed street corner on the edge of the Tiergarten. The building has a second glass facade extending over five storeys which acts like an energy-saving winter garden. The inner building has an oval ground plan on the irregular quadrilateral plot and opens up to a large atrium.

The eaves height was fixed at 18 metres. The architects went beyond this specified height by planning the streamlined "inner building" two storeys higher. These extra storeys contain the rooms of the party executive. The glass-clad gallery provides a view of the rooms below. The stone pedestal of the CDU headquarters contains the administration and the committee rooms. The ground floor has rooms for special events and press conferences, the national party executive meets on the fourth floor and the presiding committee on the sixth floor. The "glass pear" of the national Christian Democrat headquarters accommodates a staff of 150.

A property development company developed the land, which also contains the embassies of Luxembourg and Malaysia, and sold the building to the CDU.

Konrad–Adenauer–Stiftung / Konrad Adenauer Foundation

Tiergartenstraße 35
10785 Berlin

Thomas van den Valentyn, Köln

1996-1999

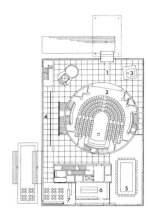

links/left: Längsseite von Westen
/Long side from the west
rechts/right: Grundriß 1.OG /
Ground plan, first floor

Das Gebäude der Konrad-Adenauer-Stiftung ist kaum halb so groß wie das ihrer sozialdemokratischen Konkurrentin. Während alle übrigen parteinahen Stiftungen Berlin zu ihrem Hauptsitz machen, baute die der CDU vis-à-vis deren Bundeszentrale nur eine Außenstelle. Die Residenz für gerade 30 der insgesamt 370 Mitarbeiter ist klein, aber fein. Kein Detail, dem in der Geschichte der modernen Architektur nicht schon ein eigenes Kapitel gewidmet worden wäre: Die Eingangstreppen gemahnen mit ihren scheinbar schwebenden Steinplatten an das Farnsworth House von Mies van der Rohe. Der Garten auf dem Dach, das wie bei Le Corbusier als fünfte Fassade ausgebildet ist, erschließt eine Rampe, die sich bereits in der Villa Savoye desselben Architekten findet. Klassisch ist nur die geometrische Ordnung des Herzstücks des Hauses: Der quadratische, zweigeschossige Veranstaltungssaal ist in einen kreisrunden, 20 Meter durchmessenden Betonzylinder eingeschnitten; wie in einem anatomischen Theater kann eine knapp 200köpfige Zuhörerschaft darin in U-Form Platz nehmen. Understatement strahlen auch die Werkstoffe aus: Innen finden sich heller Naturstein, dunkles Eichenparkett und helle Einbauten aus Ahornholz neben Sichtbeton und monochromen Wänden. Außen dominiert glattes Travertin. Wie bei Adolf Loos gibt die 40 x 28 x 13 Meter große Box nichts von ihrem Innenleben preis. Bis auf eine umlaufenden Glasattika, hinter der die Büros liegen, ist sie nahezu geschlossen. Auch wenn die an der Klingelhöferstraße geplante, schlanke Büroscheibe einmal realisiert werden sollte, dürfte der Eindruck nicht offener ausfallen. In jedem Fall könnte der Kontrast zur SPD-Stiftung, deren nicht halb so exklusiver Bau sich dem Volk geradezu entgegenwirft, kaum stärker ausfallen. (hwh)

The building of the Konrad Adenauer Foundation is hardly half the size of its Social Democratic counterpart. Whereas all other party-related foundations made their headquarters in Berlin, the CDU only set up a branch office opposite its national headquarters. The premises for just 30 of the foundation's 370 employees is small but attractive. There is hardly any detail that has not been worthy of its own chapter in the history of modern architecture. The entrance steps, with their apparently hovering stone slabs, are reminiscent of Farnsworth House by Mies van der Rohe. The garden of the roof, which is designed as a fifth facade like gardens by Le Corbusier, is reached by a ramp like the one in Villa Savoye by the same architect. The only classical element is the geometrical structure of the central feature in the building, the square two-storey main hall which is cut into a circular concrete cylinder with a diameter of twenty metres; the auditorium for almost 200 is arranged in a U shape, like an anatomy theatre. The materials also express understatement: the interior is made up of light-coloured natural stone, dark oak parquet floors, light fittings of maple with exposed concrete and monochrome walls. The exterior is dominated by the smoothness of travertine stone. Like a design by Adolf Loos, the box of 40 by 28 by 13 metres reveals nothing of its interior. It is almost a closed surface apart from a surrounding glass attic behind which there are offices. Even if the slender office block that is planned on Klingenhöferstrasse is built, it will not give the complex a more open atmosphere. In any case, the contrast with the SPD foundation, which is far less grand but throws itself wide open to the people, could hardly be more drastic. (hwh)

Friedrich-Ebert-Stiftung / Friedrich Ebert Foundation

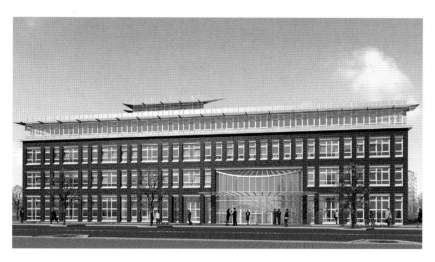

Hiroshimastr. 17-25
10785 Berlin (Tiergarten)

Fritz Novotny, Arthur Mähner, Volkhard Weber (vormals Bonn/formerly Bonn) mit Novotny Mähner & Assoziierte, Berlin

1998-2000

Blick von Westen/
View from the west

Schließt man von der Baukunst auf die Werte ihrer Auftraggeber, gelingt kaum einer Institution der Umzug vom Rhein an die Spree so mühelos wie der Friedrich-Ebert-Stiftung. Verantwortlich dafür sind die Architekten: Bekannt wurde das Büro, das damals noch Novotny Mähner und Assoziierte hieß, mit dem Entwurf für die SPD, also jener Partei, der die Friedrich-Ebert-Stiftung nahe steht. Deren Bonner Bundeszentrale gestalteten die Offenbacher in den siebziger Jahren als offenes Haus, in dem sich Vorstandssitzung und Pressekonferenzen unter den Augen der Öffentlichkeit quasi auf der Straße abspielten. Sein „hemdsärmeliges" Erscheinungsbild wurde stilprägend für die gesamte rheinische Republik. Allein diese Formlosigkeit läßt man nun in Bonn, die inhaltliche Transparenz bleibt in Berlin sehr wohl erhalten: Das naturstein- und klinkerverkleidete Stiftungshaus zwischen Hiroshima- und Hildebrandtstraße ist nur an drei Seiten so streng und steinern, wie es die Stadt verlangt. Dagegen öffnet sich der Quader, in dem auf 1300 Quadratmetern die Büros der Mitarbeiter liegen, zum Landwehrkanal mit großer, gläserner Geste. Aus dieser Schauseite stößt ein kreisrunder und komplett verglaster Vortragssaal für 500 Zuhörer. Er ist Teil eines Veranstaltungsbereichs, dessen mobile Trennwände sich aufklappen lassen, so daß sich das ganze Erdgeschoß in eine lichte, mit über 3000 Quadratmeter beeindruckend große Tagungslandschaft verwandelt. Direkter kann man sich an sein Publikum kaum wenden. Die Ironie der Geschichte liegt darin, daß die aus Bonn gewohnte Offenheit architektonisch in Berlin die große Ausnahme darstellt. (hwh)

If we deduce the client's values from their architecture, hardly any institutions are managing the move from the Rhine to the Spree as easily as the Friedrich Ebert Foundation. This is due to the architects. The office, which was then known as Novotny Mähner and Associates, became famous with its design for the SPD, the party that is close to the Friedrich Ebert Foundation. In the 1970s, the architects from Offenbach designed the SPD headquarters in Bonn as a transparent building in which executive committee meetings and press conferences took place under the public gaze, almost on the street. The building's "shirt sleeves" appearance defined the style for the Rhine republic as a whole. This informality is now being left in Bonn, but the transparency is nevertheless preserved in Berlin. Only three sides of the foundation's building between Hiroshimastrasse and Hildebrandtstrasse have an austere natural stone and brick facing as demanded by the city authorities. On the side facing the Spree, the cubic block containing the staff offices on 1,300 square metres of floor space opens up to the Landwehrkanal with a great transparent gesture. A circular and completely glazed lecture room with seats for 500 protrudes out of this open side. It is part of a public event area with mobile separating walls which can be folded open to make the whole ground floor into a bright and impressive conference landscape of over 3,000 square metres. It is an unrivalled appeal to the general public. The irony of history lies in the fact that the architectural transparency which was customary on Bonn is now the great exception in Berlin. (hwh)

Residenz des Bundeskanzlers / The Chancellor's Villa

Pücklerstraße 14
14195 Berlin (Zehlendorf)

Hermann Muthesius (Altbau/old building); Gesine Weinmiller, Berlin (Umbau/alterations)

1913, 1999

Ansicht Pücklerstraße/
View from Pücklerstrasse

In einer weißen Jugendstilvilla mit alten Bäumen in der Dahlemer Pücklerstraße, die 1913 von Hermann Muthesius erbaut wurde, wohnt die Familie des Bundeskanzlers. Muthesius hatte als Gründungsmitglied des Deutschen Werkbunds zur Verbreitung des englischen Landhausstils und seiner sachlich-schlichten Architektur in Deutschland beigetragen. Das ehemalige Gästehaus, das sich seit 1963 im Besitz des Bundes befindet, wurde nach den Wünschen des Kanzlers umgebaut und im Erdgeschoß für repräsentative Zwecke hergerichtet. Gerhard Schröder hat sich gegen einen zunächst geplanten Neubau im Park des Kanzleramtes entschieden, weil der Umbau der Amtswohnung kostengünstiger war. Sicherheitsmaßnahmen wie schußsicheres Glas waren die aufwendigsten Veränderungen, denn das Haus wurde anschlagsicher umgebaut. Beamte des Bundesgrenzschutzes bewachen die Familie von einem eigens errichteten Wachhäuschen aus rund um die Uhr.

Die Größe der Villa ist mit zehn Zimmern bescheiden. Die Wohnung der Familie im ersten Stock hat lediglich eine Küche, ein Wohnzimmer und zwei Schlafzimmer und wurde von der Berliner Architektin Gesine Weinmiller umgestaltet. Es wurden einige Wände eingerissen und neue Bäder eingebaut. Alte Möbel werden durch moderne Einrichtungsgegenstände ergänzt. „Man braucht nicht unbedingt moderne Architektur, um modernen Geist auszudrücken", so Schröder. Der Terrazzo-Boden in der Küche blieb erhalten. Die zwei hohen Salons mit Stuckdecken und das große Eßzimmer im Erdgeschoß der Dienstvilla werden als Repräsentationsräume für offizielle Anlässe genutzt. Besucher gelangen über eine Kiesauffahrt mit Springbrunnen zum Eingang.

A white Art Nouveau villa with old trees in Pücklerstrasse in Dahlem, built in 1913 by Hermann Muthesius, is the family residence of the German Chancellor. Muthesius was a founding member of the German Werkbund and contributed to the popularisation of the English country house style and its rational and plain architecture in Germany. The former guest house, which has been owned by the German government since 1963, was rebuilt to the Chancellor's wishes, and the ground floor was furnished and fitted for representation purposes. Gerhard Schröder decided against the initial plan to build a new building in the park of the Chancellery because the alterations to the official residence were less expensive. Security measures such as bullet-proof glass were the most extensive changes because the house was altered to resist attack. The family are guarded round the clock by federal border guards based in purpose-built guard houses.

The size of the villa is modest with ten rooms. The family apartment on the first floor has only a kitchen, a living room and two bedrooms and was redesigned by the Berlin architect Gesine Weinmiller. A number of walls were pulled down and new bathrooms were added. Old furniture is being supplemented by modern furnishings and fittings. "You don't necessarily have to have modern architecture to express a modern spirit", Schröder comments. The terrazzo floor in the kitchen was preserved. The two high rooms with stucco ceilings and the large dining room on the ground floor of the official villa are used as representation rooms for official occasions. Visitors reach the entrance via a gravel drive with a fountain.

Residenz des Bundespräsidenten / The Federal President's Villa

Miquelstraße 66
14195 Berlin (Zehlendorf)

Bruno Ahrends
(Altbau/old building); Gesine
Weinmiller, Berlin (Umbau/
alterations)

1912, 1999

Ansicht Miquelstraße/
View from Miquelstrasse

Nach dem Auszug eines Repräsentanten der amerikanischen Streitkräfte hatte man das Haus ursprünglich für die ehemalige Bundestagspräsidentin Rita Süssmuth erworben, die die Dienstvilla zwar umbauen ließ, sie aber selbst nur kurz bewohnte. Dann sollte es als Dienstvilla des Bundestagspräsidenten dienen, Wolfgang Thierse blieb jedoch lieber in seinem Wahlkreis im Bezirk Prenzlauer Berg wohnen. Da auch der Bundespräsident nicht in seinem Amtssitz, dem Schloß Bellevue, wohnen wollte, vereinbarte man einen Tausch. Die Wohnung dort war außerdem sanierungsbedürftig. Sie erschien der Familie unangemessen, weil Johannes Rau nicht wollte, daß seine Kinder im Schloß aufwachsen. Die Kosten für den Umbau in der Miquelstraße übernahm das Präsidialamt.

Das rote, traufenständige Backsteinhaus gehört zum Frühwerk des Berliner Architekten Bruno Ahrends, der es 1912 im norddeutschen Landhausstil für sich und seine Familie errichtete. Er gehörte in der Weimarer Republik zu den führenden Vertreter des Neuen Bauens, bevor er wegen seiner jüdischen Herkunft von den Nazis in die Emigration getrieben wurde.

Die Villa ist von einem großen Garten mit Rosenbeeten und alten Bäumen umgeben. Das Anwesen wirkt großzügig, aber nicht übertrieben prunkvoll. Der Tennisplatz dient heute als Parkplatz. Zum Schutz der Bewohner mußten in der Villa Panzerglasscheiben eingebaut und einige Bäume für das freie Sichtfeld der Videokameras im Garten gefällt werden. Für die Sicherheitsbeamten wurde ein Wachhäuschen in Form eines monumentalen Pyramidenstumpfs errichtet. Der Entwurf stammt von der Berliner Architektin Gesine Weinmiller, die auch die Umbauten im Inneren plante.

After a representative of the American forces moved out, the villa was purchased for the former parliamentary speaker, Rita Süssmuth. She had the official villa altered, but she herself only lived in it for a short time.

It was then designated as the official villa of the parliamentary speaker, but Wolfgang Thierse preferred to live in his constituency in Prenzlauer Berg. As the Federal President also did not want to live in his official residence, Bellevue Palace, an exchange was agreed. The apartment in the palace was in need of renovation and seemed inappropriate to the family because Johannes Rau did not want his children to grow up in a palace. The costs of alteration work in Miquelstrasse were borne by the Presidential office.

The red brick building with its eaves facing the street was an early work by the Berlin architect Bruno Ahrends, who built it in 1912 in the north German country mansion style for himself and his family. In the Weimar Republic he was one of the leading proponents of New Architecture before he was driven into emigration by the Nazis because of his Jewish origins.

The villa is surrounded by a large garden with rose beds and old trees. The grounds appear generous in style, but not excessively lavish. The tennis court is now used as a car park. For the protection of the inhabitants, bulletproof glass was fitted in the villa and a number of trees were felled to create a clear line of sight for surveillance video cameras in the garden. A guard house was built for the security personnel in the shape of a monumental pyramid stump. The design was by the Berlin architect Gesine Weinmiller who also planned the alterations in the interior.

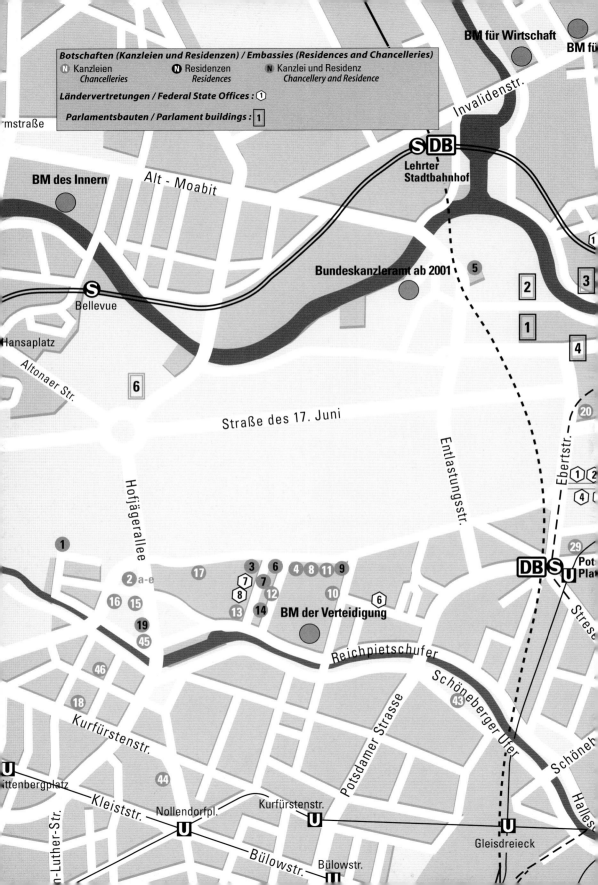

BM für Wirtschaft

BM fü

Botschaften (Kanzleien und Residenzen) / Embassies (Residences and Chancelleries)

Ⓝ Kanzleien
Chancelleries

Ⓝ Residenzen
Residences

Ⓝ Kanzlei und Residenz
Chancellery and Residence

Ländervertretungen / Federal State Offices : ①

Parlamentsbauten / Parlament buildings : 1

Invalidenstr.

S DB

Lehrter
Stadtbahnhof

BM des Innern

Alt - Moabit

S

Bellevue

Hansaplatz

Altonaer Str.

6

Straße des 17. Juni

Bundeskanzleramt ab 2001

5

2

3

1

4

20

Entlastungsstr.

Ebertstr.

①②
④

DB S U

Pot
Pla

29

Hofjägerallee

1

2 a-e

16   15

19

45

46

18

17

3   6   4 8 11   9

7

7

8

12

10

6

13   14

BM der Verteidigung

Reichpietschufer

Schöneberger Ufer

43

Strese

Schöneb

Kurfürstenstr.

U

ttenbergplatz

44

Kleiststr.

Nollendorfpl.

U

Kurfürstenstr.

U

Potsdamer Strasse

Bülowstr.

Bülowstr.

n-Luther-Str.

Halles

U

Gleisdreieck

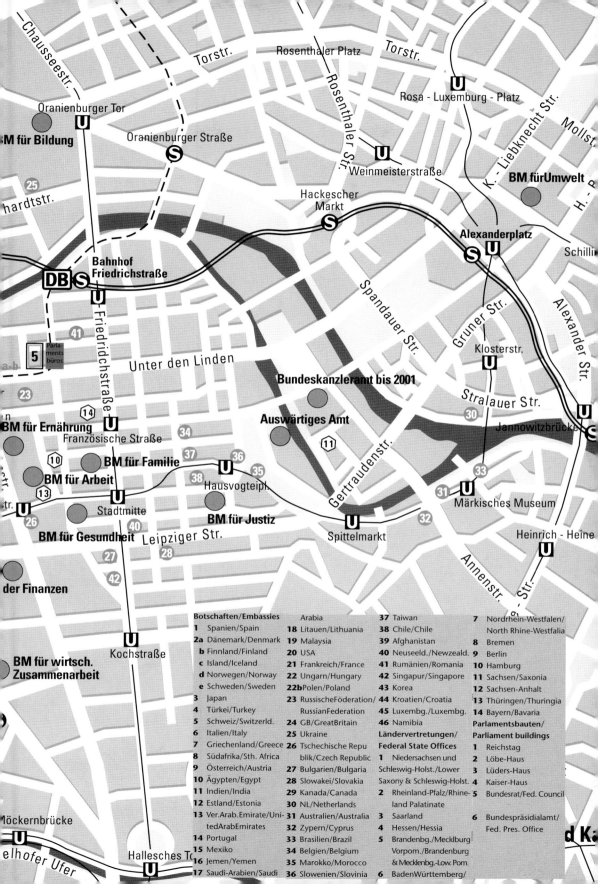

Botschaften/Embassies

1 Spanien/Spain	18 Litauen/Lithuania	37 Taiwan
2a Dänemark/Denmark	19 Malaysia	38 Chile/Chile
b Finnland/Finland	20 USA	39 Afghanistan
c Island/Iceland	21 Frankreich/France	40 Neuseeld./Newzeald.
d Norwegen/Norway	22 Ungarn/Hungary	41 Rumänien/Romania
e Schweden/Sweden	22b Polen/Poland	42 Singapur/Singapore
3 Japan	23 RussischeFöderation/ Russian Federation	43 Korea
4 Türkei/Turkey	24 GB/GreatBritain	44 Kroatien/Croatia
5 Schweiz/Switzerld.	25 Ukraine	45 Luxembg./Luxembg.
6 Italien/Italy	26 Tschechische Republik/Czech Republic	46 Namibia
7 Griechenland/Greece	27 Bulgarien/Bulgaria	**Ländervertretungen/ Federal State Offices**
8 Südafrika/Sth. Africa	28 Slowakei/Slovakia	1 Niedersachsen und Schleswig-Holst./Lower Saxony & Schleswig-Holst.
9 Österreich/Austria	29 Kanada/Canada	2 Rheinland-Pfalz/Rhineland Palatinate
10 Ägypten/Egypt	30 NL/Netherlands	3 Saarland
11 Indien/India	31 Australien/Australia	4 Hessen/Hessia
12 Estland/Estonia	32 Zypern/Cyprus	5 Brandenbg./Mecklburg Vorpom./Brandenburg & Mecklenbg.-Low. Pom.
13 Ver.Arab.Emirate/United Arab Emirates	33 Brasilien/Brazil	6 BadenWürttemberg/
14 Portugal	34 Belgien/Belgium	
15 Mexiko/Mexico	35 Marokko/Morocco	
16 Jemen/Yemen	36 Slowenien/Slovinia	
17 Saudi-Arabien/Saudi Arabia		

7 Nordrhein-Westfalen/North Rhine-Westfalia
8 Bremen
9 Berlin
10 Hamburg
11 Sachsen/Saxony
12 Sachsen-Anhalt
13 Thüringen/Thuringia
14 Bayern/Bavaria

Parlamentsbauten/ Parliament buildings

1 Reichstag
2 Löbe-Haus
3 Lüders-Haus
4 Kaiser-Haus
5 Bundesrat/Fed. Council
6 Bundespräsidialamt/Fed. Pres. Office

Ulf Meyer
Die Länder in Berlin / The Federal States in Berlin

Die Landesvertretungen in der Bundeshauptstadt sind Kontaktstellen zwischen Landes-, Bundes- und Europapolitik.

Die Mitarbeiter nehmen an Plenar- und Ausschußsitzungen teil, um Informationen in die jeweiligen Hauptstädte zu leiten und den Austausch mit Ministerien, Medien, Verbänden und Botschaften zu pflegen. Als „Schaufenster des Landes" ist es ihre Aufgabe, das Land am Sitz der Bundesregierung vorzustellen und Besuchergruppen zu empfangen. Mitunter kann ihre Beachtung von der guten Küche des Landes oder gemütlichen Clubräumen stärker abhängen als von der Statur des jeweiligen Bundeslandes. Sie sind Ausdruck, daß Deutschland auch mit der Entscheidung für die größte Stadt des Landes als Regierungssitz und Hauptstadt eine föderale Struktur behält. Die Vertretungen machen die Präsenz ihrer Länder in der Bundesrepublik mit Häusern, die die Botschaft manchen großen Staates übertrumpfen, mehr als deutlich. „Bigger is better" scheint das Motto beim Bau der Vertretungen gewesen zu sein.

In Bonn hatten sich die elf westlichen Bundesländer nach dem Zweiten Weltkrieg zumeist in Villen in der Nachbarschaft des Bundestages eingerichtet, die später häufig durch repräsentative Neubauten ersetzt wurden. Nach der Wiedervereinigung richteten sich dort auch die fünf „neuen" Bundesländer vorübergehend ein. Mit dem Umzug nach Berlin wurde die Mehrheit der Vertretungen in Bonn verkauft.

Ursprünglich war vorgesehen, alle Ländervertretungen in den ehemaligen Ministergärten zwischen Ebert- und Wilhelmstraße an der Grenze von Mitte und Tiergarten, nördlich des Leipziger Platzes unterzubringen. Von Friedrich Wilhelm I. war das Gelände als Standort für reprä-

The federal state offices in the national capital are contact points between federal state, national and European politics.

Their staff take part in plenary and committee meetings, pass information to their respective state capitals and maintain an exchange with ministries, the press, associations and embassies. They are "showcases of their federal state" and their task is to present the state at the seat of the national government and to receive groups of visitors. The attention they receive sometimes depends more on the fine cuisine of the region or the cosy club rooms in the building than on the stature of the respective state. They show that even though the largest city is now the national capital, Germany nevertheless retains a federal structure. The federal state offices make the presence of their states very clear with buildings that are grander than the embassies of some major countries. "Bigger is better" seems to have been the guiding principle in the construction of the federal state offices.

After the Second World War, most of the eleven western federal states initially set up their Bonn offices in villas near the parliament, although many were later replaced by splendid new buildings. After reunification, even the five "new" states temporarily set up premises in Bonn. With the relocation to Berlin, most federal state offices in Bonn were sold.

Originally it was planned to set up all federal state offices in the former ministry gardens between Ebertstrasse and Wilhelmstrasse on the border between Mitte and Tiergarten north of Leipziger Platz. The area was designated as the location for splendid palaces by Friedrich Wilhelm I., but it was only in the 19th century that Wilhelmstrasse became the power centre of Germany and

sentative Palais vorgesehen worden, aber erst im 19. Jahrhundert wurde die Wilhelmstraße zur Machtzentrale Deutschlands und die ehemaligen Palaisgärten zu den Ministergärten, die damals im rechten Winkel zur Wilhelmstraße parzelliert wurden. Sie dienten als Hintergarten von Auswärtigem Amt und Reichskanzlei. In den dreißiger Jahren entstanden entlang der Voßstraße Führerbunker, neue Reichskanzlei und „Adolf-Hitler-Haus". Erst mit dem Bau der Mauer begann die Enttrümmerung der unterirdischen Ruinen für die 1987 begonnenen Wohnbauten.

Der frühere Grenzstreifen bot sich nach der Wiedervereinigung als „Föderales Viertel" an. Das Architekturbüro Machleidt und Partner gewann 1993 den städtebaulichen Wettbewerb. Ihr Entwurf sah einen aufgelösten Block mit zwölf 20 Meter hohen, „autarken Würfeln" auf dem Areal vor, das jetzt längs parzelliert wurde. Am Übergang von der Friedrichstadt zum Tiergarten wurden „palaisartige Bauten in offener Bauweise" geplant, die als „städtische Kante der Wohnungsbauten an der Wilhelmstraße" dienen sollten. Die Struktur orientiert sich an den historischen Solitären. Für den Ost-West-Verkehr wurden Straßendurchbrüche vorgesehen. Die Allee in den Ministergärten gliedert das Gebiet südlich des geplanten Holocaust-Denkmals in einen kleineren nördlichen und einen größeren südlichen Teil.

Von der ursprünglichen Planung ist nicht viel übrig geblieben; teils aus übersteigertem Individualismus der Länder, teils aus praktischen Gründen. Spätestens seit die „Jewish Claims Conference" Anspruch auf ein Grundstück im Süden des Areals erhob, begann die föderale Eintracht zu bröckeln. Sachsen und Sachsen-Anhalt mußten sich daraufhin neue Grundstücke suchen.

Nur wenige Länder haben Entwürfe von „heimischen" Architekten prämiert. Beim Bau der repräsentativen Landesvertretungen besteht die Gefahr, den folkloristischen Bildern des Landes zu erliegen und gebaute Klischees zu produzieren. Weil die Architektur aber selbst nicht zum Botschafter gemacht wurde, ersetzten die obligatorischen Wein- und Bierstuben die etwaige folkloristische Architektur. Der Blick auf den Reichstag und das Brandenburger Tor hat die Architektur der Vertretungen in vielen Fällen maßgeblich geprägt.

Der Sitz des Bundesrates im Preußischen Herrenhaus stand damals noch nicht fest. Die Nähe zu den Ministergärten war ein besonders glücklicher Zufall und spielt für viele Länder eine wichtige Rolle. Die Erfahrungen aus Bonn haben gezeigt, daß weite Wege oft hinderlich sind. In fünf Gebäuden entstehen sieben Landesvertretungen

the former palace gardens became the ministry gardens, which were divided into plots at right angles to Wilhelmstrasse. They served as rear gardens for the Foreign Office and the Reich Chancellery. In the 1930s, the Fuehrer's shelter, the new Reich Chancellery and the "Adolf Hitler House" were built along Vossstrasse. When the Wall was built, the underground ruins were cleared for the residential buildings which were begun in 1987. After reunification the former border strip was a promising choice for a "federal district". The architectural office of Machleidt and Partner won the urban planning competition in 1993. Their design envisaged a loosely developed block of twelve "independent cubes" of 20 metres in height on the land which was now divided lengthwise into plots. "Palace-type detached buildings" were planned at the transition from Friedrichstadt to Tiergarten which were to serve as an "outer edge of the urban setting for the residential buildings on Wilhelmstrasse". The structure is based on the detached historical buildings. Roads were to be laid through the complex for east-west traffic. The avenue in the ministry gardens divides the area to the south of the planned Holocaust memorial into a smaller northern section and a larger southern section.

Not much remains of the original plans – partly due to excessive individualism of the federal states, partly for practical reasons. At the latest after the "Jewish Claims Conference" laid claim to a plot in the south of the area, the federal unity began to crumble. Saxony and Saxony-Anhalt had to seek new land as a result.

Only very few federal states awarded prizes to "home" architects. In the construction of the splendid federal state offices there is a risk that the design may succumb to the stylised folklore image of the respective state and that architectural clichés will be the result. And because the architecture itself is not representative, the obligatory wine and beer saloons compensate for the lack of regional character in the architecture.

In many cases, the view of the Reichstag and Brandenburg Gate had a significant impact on the architecture of the buildings.

The seat of the Federal Council in the Prussian House of Lords was not yet settled at the time. The proximity to the ministry gardens was a fortunate accident and plays an important role for many federal states. Experience in Bonn showed that long distances are often an obstacle. Five buildings with seven federal state representative offices are being built in the ministry gardens; four states are sharing with another federal state: Brandenburg and

in den Ministergärten: Brandenburg und Mecklenburg-Vorpommern sowie Schleswig-Holstein und Niedersachsen bauen jeweils zusammen. Alle haben einen gemeinsamen Garten ohne Zäune, ein durchgehendes Untergeschoß mit Garage und gemeinsame Haustechnik. Neben den Ministergärten bildet das Diplomatenviertel am südlichen Tiergartenrand einen Schwerpunkt der Ländervertretungen. Drei Bundesländer gaben diesem Quartier den Vorzug. Die übrigen Länder zogen nach Mitte in Alt- oder Neubauten.

Meckleneburg-Lower Pomerania and Lower Saxony and Schleswig-Holstein. The buildings in the ministry gardens have a joint garden without fences, a shared basement with car parking and shared utility services. Apart from the ministry gardens, the diplomatic district on the southern edge of Tiergarten contains a number of federal state offices. Three federal states decided on this area. The other states moved to old or new buildings in Mitte.

links/left: Botschaft von Malaysia/Embassy of Malaysia
unten/below: Luftaufnahme Tiergarten Dreieck (Simulation), von links nach rechts; CDU-Parteizentrale, Bürohaus, Botschaft Luxemburg, Botschaften von Malaysia, Mexiko, der Nordischen Länder, im Hg. Botschaft Jemen/ Aerial view of Tiergarten Triangle (simulation), from left to right: CDU headquarters, office building, embassies of Luxembourg, Malaysia, Mexico, in the background: Embassy of Yemen

oben/above: Botschaft Indien, Eingang Tiergartenstraße/Embassy of India, entrance on Tiergartenstrasse
unten/below: Botschaft Österreich, Modell/Embassy of Austria, model
S. 83: Botschaft Island, Hof/Embassy of Iceland, courtyard

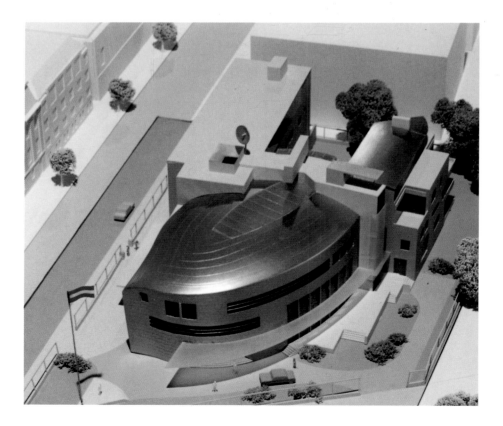

oben/above: Nordische Botschaften, das Kupferband/Embassies of the Nordic
Countries, the ribbon of copper
unten/below:Nordische Botschaften, Gemeinschaftshaus/Embassies of the
Nordic Countries,building for mutual use

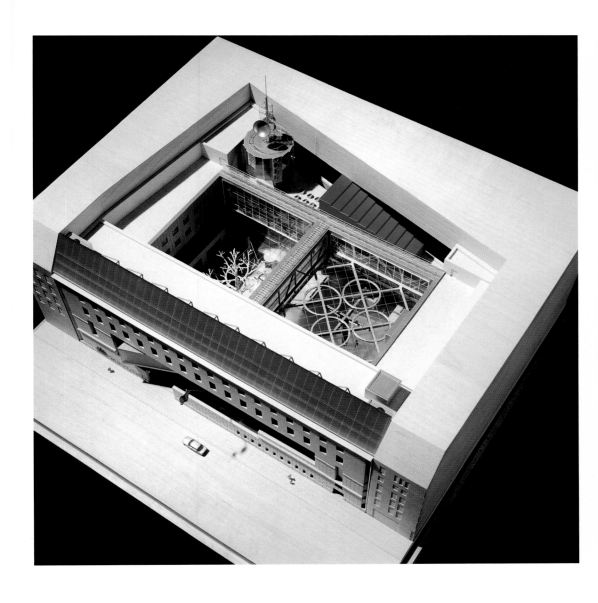

oben/above: Botschaft GB, Gesamtansicht/
Embassy of GB, general view
unten/below: Botschaft USA, Pariser Platz /
Embassy of the USA, Pariser Platz

oben/above: Botschaft Frankreich, Blick vom Pariser Platz/
Embassy of France, view from Pariser Platz
right/rechts: Botschaft Kanada, Schnitt durch die Halle/Embassy
of Canada, cross section of hall
unten/below: Botschaft Australien, Altbau Wallstraße/Embassy
of Australia, old building on Wallstrasse

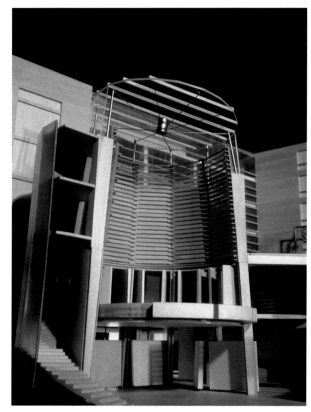

oben/above: Botschaft Brasilien (Eckhaus), Blick von der Spree/Embassy of Brazil (corner building), view from the Spree
unten/below: Botschaft Makedonien, Ansicht Hubertusallee/Embassy of Macedonia, view from Hubertusallee

oben/above: Botschaft Israel/Embassy of Israel
unten/below: Botschaft Thailand, Blick auf den Altbau/Embassy of Thailand,
view of the old building

Landesvertretung von Bayern / Federal State Offices of Bavaria

Behrenstraße 21-22/
Ecke Französische Straße
10117 Berlin (Mitte)

Ludwig Helm, Richard
Bielenberg und Josef Moser (Alt-
bau/old building); Staatliches
Hochbauamt Aschaffenburg
(Umbau/alterations)

1912, 1996-1999

links/left: Ansicht Behrenstraße/
View from Behrenstrasse
rechts/right: Atrium/Atrium

Bayern hatte bereits 1992 zwei Altbauten in Mitte günstig von der Treuhand gekauft. Weil beide Liegenschaften für Bayern zu groß waren, wurde ein Teil 1996 an eine Bank sowie die Baufirma verkauft, die als Generalunternehmer mit dem Umbau beauftragt wurde. Mit dem Verkaufserlös finanzierte Bayern den Bau seiner Vertretung und konnte als erstes der Länder schon 1998 einziehen.

Das Haus an der Französischen Straße wurde von Ludwig Helm, das an der Behrenstraße 1912 von den Architekten Richard Bielenberg und Josef Moser für den Allgemeinen Schaffhausenschen Bankverein entworfen. Zu DDR-Zeiten diente es als Haus der Außenhandelsbank und als Verkehrsministerium. Seine Elbsandsteinfassade ist reich gegliedert, und es hat eine damals hochmoderne Stahlkonstruktion, die allerdings von außen kaum wahrnehmbar ist.

Der im Wettbewerb von 1996 ausgewählte Entwurf für den Umbau stammt vom Staatlichen Hochbauamt Aschaffenburg. Das sechsstöckige Hauptgebäude, zwei Seitenflügel und ein Quergebäude gruppieren sich um einen Lichthof, der überdacht wurde und als Veranstaltungsraum dient. Der Fußboden der Halle wurde mit bayerischem Kalkstein belegt. 60 Mitarbeiter präsentieren in dem Gebäude heute bayerische Kultur, Wirtschaft und Politik. Der obligatorische Bierkeller wurde im ehemaligen Banktresor eingerichtet. Eine Lichtdecke nimmt ihm seine klaustrophobische Atmosphäre.

Im Erdgeschoß befindet sich zusätzlich eine fränkische Weinstube. Darüber liegen das Zimmer des Ministerpräsidenten, Gästewohnungen und sieben Sitzungsräume, die jeweils von einem Regierungsbezirk gestaltet wurden. Auf dem Dach wurde in einem Glaspavillon der „Club Berlin" eingerichtet.

As early as 1992, Bavaria purchased two old buildings at a good price from the government-sponsored privatisation agency. Because the two properties were too large for Bavaria, part was sold in 1996 to a bank and to the building company as the general contractor commissioned with the alteration work. Bavaria financed the construction of its offices with the proceeds of the sale and moved into its new premises in 1998 as one of the first federal states to do so.

The building in Französische Strasse was designed by Ludwig Helm, and the building in Behrenstrasse was designed in 1912 by the architects Richard Bielenberg and Josef Moser for the Schaffhausen banking association. In the GDR period it was used by the foreign trade bank and the Ministry of Transport. The facade of Elbe sandstone is richly sub-divided and the building has a steel structure which was highly modern at the time, although it is hardly visible from the outside.

The design for the alterations was selected in a 1996 competition and is by the Aschaffenburg construction authority. The six-storey main building has two wings and a transverse building grouped around a covered light courtyard which is used to hold special events. The floor of the hall is lined with Bavarian limestone. The staff of 60 now present Bavarian culture, business and politics in the building. The inevitable beer cellar is located in the former bank safe. The illuminated ceiling is designed to remedy the claustrophobic atmosphere.

The ground floor also has a Franconian wine tavern. Above that are the room of the Minister President, guest apartments and seven meeting rooms, each of which was designed by a local government district. The "Club Berlin" is located in a glass pavilion on the roof.

Landesvertretung von Thüringen / Federal State Offices of Thuringia

Mauerstraße 54-55,
Mohrenstr. 64
10117 Berlin (Mitte)

Worschech und Partner,
Erfurt

1997-1999

links/left: Ansicht Mohrenstraße/
View from Mohrenstrasse
rechts/right: Lageplan/Site plan

In unmittelbarer Nachbarschaft zum Bundesarbeitsministerium in der Friedrichstadt hat Thüringen als einziges Bundesland seine Vertretung auf einem Grundstück errichtet, das schon früher in seinem Besitz war: Auf dem Eckgrundstück an der Mohrenstraße stand seit 1933 das im Krieg zerstörte „Haus Thüringen", dessen Teilruine später abgerissen wurde.

Das fünfstöckige Gebäude, das auf zwei Seiten einen Hof umschließt, wurde vom Büro Worschech und Partner aus Erfurt entworfen und 1999 fertiggestellt. Der Bau besteht aus einem steinernen Kubus außen und einem gläsernen Baukörper innen, durch den hindurch der Blick in einen kleinen Hof mit einer Eiche fällt. Das Haus wird von Süden erschlossen, während an der Mauerstraße im Osten ein Kolonnadengang liegt. In der Mohrenstraße liegt die zweigeschossige Eingangshalle, die Raum für Ausstellungen bietet. In den darüberliegenden Geschossen befinden sich Besprechungsräume und eine kleine Bibliothek.

Zum benachbarten Kleisthaus sahen die Architekten eine Zäsur vor. In der Mauerstraße sind Büros und Appartements untergebracht. Von der Dachterrasse im sechsten Obergeschoß genießt man eine schöne Aussicht auf den Bezirk Mitte.

In der Fassade bilden horizontale Betonbänder die Geschoßdecken ab, während vertikale Streifen aus Travertin und Granit, die wiederum horizontal gefugt werden, sich mit raumhohen, bündigen Fenstern abwechseln. Eine „Thüringenstube" im Erdgeschoß soll zur „gebauten Identität" des Hauses beitragen. Dem unaufgeregten Auftritt im Straßenraum stehen wohlüberlegte Details für die Fenster, Oberflächen und die leichte Treppe gegenüber. Das Haus wirkt innen so geradlinig wie außen.

Close to the Federal Ministry of Employment in the Friedrichstadt district, Thuringia is the only federal state to build its representation offices on a plot which it formerly owned. The corner plot on Mohrenstrasse was the site of the "Haus Thüringen" which was built in 1933 and destroyed in the war – and the ruins were later demolished.

The five-storey building, which encloses a courtyard from two sides, was designed by the office of Worschech and partner from Erfurt and completed in 1999. The building consists of a stone cube on the outside and a glass structure on the inside with a view of a small inner courtyard with an oak tree. The building is entered from the south, and on Mauerstrasse there are colonnades to the east. On Mohrenstrasse lies the two-storey entrance hall which offers space for exhibitions. The storeys above the entrance hall contain conference rooms and a small library.

On the side next to the "Kleisthaus", the architects envisaged a separation. On Mauerstrasse, offices and apartments are situated. The roof terrace on the sixth floor has a fine view of the district of Mitte.

In the facade, horizontal concrete bands show the floor level of each storey, and vertical strips of travertine and granite with horizontal joints alternate with flush floor-to-ceiling windows. A "Thüringenstube" (Thuringia restaurant) on the ground floor aims to contribute to the "built identity" of the building. The sober street facade is supplemented by well designed details for the windows, surfaces and light staircase. The building is characterised by straight lines both in the interior and on the outside.

Landesvertretung von Berlin / Federal State Offices of Berlin

Wilhelmstraße 67/
Ecke Dorotheenstraße
10117 Berlin (Mitte)

Paul Spieker (Altbau/Old
building); Senatsbauverwaltung
Berlin (Umbau/alterations)

1878, 1998-1999

Dorotheen-/Ecke Wilhelmstraße/
View from the corner of Dorotheenstrasse and Wilhelmstrasse

Ob Berlin ein eigenes Gebäude für seine Vertretung beim Bund benötigt, war lange umstritten. Erst im zweiten Anlauf gelang es dem Senat, die zuständigen Haushälter zu überzeugen. Man kam zu dem Schluß, daß eine eigene Einrichtung außerhalb des Rathauses Vorteile bei der Lobby-Arbeit verspricht.

Die Landesvertretung liegt in einem Altbau an der Ecke von Wilhelm- und Dorotheenstraße, nahe Reichstag und den Bundestagsbüros im Jakob-Kaiser-Haus. Auch die kurze Entfernung von nur wenigen hundert Metern zum Bundesrat und zum Kanzleramt sollen das Land Berlin bei wichtigen Terminen einfacher in die Gastgeberrolle bringen. „Wer häufig Gastgeber ist, hat die Möglichkeit, leichter Gehör zu finden." Keine andere Landesvertretung liegt so nahe am politischen Geschehen. Der günstige Standort wiegt Nachteile auf, unter denen die Landesvertretung in Bonn litt.

Zusammen mit dem benachbarten ARD-Hauptstadtstudio bildet das Haus das Entree zur Dorotheenstadt. Der landeseigene Altbau wurde zuvor vom Institut für Arbeits- und Sozialmedizin und Epidemiologie der Charité genutzt. Er bildet den vorderen Teil eines 1878 errichteten Komplexes, in dem naturwissenschaftliche Institute der Humboldt-Universität tätig sind. Der würfelförmige, mit gelbem Ziegelmauerwerk verblendete Bau ist das ehemalige Direktorenhaus der Charité. Die Senatsbauverwaltung hatte den Direktauftrag zur Sanierung bekommen. Es wurden zwei Dutzend Büros, ein großer Sitzungssaal und mehrere Besprechungsräume eingebaut. Repräsentative Veranstaltungen müssen anderswo stattfinden, da kein adäquater Saal in der Vertretung zur Verfügung steht. Nach einer deutlichen Reduzierung des Personals dient das Haus als Arbeitsplatz für 30 Mitarbeiter.

For a long time there were arguments about whether Berlin needed a separate building for its national representation. It was only at the second attempt that the Senate convinced the auditors. It was concluded that a separate facility apart from the city hall would provide advantages for lobbying.

The Berlin offices are in an old building on the corner of Wilhelmstrasse and Dorotheenstrasse close to the Reichstag and the parliamentary offices in the Jakob Kaiser Building. The short distance of just a few hundred metres to the Federal Council and the Chancellery should enable the state of Berlin to play host more often at important events. "A frequent host can find a better hearing." No other federal state offices are as close to the centre of the political scene. The favourable location compensates for the disadvantages the Berlin representation suffered in Bonn.

With the neighbouring ARD capital city TV studio, the building forms the entrance to the Dorotheenstadt district. The building is owned by Berlin and was previously used by the occupational and social medicine and epidemiology institute of the Charité hospital. It is the front part of a complex built in 1878 which is used by the scientific institutes of the Humboldt University. The cube-like building with yellow facing bricks is the former director's building of the Charité. The Senate building administration was awarded the direct commission for the renovation and alterations. Two dozen offices, a large meeting room and several conference rooms were added. Major events must be held elsewhere because there is no suitable large room in the building. After a drastic reduction in personnel, the building now has a staff of 30.

Landesvertretung von Saarland / Federal State Offices of Saarland

📧 Allee in den Minister-
gärten
10117 Berlin (Mitte)

✏️ Peter Alt und Thomas
Britz, Saarbrücken

⚒️ 1999-2000

Blick auf den Wintergarten/
View of the wintergarden

Als einziges Bundesland hatte das Saarland 1997 einen Wettbewerb ausgelobt, zu dem nur lokale Architekten zugelassen waren. Das Büro Alt und Britz konnte den ersten Preis erringen. Ihnen gelang es nach Meinung der Jury am besten, das Saarland „in offener, freundlicher Atmosphäre zu repräsentieren".

Zusammen mit den benachbarten Vertretungen von Niedersachsen, Schleswig-Holstein und Rheinland-Pfalz werden am Standort in den Ministergärten, die den Charakter eines Villenviertels haben sollen, gemeinsam Garten, Tiefgarage und Haustechnik genutzt. Die einzelnen Häuser sollen nach Willen der Auslober nicht wie großbürgerliche Wohnhäuser wirken, sondern wie „Palais".

Die Repräsentanz des Saarlands enthält auf sechs Geschossen Büros, Gästeräume und eine Hausmeisterwohnung. Die Architekten teilen das rechteckige Baufeld in zwei Quadrate. Das vordere öffnet sich mit einer großen Halle zur Straße, das hintere verhält sich komplementär: Wo im vorderen gebäudehoher Luftraum ist, sind im hinteren Räume angeordnet und umgekehrt. So entsteht ein Spiel mit Positiv- und Negativräumen. Alt und Britz wollten sich einerseits „nahtlos in die Berliner Architekturlandschaft einfügen, andererseits den Kulturraum, den der Bau vertritt, nicht verleugnen". Das Saarland wird als „Solarland" präsentiert. Die Fassaden sind im Süden von Glas und im Norden von Muschelkalk geprägt. Über den vorgelagerten Wintergarten wird die Halle erschlossen, zum Park hin wirkt das Gebäude mit seinem disziplinierten Fassadengerüst wie mit einer Pergola gesäumt. Besonderes Gewicht erhält die Gastronomie, denn die saarländische Küche hat in Bonn Politiker begeistert.

Saarland was the only federal state which made it a condition of its competition in 1997 that only local architects could take part. The first prize was won by the architectural office of Alt and Britz. The jury considered that they had been most successful in representing Saarland "in an open and friendly atmosphere".

In the ministry gardens location, which is to have the character of a villa district, the garden, underground car park and utility services will be used jointly with the neighbouring representation offices of Lower Saxony, Schleswig-Holstein and Rhineland Palatinate. According to the will of the clients, the individual buildings should not appear like large bourgeois residential houses, but rather like "palaces". The generously proportioned representation building for Saarland will have six storeys with offices, visitors' rooms and a caretaker's apartment. The architects divide the rectangular building plot into two squares. The front square contains a large hall which opens out to the street, the rear square is complementary. Where the front square contains empty space spanning the full height of the building, the rear square contains rooms, and vice versa. Thus an interplay of positive and negative spaces arises. Alt and Britz wanted "to fit smoothly into the architectural scene of Berlin, but without betraying the cultural region which the building represents". Saarland will present itself as a "solar region". The south facades are characterised by glass, and the north facades by shell limestone. The entrance to the main hall is via a steel winter garden structure. On the side facing the park, the building with its disciplined facade framework appears almost surrounded by a pergola. The restaurant plays a special role because politicians in Bonn were enthusiastic about Saarland cuisine.

Landesvertretung von Rheinland–Pfalz /
Federal State Offices of Rhineland Palatinate

Allee in den Minister-
gärten
10117 Berlin (Mitte)

Heinle, Wischer und
Partner, Stuttgart

1999-2000

Die Vertretung von Rheinland-Pfalz in den Ministergärten liegt zwischen denen von Niedersachsen/Schleswig-Holstein und dem Saarland. Den Wettbewerb für den Bau konnte 1997 das Büro Heinle, Wischer und Partner aus Stuttgart für sich entscheiden. Der Entwurf sah eine zweigeschossige Eingangshalle vor, die von zwei unterschiedlich langen, viergeschossigen Flügeln flankiert wird. Das Gebäude umschließt von drei Seiten einen Hof. Vom Eingang an der Kleinen Querallee fällt der Blick durch das Haus in den Garten. Die mittige Glashalle soll ein heiteres Foyer bilden, von dem zur Linken verschiedene Säle, zur Rechten Empfangs- und Verwaltungsräume abgehen. Es kann auf beiden Seiten um zwei Säle vergrößert werden. Eine große Treppe führt in die Obergeschosse, in denen einhüftige, aufgereihte Büros für 50 Mitarbeiter liegen. Für den Ministerpräsidenten ist eine ganze Suite mit Dachterrasse reserviert. Besucher gelangen per Glasaufzug zum Dachgarten. Auf derselben Ebene befinden sich Besprechungszimmer und der „Panorama-Frühstücksraum". Im Ostflügel liegt der Gästetrakt, der durch eine Galerie erschlossen wird, im Erdgeschoß ist eine für das „Weinland Pfalz" unvermeidliche Weinstube vorgesehen. Die Fassaden werden von gebäudehohen, verglasten Einschnitten gegliedert und von Natursteinverkleidungen im Wechsel mit Lärchenholzlamellen geprägt. Ursprünglich waren schlichte weiße Putzflächen vorgesehen. Obwohl Kritiker den asymmetrischen Baukörper als „leicht, modern, selbstbewußt und offen" empfanden, attestierten sie ihm zugleich „fehlenden Esprit der Selbstdarstellung". „Stilvoll, aber nicht prunkvoll" und „ohne überzogenes Pathos" sollte die Landesvertretung nach dem Willen des Bauherren werden.

The representation of Rhineland Palatinate in the ministry gardens is between the buildings of Saarland and Lower Saxony/Schleswig-Holstein. The competition for the building was won in 1997 by the office of Heinle, Wischer and partner from Stuttgart. The design envisaged a two-storey entrance hall flanked by two four-storey wings of different length. The building forms three sides around a courtyard. From the entrance on Kleine Querallee, the visitor can look through the building into the garden. The central glass hall is designed as a bright foyer leading to various meeting rooms on the left and reception and administrative rooms on the right. It can be extended by two rooms on each side. A large staircase leads to the upper storeys, which contain rows of offices for 50 staff members arranged on one side of the corridor. A whole suite with a roof terrace is reserved for the Minister President. Visitors can reach the roof garden via a glass-enclosed lift. On the same level there are conference rooms and the "Panorama breakfast room". In the eastern wing is the visitor's section which is reached via a gallery, and the ground floor is designed to include a wine tavern, which is an essential feature for the "Wineland Palatinate". The facades are structured by glazed recesses spanning the height of the building and natural stone cladding alternating with larchwood segments. Originally, simple white rendered surfaces were planned. Although critics felt the asymmetric building to be "light, modern, self-confident and open", at the same time they considered that it laced a "spirit of self-presentation". The client wanted the federal state offices to be "stylish but not grand" and "without exaggerated pathos".

Landesvertretung von Brandenburg und von Mecklenburg-Vorpommern / Federal State Offices of Brandenburg and Mecklenburg-Lower Pomerania

 Allee in den Ministergärten
10117 Berlin (Mitte)

von Gerkan, Marg und Partner (gmp), Hamburg

1999-2000

Brandenburg baut zusammen mit Mecklenburg-Vorpommern eine Vertretung in den Ministergärten. Die Ausschreibung für den Wettbewerb 1998 sah „zwei verbundene Gebäude auf einem Grundstück" vor. Daß sich diese beiden Länder zusammengefunden haben, liegt weniger an ihrer räumlichen Nachbarschaft, als viel mehr an der Sparsamkeit und dem Wunsch, „besonders kleine" Vertretungen zu errichten.

Den ersten Preis errang zwar das Büro Mai, Zill und Kuhsen aus Lübeck, der Auftrag ging aber an das zweitplazierte Büro von Gerkan, Marg und Partner aus Hamburg, deren funktionaler erscheinender Entwurf wegen Mängeln in der Qualität der Fassaden überarbeitet wurde.

Beide Vertretungen haben Häuser mit eigener Identität. Sie werden durch eine mehrgeschossige Halle verbunden und durch ein gemeinsames Foyer und die einheitliche Fassade zusammengefaßt. Die Strenge der „Palais" kontrastiert mit der Transparenz der Halle, um die sich die beiden ungleichen Winkel legen. Ein Flügel ist um ein Geschoß niedriger. Von der Straße aus betritt man das zweigeschossige gläserne Foyer mit Blick zum Garten und den repräsentativen Gemeinschaftsräumen. Im Erdgeschoß liegen die Veranstaltungsräume, die „Fontaneklause" und „Kajüte", in den Geschossen darüber die Büros und Wohnräume. Sie bilden sich mit Lochfassaden nach außen ab. Der Entwurf sucht die Individualität der Bundesländer in der Wahl landestypischer Materialien auszudrücken: Die Außenflächen werden mit „brandenburgisch-preußischen" Muschelkalkplatten verkleidet und die Innenfassaden mit „nordischem" Holz. Auch der Garten soll durch sanfte Hügel, Wasserflächen und märkische Kiefern Bezüge zu den Landschaften der beiden Bundesländer schaffen.

Brandenburg is combining with Mecklenburg-Lower Pomerania to build federal state offices in the ministry gardens. The competition tender in 1998 stipulated »two linked buildings on a single plot«. The fact that the two states cooperated in this project was due not so much to their geographical proximity, but rather to economies and their wish to build »especially small« representation offices.

Although the first prize was won by the architectural office of Mai, Zill and Kuhsen from Lübeck, the commission was awarded to the second-placed office of von Gerkan, Marg and Partner from Hamburg. However, their design with its functional appearance had to be revised because of defects in the quality of the facades.

Both buildings have their own identity. They are linked by a multiple-storey hall and combined by a joint foyer and the uniform facade. The austerity of the "palaces" contrasts with the transparency of the hall around which the two unequal wings are arranged at an angle. One wing is a storey lower. From the street, the visitor first enters the two-storey glass foyer with its view of the garden and the impressive shared rooms. The ground floor contains the rooms for public events, the »Fontaneklause« and »Kajüte«, and the upper storeys contain office and residential accommodation. The exterior consists of a perforated facade. The design seeks to express the individuality of the federal states in the selection of typical regional materials: the outer facades are clad with »Brandenburg-Prussian« shell limestone panels, and the interior facades with »Nordic« wood. Even the garden is planned to contain gentle hills, water areas and the typical pine trees of the region to create a reference to the landscape in the two federal states.

Landesvertretung von Hessen / Federal State Offices of Hessia

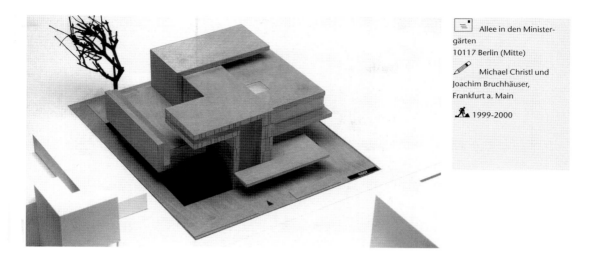

Allee in den Minister-
gärten
10117 Berlin (Mitte)

Michael Christl und
Joachim Bruchhäuser,
Frankfurt a. Main

1999-2000

Hessen hatte als erstes Bundesland ein Grundstück in den Ministergärten erworben, nachdem es seine Liegenschaft auf dem Tiergarten-Dreieck an Dänemark verkauft hatte. Michael Christl und Joachim Bruchhäuser aus Frankfurt, die den Architekturwettbewerb von 1998 gewannen, wollten dem fünfgeschossigen Gebäude durch eine plastische Ausformung eine einprägsame Gestalt geben. Bei fast maximaler Ausnutzung des Grundstücks gruppieren sich unterschiedliche Baukörper zu einer kubischen Komposition. Ein weit auskragendes Vordach schützt den Eingang zur Allee.

Die wichtigsten Räume liegen entlang einer in Nord-Süd-Richtung verlaufenden Erschließungsachse. Das Foyer weitet sich bis zum Garten und bietet Platz für Veranstaltungen. Im ersten Geschoß liegen Gästeräume, Büros und eine Weinstube, darüber die Verwaltung. Im auskragenden fünften Geschoß sind Appartements untergebracht. Scheibenartige Auskragungen und die Fensterbänder gliedern die Fassade horizontal. Große Überstände und heller Mainsandstein bestimmen die Fassaden, während im Inneren Holz dominiert.

Die auskragenden Teile liegen wie „Äste" um einen Versorgungsturm mit Lichtschacht als „Stamm". Diese Baumsymbolik steht nach Ansicht der Architekten für „Wachstum, Veränderung und Lebendigkeit", brachte dem Entwurf aber auch heftige Kritik ein. Die hessischen Grünen waren entsetzt über die „mißglückte Adaption des Bauhauses, die an die überwunden geglaubte sozialdemokratische Architektur der 60er Jahre" erinnere.

Die Diskriminierung des Entwurfs als „klotzige, massive Betonquader« verriet ideologische Scheuklappen. Das Spiel der versetzten Kuben verspricht, einem reizvollen Gebäude Gestalt zu geben.

Hessia was the first federal state to purchase a plot in the ministry gardens after selling its land in the Tiergarten Triangle to Denmark. Michael Christl and Joachim Bruchhäuser from Frankfurt, who won the 1998 architectural competition, wanted to give the five-storey building a distinctive appearance with its expressive facade style. In an almost maximum utilisation of the land, different buildings are grouped to form a cubic composition. The entrance on Queralle is protected from the weather by an overhanging porch.

The most important rooms are situated along a north-to-south access line. The foyer extends to the garden and offers space for official events. The first floor contains guest rooms, a wine tavern and offices, and the higher storeys contain the administration. The overhanging fifth floor contains apartments. Slab-like protusions and the rows of windows structure the facade horizontally. The elevation is characterised by wide projections and light-coloured sandstone from the Main valley, whereas wood dominates the interior.

The protruding sections are arranged like "branches" around a supply tower with a light shaft as the "trunk". The architects consider that this tree symbolism stands for "growth, change and dynamism", but it also came in for fierce criticism. The Green party in Hessia was horrified at the "unsuccessful adaptations of the Bauhaus style which are reminiscent of the Social Democratic architecture of the 1960s which we thought had been overtaken by history".

The criticism of the design as a "solid square chunk of concrete" betrays an ideological bias. The interplay of the staggered cubes promises to give form to an attractive building.

Landesvertretung von Niedersachsen und von Schleswig–Holstein / Federal State Offices of Lower Saxony and Schleswig–Holstein

Allee in den Minister-
gärten
10117 Berlin (Mitte)

Cornelsen + Seelinger/
Seelinger + Vogels, Amsterdam/
Darmstadt

1999-2000

links/left: Ansicht
Fassade/Facade
rechts/right: Grundriß EG/
Ground plan, ground floor

Niedersachsen und Schleswig-Holstein werden zusammen eine Ländervertretung neben den Häusern von Rheinland-Pfalz und dem Saarland in den ehemaligen Ministergärten errichten: Beim Wettbewerb 1997 wurden zwei erste Preise an die Büros Böge/Lindner-Böge aus Hamburg und Cornelsen und Seelinger vergeben; erst in einem zweiten Anlauf konnte sich der Bauherr für das junge Büro aus Darmstadt entscheiden.

„Eine Mitte ohne Masse" zu bilden, ist das Ziel der Architekten für das Haus der beiden Bundesländer. Auf einem quadratischen Grundriß entwarfen sie zwei schmal parallelliegende sechsgeschossige Riegel mit einer gläsernen Halle dazwischen, in dem der große Saal und die Cafeteria wie ein „Haus im Haus" stehen. Sie sind mit Lärchenholz verkleidet. Die beiden gleichwertigen Gebäudeteile nehmen jeweils eine Landesvertretung auf. Die „einladende Geste des attraktiven, großzügigen Entrees" hat den Bauherren besonders überzeugt. Vereinzelte eingestellte Wände trennen das Foyer vom Saal. Durch das große, baumbestandene Atrium hindurch fällt der Blick auf das Brandenburger Tor und den Reichstag. Die beiden Gaststätten „Pesel" und „Friesenstube" sind im Erdgeschoß untergebracht. Ein in die Halle eingestellter Saal bietet auf seiner Dachterrasse Platz für ein Café. Die Wohn- und Arbeitsräume der beiden Ministerpräsidenten liegen auf der Gartenseite. Die Büros bilden den Hintergrund für die Halle, den die Architekten poetisch als „espace imaginaire" interpretieren. Die massiven Riegel nehmen weniger als die Hälfte des Grundstücks ein. Ihre Fassaden werden von grauem italienischen Sandstein und schmalen, hohen Holzfassaden geprägt.

Lower Saxony and Schleswig-Holstein will build a federal state representation together next to the buildings for Rhineland-Palatinate and Saarland in the former ministry gardens. In the competition in 1997, two first prizes were awarded to the offices of Böge/Lindner-Böge from Hamburg and Cornelsen and Seelinger; it was only in the second stage that the client decided in favour of the young office from Darmstadt.

The aim of the architects for the building of the two federal states was to create »a middle without a mass«. On a square ground layout they designed two narrow parallel six-storey blocks with a glass hall between them which contains the large hall and the cafeteria like a "building within a building". They are clad with spruce wood. The two parts of the building are equal in significance, and each will accommodate the offices of one federal state. The »inviting gesture of the attractive and generous entrance« especially convinced the clients. Single walls are inserted to separate the foyer from the main hall. Through the large atrium with its trees there is a view of the Brandenburg Gate and Reichstag. The two restaurants »Pesel« and »Friesenstube« are located on the ground floor. A room inserted into the main hall offers space for a café on its roof terrace. The residential and working rooms of the two Minister Presidents are on the side facing the garden. The offices form the background to the main hall, which the architects poetically interpret as an »espace imaginaire«. The solid block structures occupy less than half of the land. Their facades are characterised by grey Italian sandstone and narrow, high wooden facades.

Landesvertretung von Baden-Württemberg /
Federal State Offices of Baden-Württemberg

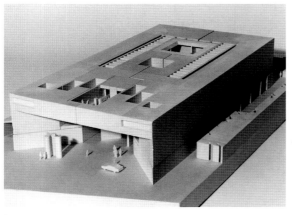

Tiergartenstraße 15
10785 Berlin (Tiergarten)

Dietrich Bangert, Berlin

1998-2000

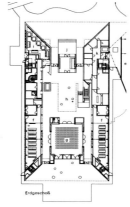

Erdgeschoß

links/left: Eingang Tiergarten-
straße/Entrance Tiergartenstrasse
rechts/right: Grundriß EG/
Ground plan, ground floor

Für seine Residenz hat Baden-Württemberg ein Grundstück in der Tiergartenstraße in unmittelbarer Nähe zu den Botschaften von Österreich, Indien und Ägypten erworben. Der im Wettbewerb von 1997 prämierte Entwurf stammt vom Büro Dietrich Bangert aus Berlin. Obwohl die Parzelle besonders groß ist, wird das Grundstück fast maximal ausgenutzt. Der wuchtige Bau steht mittig auf dem Baufeld und ist unter dem Dachgeschoß trapezförmig eingeschnitten. Auf rechteckigem Grundriß haben die Architekten eine Raumfolge von Foyer, Saal mit Oberlicht, Loggia, Terrasse und Hof geschaffen, die sich zu Straße und Garten gleichermaßen öffnet. Die Wände, die den Eingang bilden, reichen durch das ganze Haus bis zum Garten. Große, bewegliche Holzelemente erlauben die flexible Nutzung des Foyers und schaffen einen fließenden Raumzusammenhang. Ein dreigeschossiger Saal und ein weiterer Lichthof durchschneiden die Baumasse in vertikaler Richtung.

In den ersten zwei Etagen liegen Büros, Wohn- und Gästeräume, die entlang der seitlichen Gärten aufgereiht sind. Der Leitungsbereich orientiert sich zur Straße und erhält einen eigenen Zugang von der Halle. Von der Dachterrasse fällt der Blick auf die Stadt. Im Garten wurden den Räumen Außenbereiche zugeordnet, die das Anwesen einfassen und durch Hecken intime Räume schaffen. Die wohlproportionierten, schlichten Putzfassaden verraten die dahinterliegenden Funktionen. Das Haus wurde als „überteuerter Prachtbau" und „eine Nummer zu groß geraten" kritisiert. Tatsächlich übertrifft der räumliche Reichtum alle anderen Ländervertretungen, so daß sich Baden-Württemberg nicht allein auf die Überzeugungskraft der badischen Weinstube und des Bierkellers im Untergeschoß verlassen muß.

For its official offices, Baden-Württemberg acquired a plot in Tiergartenstrasse close to the embassies of Austria, India and Egypt. The winning design in the 1997 competition was from the office of Dietrich Bangert in Berlin. Although the plot is large, it is used almost to the maximum extent. The bulky structure is in the middle of the plot and is cut away in a trapezoidal pattern below the attic. On a square ground layout, the architects created a sequence of rooms consisting of the foyer, the hall with a skylight, loggia, terrace and courtyard which opens equally to the street and the garden. The walls which form the entrance extend through the building to the garden. Large, mobile wooden elements permit flexible use of the foyer and create a flowing interrelationship between the rooms. A three-storey hall and a light courtyard create a vertical penetration through the building.

The first two storeys contain the offices, residential and guest rooms which are arranged facing the side gardens. The management section faces the street and has a separate entrance from the hall. There is a view of the city from the roof terrace. The rooms are assigned to outdoor areas in the garden which encloses the grounds and has hedges to create intimate areas.

The well-proportioned, simple rendered facades betray the purpose of the interior rooms. The building has been criticised as an allegedly "over-expensive extravagant building" which is "several sizes too big". In fact the spatial richness is greater than in all other federal state offices, so that Baden-Württemberg does not need to rely solely on the persuasive powers of the Baden wine tavern and the beer cellar in the basement.

Landesvertretung von Nordrhein-Westfalen / Federal State Offices of North Rhine-Westfalia

Hiroshimastr. 22-26
10785 Berlin (Tiergarten)

Petzinka, Pink und Partner, Düsseldorf

2000-2001

links/left: Fassade/Facade
rechts/right: Grundriß 1.OG/
Ground plan, first floor

Nordrhein-Westfalen baut seine Vertretung in der Hiroshimastraße am Tiergartenrand. Die Botschaften von Japan und den Arabischen Emiraten werden die Nachbarn sein. Die Entscheidung für den Bau fiel spät. „Wir konnten nicht zu früh entscheiden, weil wir damit gezeigt hätten, daß wir glauben, daß Bonn nicht mehr Hauptstadt bleibt", hieß es dazu von der Landesregierung. Zwischenzeitlich wurde erwogen, nicht neu zu bauen, sondern die Landesvertretung in einem Altbau Unter den Linden 26 unterzubringen und von einer Bank zu mieten. Eine Wirtschaftlichkeitsberechnung ergab, zu mieten sei billiger als zu bauen, obwohl schon ein Grundstück gekauft worden war. Ein zweites Gutachten kam überraschenderweise zu dem Schluß, daß ein Neubau „langfristig wirtschaftlicher" sei.

1997 wurde ein Architekturwettbewerb veranstaltet, bei dem vier Entwürfe in die engere Auswahl gekommen waren. Der Wettbewerb ergab nur ein vorläufiges Ergebnis. Erst nach einer Überarbeitung entschied sich das Bundesland 1999 ein Haus mit viel Glas und Holz nach den Entwürfen des Düsseldorfer Architekturbüros Petzinka Pink und Partner zu bauen. Innovative Konstruktionen und umweltfreundliche Baustoffe waren dem Bauherren besonders wichtig, um eine „großzügige, funktionale und freundliche Architektur« entstehen zu lassen.

Das rechteckige Gebäude im Diplomatenviertel hat nur an der östlichen Seite einen Eingang. Eine Doppelfassade aus Glas und Stahl sorgt für natürliche Belüftung und wandelt Solarenergie mit Hilfe von Brennstoffzellen in Strom und Kälte um. Neben den Büros und Appartements befinden sich Repräsentationsräume für Empfänge und Ausstellungen in der Vertretung, die „Offenheit und Vielfalt verkörpern" will.

North Rhine-Westfalia is building its representation in Hiroshimastrasse on the edge of the Tiergarten. The embassies of Japan and the Arab Emirates will be the neighbours. The decision to build was taken late. "We could not decide too early because that would have implied that we did not believe that Bonn would remain the capital", commented the federal state government. For a time, the federal state considered the possibility of locating its representation offices in an old building at Unter den Linden 26 and renting them from a bank instead of building a new building. An economic feasibility study concluded that renting would be cheaper than building, although a plot had already been purchased. A second study surprisingly concluded that a new building would be "more economical in the long term".

In 1997 an architectural competition was held, and four designs were shortlisted. The competition only produced a provisional result. It was only after a revision of the plans that the federal state decided to build a house with much glass and wood to the plans of the Düsseldorf architectural office of Petzinka Pink und Partner. Innovative designs and environmentally compatible building materials were particularly important to the client in order to create a "generously sized, functional and friendly architecture".

The rectangular building in the diplomatic district only has a entrance on the eastern side. A double facade of glass and steel provides natural ventilation and transforms solar energy into electricity and refrigeration with the aid of fuel cells. In addition to the offices and apartments, the building contains representation rooms for receptions and exhibitions and aims to embody a spirit of "openness and variety".

Landesvertretung der Freien und Hansestadt Bremen / Federal State Offices of the Hanseatic city of Bremen

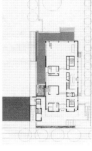

Hiroshimastr. 22-26
10785 Berlin (Tiergarten)

Léon Wohlhage
Wernik Architekten, Berlin

1998-1999

links/left: Eingang Hiroshima-
straße/Entrance Hiroshimastrasse,
rechts/right: Grundriß EG/
Ground plan, ground floor

Als kleinstes und armes Bundesland hat Bremen eine großzügige Vertretung nach Plänen von Léon Wohlhage Wernik Architekten aus Berlin im ehemaligen Diplomatenviertel in Tiergarten errichtet.

Der Wettbewerb war auf je sieben Büros aus Bremen und Berlin beschränkt. Die Vertretung, aus zwei Baukörpern bestehend, vermittelt zwischen der geschlossenen Bebauung am Reichpietschufer am Landwehrkanal und dem Villenensemble an der Hiroshimastraße. Sie sucht Kontakt zur historischen Struktur des Viertels. Während das achtgeschossige Gästehaus einen kopfartigen Endpunkt der zukünftigen Blockrandbebauung bildet, ist das viergeschossige Hauptgebäude wie eine Villa konzipiert. Das Gästehaus bildet eine schmale Brandwandbebauung zum Nachbargrundstück, und die Vertretung steht als Solitär, zurückgesetzt von der Straße, im Garten.

Die „Offenheit entspricht Bremischer Identität", befand das Preisgericht. Beide Gebäudeteile werden getrennt erschlossen.

Die Fassaden sind von einer Edelputzoberfläche geprägt, in die in scheinbar freier Anordnung Fenster, Eingang und Loggien tief eingeschnitten sind. Die Anordnung der Stahlfenster folgt einer spielerischen Komposition. Der rötlich gefärbte Putz erinnert an die hanseatische Backsteinarchitektur. Die ersten beiden Geschosse des traditionellen Mauerwerksbaus sind über versetzte Splitlevel miteinander verbunden und ergeben eine großzügige Raumfolge. Einen privilegierten Blick genießt man im Sitzungssaal in der obersten Etage. Die Außenanlagen wurden mit Wasserflächen, Pergola und Terrasse subtil auf die Architektur abgestimmt. Das Gebäude wird auch für große Feste und Veranstaltungen genutzt. Es bietet Büros, Konferenzsäle und Übernachtungsgelegenheiten für Gäste.

Bremen is the smallest and one of the least affluent federal states, but it has built a generously sized representation building in the former diplomatic district in Tiergarten to plans by the Berlin architects Léon, Wohlhage and Wernik.

The competition was restricted to seven offices from Bremen and seven from Berlin. The representation building, which consists of two structures, mediates between the closed building structure on Reichpietschufer by the Landwehrkanal and the villa ensemble on Hiroshimastrasse. It seeks to follow on from the historical structure of the district. Whereas the eight-storey visitors' building marks the end of the future block edge development, the four-storey main building is more like a villa in its design. The visitors' building forms a narrow structure against the fire wall to the adjacent plot, but the representation building is a solitary structure in the garden, set back from the road.

The jury decided that the "openness corresponds to Bremen's identity". Each building has a separate entrance.

The facades are characterised by a coloured rendered surface into which windows, the entrance and loggias are deeply recessed in an apparently random pattern. The arrangement of the steel windows is playful in its design. The reddish plaster is reminiscent of the Hanseatic brick architecture. The first two storeys of the traditional masonry building are linked by off-set split levels, which creates a generous sequence of rooms. A privileged view can be enjoyed in the conference room on the top floor. The grounds subtly match the architecture with water areas, a pergola and a terrace. The building is also used for large festivals and events. It offers offices, conference rooms and overnight accommodation for guests.

Hans Wolfgang Hoffmann
Der Festplatz der Völkerfamilie: Die Botschaften in Berlin /
A Gala for the Family of Nations: The Embassies in Berlin

Berlin als Festplatz der Völkerfamilie – diese Botschaft der Botschaftsbauten in der Kapitale des vereinten Deutschlands steht unter einem Vorbehalt: Im Gegensatz zum deutschen Teil des Hauptstadtprojekts ist die Niederlassung der Nationen noch längere Zeit nicht abgeschlossen. Mit dem Tempo des gastgebenden Landes konnten viele der gut 150 Staaten, die zur Bundesrepublik diplomatische Beziehungen unterhalten, offensichtlich nicht Schritt halten. Selbst die Vertretung der Supermacht USA ist immer noch nicht mehr als ein Vorhaben. Nachdem zunächst eine Immoblienbaisse die Verwirklichung des Botschaftsneubaus, der durch Verkauf anderer staatseigener Liegenschaften finanziert werden sollte, hinauszögerte, droht das Projekt derzeit an Sicherheitsbedenken zu scheitern. Die US-Adminstration verlangt einen Schutzstreifen von 30 Metern um jede ihrer Botschaften – eine Forderung, die Berlin nicht akzeptieren kann, ohne sich selbst zu verleugnen: Ihre Umsetzung würde am Pariser Platz die Verlegung ganzer Straßen nach sich ziehen und dem Ort genau jenen Sperrgebiets-Charakter zurückgeben, der durch die deutsche Einheit gerade erst gefallen war.

Die US-Botschaft stellt freilich einen Einzelfall dar. Vergleichbare Probleme bereitet nicht einmal die Vertretung Isreals – eines Landes mit vergleichbar sensiblem Sicherheitsbedürfnis. Weniger spektakulär, doch in der Summe bedeutsamer sind dagegen die Schwierigkeiten all der Mittelmächte und Zwergstaaten, die vorerst aus Finanznot in Bonn bleiben müssen. Obwohl sich der Berliner Senat mit einer Botschaftsbörse redlich bemüht, Umzugshindernisse aus dem Weg zu räumen, haben erst zehn asiatische, sieben afrikanische und drei lateinamerikanische Länder eine Adresse in der deutschen Haupt-

Berlin as a gala for the family of nations – this is the message of the embassy buildings in the capital of the reunified Germany, but it is subject to one reservation. By contrast with the German side of the capital city project, the relocation of the nations will not be completed for some time. Many of the 150 or so countries which maintain diplomatic relations to Germany were evidently unable to keep pace with the host country. Even the embassy of the superpower USA has not progressed beyond the planning stage. After the realisation of the new embassy project was delayed by a slump in the property market because the financing was dependent on the sale of other state-owned properties, the project may now fail because of qualms about security. The US administration demands a protective zone of 30 metres around every US embassy – a demand which Berlin is unable to accept without denying itself. At Pariser Platz it would mean relocating whole streets, and it would turn the location into a fortified zone – only a few years after the fortifications were removed in the process of German reunification.

However, the US embassy is an exception. Not even the embassy of Israel caused similar problems, although Israel is a country that is equally sensitive to security. Less spectacular, but more significant in their volume, are the difficulties of the medium-sized powers and minor states which initially have to stay in Bonn for lack of finance. Although the Berlin Senate is making every effort to remove obstacles to relocation with an embassy exchange programme, only ten Asian countries, seven African countries and three Latin American countries have an address in the German capital. That means that the distribution of diplomatic missions between Bonn and

stadt. Damit entspricht die Verteilung der diplomatischen Vertretungen zwischen Bonn und Berlin zwar in etwa jener der Regierungsdienststellen – doch repräsentiert sie nicht föderale Überzeugung, sondern die Finanzkraft der Nationen.

Doch genug der Einschränkungen. Im Jahr des Umzugs haben nahezu hundert Staaten eine Repräsentanz in der Kapitale des vereinten Deutschlands. Damit wurde die Stadt schneller international als jemals zuvor. In der fast 75jährigen Epoche, in der Berlin zuletzt Hauptstadt eines geeinten Deutschlands war, hatten hier gerade zwei Drittel der zu jener Zeit nur 83köpfigen Staatenfamilie eine Vertretung aufgebaut. Noch deutlicher unterstrich die Architektur den damals geringeren Stellenwert der Botschaften. Bis zur Weimarer Republik baute kaum ein Staat selbst, sogar Nachbarländer wie Frankreich, die Schweiz oder Österreich erwarben für andere Zwecke errichtete Gebäude. Ihre Stadtpalais war zwar durchaus repräsentativ, schlossen aber die Möglichkeit, die Baukunst selbst zum Botschafter zu machen, von vornherein aus. Einen weiteren Beweis des damals weniger ausgeprägten Selbstbewußtseins ausländischer Mächte stellte die Vertreibung der Repräsentanzen aus dem Stadtzentrum während des Nationalsozialismus dar. Für die Speerschen Germania-Planungen wurden die Gesandtschaften, die bis dahin mehrheitlich nahe der administrativen Magistrale der Wilhelmstraße bzw. nahe des Reichstags im Alsenviertel residierten, in den südlichen Tiergarten verlagert. In dem neuen Diplomatenviertel wurde die Botschaft zwar erstmals zu einer eigenen Bauaufgabe, doch bis heute bezeugen die Gesandtschaften der damaligen Bündnispartner Spanien, Italien und Japan, daß sich die Architekten zu jener Zeit mehr einer „einheitlichen Baugesinnung" als der Darstellung nationaler Besonderheiten verpflichtet fühlten.

Das blieb auch in der Nachkriegszeit so. Die Architektur der Botschaften, die in der Hauptstadt der DDR neu gebaut wurden, gaben sich mehr zeitgenössisch als patriotisch. Den Anfang machte die ehemalige UdSSR, die schon 1953 Unter den Linden anstelle des kriegszerstörten russischen Gesandtschaftshotels durch die Architekten Stryshewski, Lebedinski, Sichert und Skujin eine Ehrenhofanlage (Seite 102) errichten ließ. So wie ihre neoklassizistischen Schmuckelemente die bis in die späten Fünfziger verbindliche Baudoktrin der „nationalen Tradition" vorgaben, folgten die in den Sechzigern vis-à-vis ausgeführten Neubauten Polens und Ungarns dem dann weltweit gültigen Ideal des International Style, gaben Vera Machoninova, Vladimir Machonin mit Klaus Pätz-

Berlin is approximately the same as for German government departments – but this does not reflect an approval of the federal system, it is merely due to the financial power of the countries.

But enough of restrictions. In the year of the relocation, almost 100 countries have a diplomatic address in the capital of the unified Germany. That means that Berlin has become international more quickly than ever before. In the almost 75 year era when Berlin was previously the capital of the united Germany, only two thirds of the family of nations, which then comprised only 33 countries, had a diplomatic mission here. The architecture underlined even more clearly the low prestige of embassies at the time. Until the Weimar Republic, hardly any countries built their own embassies, and even neighbouring countries such as France, Switzerland and Austria acquired buildings designed for other purposes. Their palatial buildings were certainly worthy, but from the outset they excluded the possibility of making architecture itself into an ambassador. The way the diplomatic missions were driven out of the city centre during the National Socialist era is further evidence of the lesser self-esteem of foreign powers. Until then the embassies were mainly near the administrative buildings around Wilhelmstrasse or in the Alsen district close to the Reichstag, but they were moved to the southern part of Tiergarten to make way for Speer's plans for Germania. It is true that the embassies in the diplomatic district were separate architectural entities for the first time, but the embassies of the allies of the time, Spain, Italy and Japan, show that the architects were more concerned to adhere to a "united architectural spirit" than they were to reflect the national character of the country.

That also remained true in the post-war period. The architecture of the new embassies which were built in the capital of the GDR were in the contemporary spirit rather than patriotic. This began with the USSR, which built a building with a courtyard of honour on Unter den Linden in 1953 to designs by Stryshevski, Lebedinski, Sichert and Skujin (p.102) in place of the Russian diplomatic hotel destroyed in the war. Its neo-classical decorative elements followed the architectural doctrine of the "national tradition" which was dominant until the late 1950s. The new embassies of Poland and Hungary on the other side of the street followed the ideal of the international style which was valid throughout the world in the 1960s. Then Vera Machoninova, Vladimir Machonin and Klaus Pätzmann gave the Czech embassy

Russische Botschaft, Unter den Linden/Russian embassy, Unter den Linden

mann der Botschaft der ČSSR (Seite 103) auf dem Wilhelmplatz eine brutalistische Gestalt, wie sie dem Zeitgeist der siebziger Jahre entsprach.

Der eigentliche Bedeutungsgewinn, den die ausländischen Repräsentanzen in der Nachkriegszeit erlebten, war nicht baukünstlerischer, sondern funktionaler Natur: Kulturzentren entstanden, in denen Künstler die Botschaft ihres Landes ungleich deutlicher formulierten als die Architekten und dabei ein weit größeres Publikum fanden als die Diplomaten. Allerdings agierten sie geographisch getrennt von deren Residenzen und in meist nur angemieteten Räumen (die UdSSR unterhielt in der Friedrichstraße ab Mitte der achtziger Jahre zum Zwecke des wissenschaftlichen und kulturellen Austauschs ein eigenes Gebäude). Freilich verfügten nur die wichtigsten „Bruderstaaten" der DDR sowohl über ein ansehnliches Botschaftsgebäude wie über ein Kulturhaus im Machtzentrum Ostdeutschlands. Die Mehrzahl der diplomatischen Vertretungen kam in Ost-Berlin nicht über eine Briefkastenadresse hinaus. Eigene Gebäude ließ die DDR fast ausschließlich in Pankow zu, wo sie dem diplomatischen Corps auch abgeschlossene Wohnanlagen errichtete. In jedem Fall wurden den Nationen nur Nutzungsrechte, nicht aber Besitztitel an ihren Immobilien zugestanden. Obgleich in der westdeutschen Kapitale keine derartigen Repressionen bestanden, war die Außenwirkung der Botschaften dort kaum größer. Keine einzige Repräsentanz brachte es zu überlokaler Ausstrahlung: Der provisorische wie kleinstädtische Charakter Bonns motivierte die Nationen nicht eben zu Kraftakten.

Das einzige, was viele Nationen von diesem Erbe in der Hauptstadt des vereinten Deutschlands beibehalten, sind ihre Standorte. Wer kann, kehrt auf die alten Grund-

(p.103) on Wilhelmplatz a brutalist form which corresponded to the spirit of the 1970s.

The gain in significance which foreign diplomatic buildings saw in the post-war period was functional rather than architectural in nature. Cultural centres arose in which artists formulated the character of their countries more clearly than the architects and reached a far wider public than the diplomats. But these cultural centres were separate from the embassies and often only in rented premises (the USSR maintained its own building for cultural exchange in Friedrichstrasse from the mid-1980s). But only the most important partner states of the GDR had both a substantial embassy building and a cultural centre in the power centre of East Germany. The majority of diplomatic missions in East Berlin were no more than letter box addresses. The GDR permitted them their own buildings almost only in Pankow where it also built separate residential complexes for the diplomatic corps. And in every case the countries were only permitted usage rights, not ownership of their properties. Although there were no such repressions in the west German capital, the public impact of the embassies was hardly greater there, either. Not one of the embassies was able to have an impact on more than a local level: the provisional and small town character of Bonn did not motivate other countries to invest a great deal of effort.

The only thing which many countries have retained from their heritage in the united German capital is their location. Those countries which are able to return to their old land properties do so. And even the few states which once had their residence in the west of the city and sold their properties in the divided city are returning

Botschaft der Tschechischen Republik, Wilhelmstraße/
Embassy of the Czech Republic, Wilhelmstrasse

stücke zurück. Selbst die nicht wenigen Staaten, die einst im Westen der Stadt residierten und ihre Liegenschaften angesichts deren Wertlosigkeit in der Teilungszeit veräußerten, lassen sich in der vertrauten Umgebung nieder. Neu ist dagegen die Leidenschaft, mit der Neubauten zum Mittel der Selbstdarstellung werden – selbst im internationalen Vergleich. Stärker als jemals zuvor führen die Botschaftsbauten die genuinen Baugewohnheiten ihrer Mutterländer vor. Auch, wo sich die Architektur mit den von Berliner Seite vorgegebenen Regularien auseinandersetzen muß, entstehen zukunftsweisende Lösungen – wofür die Französische Botschaft am Pariser Platz nur eines von vielen Beispielen ist. Doch das Geschenk an Berlin ist mehr als nur eine internationale Bauausstellung. Den eigentlichen Gewinn läßt die Bautypologie der Projekte erkennen: Kulturabteilungen sind nun durchweg fester Bestandteil der Botschaften. Selbst Zwergstaaten, wie der Vatikan oder Island, errichten regelrechte Festspielhäuser, in denen das diplomatische Parkett schwellenloser in den Stadtraum übergeht denn je: Berlin wird zum Festplatz der Vereinten Nationen.

to familiar surroundings. A new element, however, is the passion with which new buildings are becoming a means of self-presentation – even in an international comparison. More than ever before, embassy buildings are showing the original building customs of their home countries. Even where the architecture needs to fit in with the regulations imposed by Berlin, progressive solutions are being developed – with the French Embassy on Pariser Platz as just one of the examples. But the benefit for Berlin is more than just an international exhibition of building. The real gain can be seen in the type of projects that are being built. Cultural departments are now a firm element in embassies. Even minor states such as the Vatican and Iceland are building veritable festival houses in which the diplomatic scene overflows into the urban setting more than ever before – Berlin is becoming a gala location of the United Nations.

Botschaft der Republik Frankreich / Embassy of France

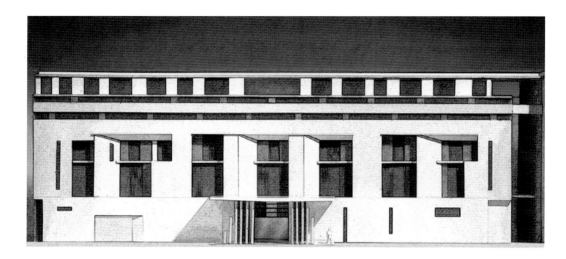

Bis zum Jahr 2001 wird am Pariser Platz die Französische Botschaft entstehen – just an der Stelle, an der die Gesandtschaft bereits bis 1945 ihren Sitz hatte. Sie residierte in einem 1735 fertiggestellten Stadtpalais, dessen markantestes Element eine Säulenhalle mit Terrasse im ersten Obergeschoß darstellte, die Schloßarchitekt Friedrich August Stüler Mitte des 19. Jahrhunderts hinzugefügt hatte. Sein Erwerb durch den französischen Staat entzog die Immobilie 1860 der Spekulation, so daß sie als einziger dreigeschossiger Barockbau am Platz die Ende des Jahrhunderts einsetzende Modernisierung und bauliche Verdichtung überlebte, aber nicht die Bomben des Zweiten Weltkriegs. Die Überreste wurden 1960 abgetragen.

Durch einen Grundstückstausch mit der Bundesrepublik Deutschland wurde nach der Wende aus dem ursprünglich quadratischen ein L-förmiges Areal, wodurch die Botschaft einen zweiten Zugang an der Wilhelmstraße bekam, wo zukünftig der öffentliche Eingang liegen wird. Der Neuzuschnitt erschwerte allerdings die räumliche Organisation, so daß die Aufgabe, Kanzlei, Empfangssäle, das Centre Culturel sowie die Residenzen des Botschafters und seines Sicherheitspersonals auf dem schmalen Streifen unterzubringen, mit zu der größten Herausforderung für die sieben Architekten wurde, die 1996 die Einladung zu einem zweistufigen Wettbewerb ereilte. Christian de Portzamparc entwarf dabei eine Hoflandschaft, in die er die verschiedenen Nutzungen in Form von Pavillons einstellte. Über einem einhüftigen Büro-„Viadukt" schlug er einen vertikalen Garten vor, der sich entlang der 130 Meter langen Brandwand des angrenzenden Jakob-Kaiser-Hauses emporranken soll. In die Lücke der Bauflucht an der Wilhelmstraße stellte

The French Embassy will be completed in 2001 on Pariser Platz in the same place where it was situated up to 1945. It occupied a city palace which was opened in 1735 and which featured a portico with terraces on the first floor which was added by the palace architect Friedrich August Stüler in the middle of the 19th century. The purchase of the building by France in 1860 saved it from commercial speculation so that it was the only three-storey baroque building on Pariser Platz which survived the wave of modernisation and denser building which began at the end of the century – but not the bombs of the Second World War. The ruins were cleared in 1960.

In an exchange of land with the Federal Republic of Germany after the fall of the Wall, the original land became an L-shaped plot giving the embassy a second entrance on Wilhelmstrasse, where the public entrance will be in future. But the new layout made spatial organisation more difficult, so the task of accommodating the embassy, reception rooms, cultural centre and the residence of the ambassador and his safety personnel on the narrow strips of land was one of the greatest challenges for the seven architects who were invited to take part in a two-phase competition in 1996. Christian de Portzamparc designed a courtyard landscape into which he placed the various functional units in the form of pavilions. Above an office "viaduct" with rooms on one side of a corridor, he proposed a vertical garden which was to grow up along the 130 metre long fire wall of the adjoining Jakob-Kaiser building. Portzamparc inserted a tower into the gap in the alignment line on Wilhelmstrasse, and the eight storeys of this tower will be used for the cultural department and parts of the administra-

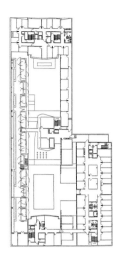

Pariser Platz 5/Wilhelm-
straße
10117 Berlin (Mitte)

Christian de Portzamparc,
Paris mit Steffen Lehmann, Berlin

1999-2001

S.104: Ansicht Pariser Platz/
View from Pariser Platz
S.105 links/left: Grundriß 1.OG/
Ground plan, first floor
rechts/right: Fassade/Facade

Portzamparc einen Turm, auf dessen acht Geschossen die Kulturabteilung sowie ebenfalls Teile der Verwaltung unterkommen. Ob dieses Arrangement die Enge des Terrains vergessen machen läßt, bleibt abzuwarten.

Aus Sicherheitsgründen verlangte die Französische Botschaft von ihren Nachbarn am Pariser Platz den Verzicht auf Fenster – ein Wunsch, dem nachgekommen wurde.

Kaum Zweifel läßt der Entwurf des Haupthauses zu, wegen dessen Fassadenqualitäten Portzamparc den Wettbewerb letztlich gewann. Im Erdgeschoß ist die Front bis auf den mittig plazierten Eingangsportikus geschlossen. Die beiden Geschosse über diesem Sockel werden von einer Reihe aus sieben kolossalen Fenstern zusammengefaßt. Ihre Laibung ist so angeschrägt, daß aus allen Kanzlei- und Empfangsräumen der Blick auf das „Wahrzeichen des neuen Deutschlands" – das Brandenburger Tor – gewahrt bleibt. Ihren horizontalen Abschluß findet die Fassade in einem leicht zurückgesetzten, vollkommen verglasten Dachgeschoß, das die Residenz des Botschafters aufnimmt. Mit den Mitteln der formalen Abstraktion, die eindeutig der Moderne zugehörig sind, entsteht eine nachgerade klassisch gegliederte Fassade, die das alte Stadtpalais reflektiert. Der Entwurf für die Französische Botschaft verspricht, den Spagat zwischen Vergangenheit und Gegenwart weitaus kraftvoller zu bewältigen als alle übrigen Bauten am Pariser Platz. (hwh)

tion. It remains to be seen whether this arrangement will be sufficient compensation for the narrowness of the terrain.

For security reasons the French Embassy demanded that its neighbours should omit windows – a wish that has now been complied with.

The design of the main building – with its facade which was the reason why Portzamparc finally won the competition – leaves little room for doubt. Apart from the centrally placed entrance portico, the ground floor facade is closed. The two storeys above this base are held together by a row of seven colossal windows. The window jambs are angled so that there is a clear view of the "symbol of the new Germany" – the Brandenburg Gate – from all embassy and reception rooms. The top of the facade is formed by a slightly receding and completely glazed roof storey which contains the residence of the ambassador. By means of a formal abstraction which is clearly modernist in style, a facade with a classical subdivided structure is created which reflects the old city palace. The design for the French Embassy promises to span the tension between the past and the present in a far more dynamic way than any other building on Pariser Platz. (hwh)

Botschaft der Vereinigten Staaten von Amerika / Embassy of the USA

Ansicht Ebertstraße/
View from Ebertstrasse

1930 erwarben die USA das barocke, 1870 von Karl Richter umgebaute Palais Blücher am Pariser Platz, das 1931 völlig ausbrannte. Erst 1939 konnte die Botschaft ihre Arbeit im wiederaufgebauten Haus aufnehmen, mußte sie aber bereits 1941 mit Kriegseintritt der USA erneut aufgeben. Das Haus wurde 1957 abgerissen.

Nach der deutschen Wiedervereinigung entschieden sich die USA, einen Neubau auf dem Gelände zu errichten. Der Wettbewerb war der erste seit vierzig Jahren, den das US-Außenministerium für eine Botschaft ausgeschrieben hat. Die Jury entschied sich 1995 einstimmig für den Entwurf des kalifornischen Büros Moore Ruble Yudell, das in Berlin bereits die Vorstadt Karow-Nord geplant hat.

Das grundlegende Dilemma des Entwurfs ist es, einerseits „Symbol einer offenen Gesellschaft" sein zu wollen, sich andererseits aber wegen des Sicherheitsrisikos „einigeln" zu müssen. Das „Antiterrorismus-Gesetz" von 1986 machte aus den neuen amerikanischen Botschaften wahre Festungen. Der Entwurf paßt sich diplomatisch den am Pariser Platz geltenden Gestaltungsregeln an, obwohl der Bauherr größere Freiheit gehabt hätte. Die Sicherheitsvorschriften geboten eine Verminderung der Verglasung, so daß das Verhältnis von Glas zu Stein fast jenen strengen Vorschriften entspricht.

Das Haus ist voller pathetischer Anspielungen. Der Eingang am Pariser Platz wird von einer Rotunde mit geschwungenem Glasvordach markiert, die den amerikanischen „Schmelztiegel der Nationen" symbolisieren soll. Darüber fällt das Licht von Süden durch einen Schlitz in der Fassade direkt auf die amerikanische Flagge, die für eine „sonnige und leuchtende amerikanische Zukunft" steht. Eine stets beleuchtete Laterne auf

In 1930 the USA purchased the Palais Blücher on Pariser Platz (a baroque palace altered in 1870 by Karl Richter) which was completely destroyed by fire in 1931. The embassy only started work in the rebuilt building in 1939, but had to give it up again in 1941 when the USA entered the war. The building was pulled down in 1957. After German re-unification, the USA decided to erect a new building on the land. The competition was the first such competition declared by the US Foreign Ministry for an embassy for 40 years. In 1995 the jury decided unanimously on the design by the Californian office of Moore Ruble Yudell which had already planned the new suburb of Karow-Nord. The fundamental dilemma of the design is that on the one hand it aims to be a "symbol of an open society", but on the other hand it must encapsulate itself in view of the security risk. The "Anti-terrorism Act" of 1986 made the new American embassies into veritable fortresses. The design diplomatically adjusts to the design regulations for Pariser Platz although the client could have claimed greater freedom. The security regulations required a reduction in the amount of glass, so that the proportion of glass to stone almost complies with the strict regulations.

The building is full of sentimental touches. The entrance on Pariser Platz is dominated by a rotund with a curved glass porch which is designed to symbolise the American "ethnic melting pot". Above it, light from the south falls through a crack in the facade directly onto the US flag, symbolising a "sunny and shining American future". A permanently illuminated lantern on the roof pavilion aims to symbolise "common democratic values". The four-storey office wings, the conference rooms and the residence face the courtyard. The consu-

Pariser Platz 2, Ebert-
straße, Behrenstraße
10117 Berlin (Mitte)

Moore Ruble Yudell,
Santa Monica mit Gruen Associates, Los Angeles

ab 2000

Ansicht von Südwesten
View from the southwest

dem Dachpavillon soll ein Zeichen „gemeinsamer demokratischer Werte" setzen. Zum Hof orientieren sich die
viergeschossigen Bürotrakte, Konferenzräume und die
Residenz. Der konsularische Eingang im Süden wirkt wie
eine Veranda. Der „South Lawn" ist eine Anspielung auf
den Rasen vor dem Weißen Haus, der Garten zitiert die
„Plains" und Gärten der Südstaaten.

Der langgestreckte Blockrand bildet einen Hof. Eine Basis aus Kalkstein umfaßt das gesamte Gebäude. Wegen
der Größe des Grundstücks wurden die Fassaden unterschiedlich gestaltet. Die steinerne Lochfassade zum Platz
erinnert an die frühere Botschaft. Die lange Fassade an
der Ebertstraße gehorcht in ihrer formalen Strenge den
Vorgaben der kritischen Rekonstruktion, während die
Südfassade mit hellem Putz, „Arkaden und Pergolen"
leicht und abstrakt wirkt. Alle Fassaden sind dreigeglie-
dert.

Dachpavillon, Loggien, Garten, Dachterrasse sind unterschiedlich gestaltet und stehen für „das soziale und kulturelle amerikanische Mosaik". Der traditionell postmo-
derne Entwurf zitiert die Baugeschichte und mischt sie
zu einer eklektischen Collage. Die Architekten begründen ihn damit, daß Amerika seine Stärke „aus der Integration vielfältiger Ideen" beziehe. Ziel des Entwurfs sei
eine Botschaft als „Schaukasten amerikanischen Designs,
Baukunst und Technologie".

Nachdem die Finanzierung gesichert werden konnte,
verzögert sich der Bau wegen eines geforderten Sicher-
heitsabstands zur Straße, der zu erheblichen städtebaulichen Problemen führt. Er macht umfangreiche Absper-
rungen, eine Straßenverlegung und Verkleinerung des
Grundstücks, auf dem das Holocaust-Mahnmal errichtet werden soll, nötig.

lar entrance to the south is like a veranda. The "south
lawn" is a reminder of the lawn of the White House, and
the garden is reminiscent of the plains and gardens of
the southern states.

The elongated edge of the block encompasses an inner
courtyard. A limestone base surrounds the whole building. Because of the size of the building, the facades differ
in their design. The stone perforated facade facing
Pariser Platz recalls the former embassy building. The
long facade along Ebertstrasse complies in its formal
austerity with the requirements of critical reconstruction, whereas the southern facade with its light-
coloured rendering, "arcades and pergolas" appears
weightless and abstract. All facades are sub-divided into
three parts.

The roof pavilion, loggias, garden and roof terrace are
different in their design and represent the "social and
cultural American mosaic". The traditionally post-modernist design combines elements from architectural history to form an eclectic collage. The architects argue
that America draws its strength "from the integration of
a variety of ideas". The design aims to create an embassy
which is a "showcase of American design, architecture
and technology".

The financing for the project has been secured, but
construction is delayed because of the demand for a safe
distance to the road, which leads to considerable urban
planning problems. It necessitates extensive barriers, re-
routing of roads and a reduction in the size of the land
on which the Holocaust memorial is to be constructed.

Botschaft des Vereinigten Königreichs von Großbritannien und Nordirland / Embassy of the United Kingdom of Great Britain and Northern Ireland

Der Neubau der britischen Botschaft entsteht neben dem Hotel Adlon in der Wilhelmstraße, dort, wo einst das Palais Strousberg (Architekt: August Orth, 1868) stand, das Großbritannien im 19. Jahrhundert erworben hatte und das im Krieg von britischen Bomben zerstört worden war. Das Grundstück blieb jedoch im Besitz Großbritanniens, ein angrenzendes wurde unlängst dazugekauft. Es ist auf drei Seiten von Brandwänden umgeben, nur zur Wilhelmstraße hin hat es eine Straßenfassade.

Der Entwurf vom Büro Michael Wilford & Partners, das auch das Wissenschaftszentrum am Reichpietschufer entwickelte, konnte sich im Wettbewerb 1995 durchsetzen. Der Partner des verstorbenen James Stirling plante eine ausgeklügelte Staffelung von Räumen. Die Straßenfassade aus Sandstein gliedert sich wie bei einem Palazzo in drei horizontale Zonen: Basis, Piano Nobile und Bürogeschosse. In der Mitte über dem geschlossenen Sockel wurde eine große Öffnung in die Lochfassade eingeschnitten, die den Blick in das Innere freigibt. Für die Fassade galten die strengen Vorgaben der Gestaltungssatzung für den Pariser Platz: ihre Höhe ist auf 22 Meter beschränkt, und auch der hohe Anteil geschlossener Fläche war vorgeschrieben. Mit der großzügigen Bel Etage versuchte der Architekt, dennoch eine repräsentative Empfangssituation zu schaffen. Durch eine Zufahrt von der Wilhelmstraße gelangt man in einen quadratischen offenen Hof, in dem eine englische Eiche steht. Von dort führt eine repräsentative Treppe an einem abstrahierten „Union Jack" vorbei in den Wintergarten des zweiten, gedeckten Hofes. Er entspricht in der Größe dem Eingangshof und dient den angrenzenden Sälen als Foyer. Der zeremonielle Weg führt weiter in die Kanzlei des Botschafters. Die über dem Zugang von der Straße liegende

The new building for the British Embassy is being built next to Hotel Adlon in Wilhelmstrasse where Palais Strousberg once stood (Architect: August Orth, 1868) – the building which Britain acquired in the 19th century and which was destroyed by British bombs in the war. But the land remained the property of Britain, and a neighbouring plot was recently purchased. It is enclosed by fire walls on three sides and only has a street facade facing Wilhelmstrasse.

The design by the office of Michael Wilford & Partners, which also developed the Science Centre on Reichpietschufer, was the winner in the 1995 competition. The partner of the late James Stirling planned a sophisticated staggering of rooms. The sandstone street facade is sub-divided into three horizontal zones like a "palazzo": the base, the "piano nobile" and the office storeys. In the middle, above the closed pedestal, a large opening is cut into the perforated facade, giving a view of the interior. The facade was subject to the strict design rules for Pariser Platz, with the height limited to 22 metres and a prescribed proportion of closed surfaces. With the generously sized main storey, the architect tried to create an impressive reception area in spite of the restrictions. An entrance drive from Wilhelmstrasse leads into a square open courtyard containing an English oak tree. Then a splendid flight of stairs leads past an abstract "Union Jack" into the winter garden of the second covered courtyard. It is the same size as the entrance courtyard and serves as a foyer for the adjoining rooms. The visitor then comes to the ambassador's official rooms. The business department and library above the street entrance stand for the trading relationships between Britain and Germany. The embassy's security zone be-

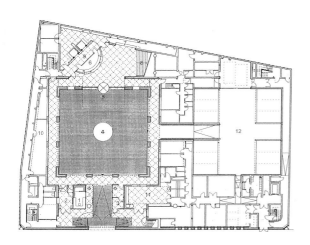

Wilhelmstraße 70-71
10117 Berlin (Mitte)

Michael Wilford & Partners, London/Stuttgart

1998-2000

S.108 links/left: Blick in den Hof/
View into the courtyard
rechts/right: Eingang Wilhelmstr./Entrance on Wilhelmstr.
S.109: Grundriß EG/Ground
plan, ground floor

Wirtschaftsabteilung und Bibliothek steht für die Handelsbeziehungen zwischen Deutschland und Großbritannien. Erst im vierten Geschoß beginnt die Sicherheitszone der Botschaft. U-förmig liegen die Büros um die beiden Höfe herum. Sie sind über vier in den Ecken liegende Treppenhäuser erreichbar. Um Besuchern Einblick und den Mitarbeitern Ausblick zu geben, öffnen sich die Bürogeschosse mit Balkonen zu den Höfen. Ziel des Entwurfs war es, „nicht geheimnisvoll" zu wirken und der Öffentlichkeit Zugang zu den Ausstellungsräumen, einem Auditorium und einem Café zu geben. Wie das benachbarte Hotel hat die Botschaft ein vorpatiniertes, grünes Kupferdach. Hinter der potemkinschen Konstruktion befindet sich jedoch kein Dachgeschoß, sondern ein Flachdach.

Der Neubau gilt als erste privat finanzierte Botschaft der Welt. Ein deutsches Firmenkonsortium finanziert die Vertretung und vermietet sie für 30 Jahre mit Verlängerungsoption. 125 Angestellte arbeiten in dem Gebäude.

Britische Architekten haben Berlin nach dem Fall der Mauer mitgeprägt: Norman Foster mit dem Reichstagsumbau, Nicholas Grimshaw mit dem Erhard-Haus und Richard Rogers mit Wohnbauten am Potsdamer Platz – Bauten, die eine kühle, technische Entwurfssprache sprechen. Für die britische Botschaft hingegen hat sich ein nach außen konventioneller Entwurf durchgesetzt, der zur Straße steinern-streng wirkt, während im gläsernen Hof mit seiner Collage aus rundem Turm und farbigen Metallplatten das ganze Repertoire einer unverkennbar postmodernen Architektur ausgespielt wird. Ein avantgardistischerer Entwurf von Alsop und Störmer wurde vom britischen Establishment als „zu radikal" verworfen.

gins on the fourth floor. The offices are arranged in a U shape around the two courtyards and are reached via four staircases situated at the corners. To allow visitors to look in and the staff to look out, the office storeys have balconies overlooking the courtyards. The design aimed not to appear "secretive" and to allow the public access to the exhibition rooms, an auditorium and a café. Like the adjoining hotel, the embassy has a pre-patinated green copper roof. However, behind the pretentious structure there is just a flat roof instead of an attic.

The new building is the first privately financed embassy in the world. A German consortium of companies is financing the building and letting it for 30 years with an extension option. The building has a staff of 125.

British architects have left their mark on Berlin since the fall of the Berlin Wall: Norman Foster with the alterations to the Reichstag, Nicholas Grimshaw with the Erhard building and Richard Rogers with residential buildings on Potsdamer Platz – buildings which are reserved and technical in their architectural style. But the design for the British Embassy is conventional on the outside, appearing as an austere stone street facade, whereas the glass courtyard with its collage of the round tower and coloured metal panels seems to draw on the entire repertoire of an unmistakably post-modernist architecture. An avant garde design by Alsop and Störmer was rejected as "too radical" by the British establishment.

Botschaft des Königreichs Belgien / Embassy of the Kingdom of Belgium

 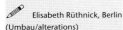 Jägerstraße 52-54
10117 Berlin (Mitte)

 Elisabeth Rüthnick, Berlin
(Umbau/alterations)

1967; 1999-2001

Ansicht Jägerstraße/
View from Jägerstrasse

Belgien richtet seine Botschaft als einziges Land in einem DDR-Plattenbau in Mitte ein. Auf dem Grundstück in der Nähe des Gendarmenmarkts befand sich bis zum Zweiten Weltkrieg die Belgische Botschaft in einem 1884 errichteten Gebäude, das im Krieg zerstört wurde. Der in den 60er Jahren errichtete Plattenbau diente der Volkspolizei der DDR. Die jüngste Geschichte des Hauses wird nicht vertuscht.

1999 wurde ein Wettbewerb ausgelobt, bei dem sich die Architektin Elisabeth Rüthnick aus Berlin durchsetzen konnte. Belgien gehört damit zu den wenigen Ländern, deren Botschaft nicht von einem Landeskind geplant wird. Aus Kostengründen wurde die Konstruktion des Gebäudes weitgehend erhalten. Die bestehenden fünf Geschosse wurden in Grundriß und Fassade neu konzipiert und um ein Geschoß aufgestockt. Städtebauliche Disziplin und „Respekt vor der Geschichte" waren die Vorgaben. Die Fassade an der Jägerstraße wird zwar stellenweise aufgebrochen, der Entwurf übernimmt aber mutig die Fassadenstruktur des Plattenbaus. Sie erhält einen anthrazitfarbenen Anstrich und markante Kastenfenster. Einschnitte in den unteren Geschossen schaffen ein „Fenster zum Hof". Fensterbänder und Ausschnitt markieren die unterschiedlichen Räume der Botschaft. Die schlichte Aufstockung war durch die Tragfähigkeit des Plattenbaus beschränkt.

Vom Empfangssaal im Erdgeschoß gelangt man in den Hof, der mit Buchenhecken und Rasenhügeln als „Festgarten" gestaltet ist. Da er von hohen Brandwänden umgeben ist, hilft eine Wasserwand durch Reflexion bei der Belichtung der Arbeitsräume. Im Hof entsteht ein ovaler Veranstaltungsraum. Der freistehende, eingeschossige, orange Saal steht auch für Konferenzen zur Verfügung.

Belgium is the only country which will occupy a GDR concrete slab building in Mitte.

Until the Second World War, the Belgian Embassy was situated on the plot near Gendarmenmarkt in a building erected in 1884 which was destroyed in the war. The concrete slab building dates from the 1960s and was used by the police of the GDR. No attempt is made to conceal the recent history of the building.

A competition was declared in 1999 and was won by the architect Elisabeth Rüthnick from Berlin. Belgium is thus one of the few countries to have an embassy which was not designed by a national of the country. The existing five storeys were completely redesigned in their layout and facade, and an extra storey was added. Discipline of urban design and "respect for history" were the guiding principles. The facade on Jägerstrasse is partly broken up, but the design boldly takes over the facade structure of the concrete slab building, with an anthracite colour coating and striking box-type windows. Cutaway areas in the lower storeys create a "window onto the courtyard". The rows of windows and the cutaways show the different rooms in the embassy. The plain extra storey was limited by the load-bearing capacity.

The reception room on the ground floor leads into the courtyard, which is designed as a "festival garden" with beech hedges and grassy mounds. Because the courtyard is surrounded by high fire walls, a wall of water provides reflections to help illuminate the offices. An oval room for meetings is being created in the courtyard. The single-storey free-standing orange room is also available for conferences.

Botschaft der Föderativen Republik Brasilien / Embassy of Brazil

Wallstraße 56-59, Märkisches Ufer 38-42
10179 Berlin (Mitte)

PSP Pysall, Stahrenberg & Partner, Berlin

1998 - 2000

links/left: Blick von der Spree/
View from the Spree
rechts/right: Grundriß, EG/
Ground plan, ground floor

Brasilien baut seine neue Botschaft direkt an der Spree, in unmittelbarer Nachbarschaft zum Märkischen Museum und den Botschaften von Australien und den Niederlanden. Die Architekten Pysall, Stahrenberg & Partner aus Berlin haben das Haus entworfen. Der Neubau liegt am südlichen Flußufer gegenüber dem Köllnischen Park und bildet den Kopfbau eines aus drei Gebäuden bestehenden Geschäftshauskomplexes. Die Berliner Repräsentanz ist eine der weltweit größten Brasilianischen Botschaften. Brasilien wird jedoch nicht Bauherr sein, sondern Mieter „in einem ganz normalen Bürohaus". Neben der Botschaft entstehen zwei ebenfalls 22 Meter hohe Bürogebäude mit Wohnungen in den Dachgeschossen. Das neue Ensemble bildet den Abschluß eines Bürohausriegels aus den zwanziger Jahren mit dem Haus der Gewerkschaft von Max Taut. Für den Neubau mußte das im Jahr 1969 errichtete Spreehotel (Architektenkollektiv Pätzmann/Boy), das als Gästehaus des SED-Zentralkomitees diente, abgerissen werden. Die Kopfseite des Gebäudes orientiert sich zur Grünanlage „Märkischer Platz", an der ein eigener Vortritt der Botschaft entsteht. Die Fassade lebt vom Spiel unterschiedlich weit geöffneter Schiebeläden aus grauen Lärchenholzlamellen als Sonnenschutz. In dem siebengeschossigen Gebäude liegen in den unteren vier Etagen Büros und die Veranstaltungsräume der Kanzlei. Die Geschosse darüber mit den Repräsentations- und Wohnräumen zeigen sich in der Fassade mit Balkonen. In der Fassade werden durch verschiedene Fenstergrößen und Proportionen die unterschiedlichen Nutzungen deutlich. Eine „Krone" bildet den Dachabschluß. Raumhohe Fenster geben dem Haus Transparenz.

Brazil is building its embassy next to the Spree close to the Märkisches Museum and the embassies of Australia and the Netherlands. The building was designed by the architects Pysall, Stahrenberg & Partner from Berlin. The new building is situated on the southern bank of the river opposite Köllnischer Park and forms the end of a commercial building complex. The building in Berlin is one of the largest Brazilian embassies in the world. But Brazil will not be the client for the building work, merely a tenant "in a normal office building". Next to the embassy, two office buildings are being built which have the same height of 22 metres and contain apartments in the attics. The new ensemble completes a long block-type office complex dating from the 1920s, with the trades union building by Max Taut. To make room for the new building, the Spree hotel built in 1969 (architectural collective of Pätzmann/Boy), which was the guest house of the central committee of the ruling SED Communist party, had to be pulled down. The end of the embassy faces the small park "Märkischer Platz" to which the embassy has its own access. The facade is enlivened by the interplay of "drawers" of grey larch slats which are opened to different degrees and give shade. The lower four storeys of the seven-storey building contain offices and the official meeting rooms of the embassy. The higher storeys with their representation and residential facilities are shown in the facade with balconies. The different functions are apparent in the facade due to the different window sizes and proportions. The roof forms a "crown", and floor-to-ceiling windows make the building appear transparent.

Australische Botschaft / Australian Embassy

 Wallstraße 76-79,
Märkisches Ufer 6-8
10179 Berlin (Mitte)

 Fritz Crzellitzer(Altbau/old
building); Bates Smart, Mel-
bourne; Braun, Schlockermann
& Partner, Berlin (Umbau/altera-
tions)

 1886, 1913, 1999

links/left: Ansicht Märkisches
Ufer/View from Märkisches Ufer
rechts/right: Grundriß EG/
Ground plan, ground floor

Australien baut für seine Botschaft zwei benachbarte Alt-bauten an der Spree, nahe der Fischerinsel, in Mitte um. Sie werden nach Plänen der Architekten Bates Smart und Braun, Schlockermann & Partner renoviert. Die Gebäu-de sind bereits mehrfach umgebaut worden. Der größere Jugendstilbau an der Wallstraße von 1913 (Architekt: Fritz Crzellitzer) diente als Gewerberaum für Textil-manufakturen. Der Grundriß kommt mit nur vier In-nenstützen aus und erwies sich beim Umbau als beson-ders flexibel. Die detailreiche Majolika-Fassade an der Wallstraße wurde liebevoll saniert. Die weißglasierte me-diterrane Keramikfassade verrät in ihrer Stringenz be-reits eine Ahnung der beginnenden Moderne. Sie gehört zu den wenigen erhaltenen Fassaden ihrer Art in Berlin.

In den dreißiger Jahren zogen die Tischlerinnung und der Verlag „Das Deutsche Holzgewerbe" in das Haus. Nach dem Zweiten Weltkrieg, den das Haus weitgehend unbeschadet überstanden hatte, diente es vorüberge-hend der KPD und verschiedenen SED-eigenen Verla-gen. Die SED hatte Ende der vierziger Jahre das benach-barte Wohnhaus am Märkischen Ufer von 1886 zusätz-lich erworben und zu einem Gästehaus umbauen lassen. Australien hat beide Gebäude 1996 gekauft und einen Wettbewerb ausgeschrieben. Zwischen beiden Häusern liegen ein Hof und ein Quergebäude. Im Haus am Mär-kischen Ufer befinden sich die Wohnungen, die Büros und das Konsulat im fünfgeschossigen Haus an der Wall-straße. Im Erdgeschoß liegt ein Veranstaltungssaal und im Dachgeschoß Konferenzräume.

Beide Häuser behalten ihre eigenen Zugänge. Im Hof wer-den sie durch einen fünf Meter hohen, dekonstruktivisti-schen Kubus aus rahmenloser Verglasung verbunden.

For its embassy, Australia is carrying out alterations to two adjoining old buildings by the Spree near Fischerin-sel (fishers' island) in Mitte. They are being renovated to plans by the architects Bates Smart and Braun, Schlock-ermann & Partner. The buildings have already been al-tered several times. The larger building in Art Nouveau style at the Wallstrasse (architect: Fritz Crzellitzer) dates from 1913 and was used as industrial premises for textile manufacturers. The ground layout includes only four in-terior supports and was particularly flexible in the reno-vation. The Majolika facade on Wallstrasse with its rich details was carefully restored. The white glazed Mediter-ranean ceramic facade has a stringency which foreshad-owed the onset of Modernism. It is one of the few re-maining facades of its kind in Berlin.

In the 1930s, the guild of joiners and the specialist timber trade publisher "Das Deutsche Holzgewerbe" moved into the building. After the Second World War, which it survived with little damage, it was mainly used by the Communist party and various publishers operated by the ruling SED party. At the end of the 1940s, the SED party also acquired the adjoining residential building on Märkisches Ufer dating from 1886 and had it rebuilt as a guest house.

Australia purchased both buildings in 1996 and de-clared a competition. Between the two buildings are a courtyard and a connecting building. The building on Märkisches Ufer contains the apartments, and the of-fices and consulate are in the five-storey building on Wallstrasse. The ground floor contains a room for official occasions, and the attic contains conference rooms.

Both buildings retain their own entrances. In the court-yard they are linked by a five metre high, deconstruc-

Botschaft des Königreichs Marokko / Embassy of the Kingdom of Morocco

Niederwallstraße 39
10117 Berlin (Mitte)

Hermann Friedrich Wae-
semann (Umbau/alterations);
GFB Gesellschaft für Planung
und Projektsteuerung, Berlin,
und Manuel Alvarez, Berlin
(Sanierung/renovation)

1688, 1857, 1998-99

Ansicht Niederwallstraße/
View from Niederwallstrasse

Der Altbau, in dem Marokko seine Botschaft einrichtet, wurde als „Kurfürstlicher Jägerhof" 1688 erbaut und diente um 1750 als Gericht. Das dreigeschossige Haus mit Lochfassade hatte ehemals einen mittigen Eingang und wurde im gleichen Stil mehrmals erweitert. Ende des 18. Jahrhunderts hatte die von Friedrich dem Großen gegründete „Giro- und Lehnbanc" in dem Gebäude ihren Sitz, gefolgt vom Königlichen Forstdepartement. 1834 zog die Preußische Regierung ein, für die das Haus 1857 von Hermann Friedrich Waesemann umgebaut wurde. 1901 folgte ihr die Deutsche Reichsbank. Sie vereinnahmte sukzessive den gesamten Block. Das Haus ist damit der einzige erhaltene Teil der alten Reichsbank.

1998 erwarb ein Investor das denkmalgeschützte Gebäude und begann mit der Sanierung. Nach den Entwürfen vom Büro GFB und Manuel Alvarez aus Berlin wird die Fassade neu verputzt und die Fenster ersetzt. Das Dach wird neu gedeckt und bekommt Gauben. Innen werden der Bodenbelag und die Haustechnik erneuert und flexible Trennwände eingebaut. Treppenhaus und Durchfahrt werden im ursprünglichen Stil wiederhergestellt.

The old building in which Morocco is setting up its embassy was built in 1688 as the "Electoral hunting tavern" and served as a court around 1750. The three-story house with a perforated facade formerly had an entrance in the middle. It was extended several times in the same style. At the end of the 18th century it was the headquarters of the "giro and lending bank" founded by Friedrich the Great, and it was later used by the royal forestry department. In 1834 the Prussian government moved in, and the building was altered in 1857 by Hermann Friedrich Waesemann. In 1901 the Deutsche Reichsbank moved into the building and successively occupied the entire block. It is thus the only remaining part of the old Reichsbank.

In 1998 an investor purchased the building, which is a listed monument, and began renovation work. The facade rendering and windows are being replaced to plans by the office GFB and Manuel Alvarez from Berlin. New roof tiles are being fitted and gable windows integrated. The floor covering and utilities are being replaced and flexible dividing walls fitted. The staircase and vehicle entrance are being restored in the original style.

Botschaft des Königreichs der Niederlande / Embassy of the Netherlands

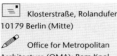 Klosterstraße, Rolandufer
10179 Berlin (Mitte)

Office for Metropolitan
Architecture (OMA); Rem Koolhaas , Erik Schotte, Gro Bo-
nesmo, Rotterdam

1999-2001

Spreeuferansicht/
View from the Spree

Exzentrisch wie keine zweite Botschaft in Berlin gibt sich die niederländische Gesandtschaft. Das beginnt mit dem Standort: Fernab des übrigen diplomatischen Corps residiert man am Rolandufer im ältesten Teil der Stadt, in dem seit vielen Jahrzehnten riesige Administrationen dominieren, die keine Botschaft an die Öffentlichkeit tragen wollen. Zudem verschließt sich die hier geplante Baulichkeit auf den ersten Blick vordergründigen Assoziationen an das Land, das sie in Auftrag gibt. Tatsächlich ist sie vor allem ein Meilenstein der Baukunst: Ausgerechnet in Berlin, wo man seine Anliegen nie teilte, verwirklicht Rem Koolhaas, weltweiter „mastermind" der Avantgarde-Architekten, einen Raum-Traum, dem er seit Ende der achtziger Jahre nachhängt, aber nie in die Realität retten konnte: ein Gebäude, in dem eine einzige, vielfach gefaltete Ebene den traditionellen Stapel aus Geschossen ersetzt.

Um das zu verwirklichen, braucht man zunächst eine für sich stehende Hülle. Um sie, wie von der Stadtregierung gefordert, doch in den Block einzupassen, griff Koolhaas zu einem Trick: Mit einem schmalen, einhüftigen Riegel, in dem die Appartments der Botschaftsbediensteten liegen, geht der Glasquader mit je 27 Meter Kantenlänge knapp auf Tuchfühlung zu seinen Nachbarn, zum Wasser bleibt ein erhöhter Garten frei. Durch alle acht Geschosse des Würfels windet sich eine Binnenstraße vom Eingang bis zum Dach: Vom zweiten bis zum dritten Stock erhebt sich die Promenade wie ein Erker über die Klosterstraße, der das Haus in die Stadt verlängert. Traditionelle Baukategorien – Körper und Raum, Solitär und Block, innen und außen, Öffentlichkeit und Privatwelt – geraten durcheinander. Und diese Unkonventionalität ist dann doch wieder typisch Niederländisch. (hwh)

The embassy of the Netherlands is more eccentric than any other embassy in Berlin. That begins with the location, far from the rest of the diplomatic corps it is set on Rolandufer in the oldest part of the city where for decades there were enormous administrations which did not want to pass any information to the public. At first sight, the building planned here does not offer any obvious associations with the country that commissioned it. But in fact it is a milestone in architecture: in Berlin of all places Rem Koolhaas, the world's "mastermind" of avant garde architecture, is realising a spatial dream which he has pursued since the end of the 1980s but never been able to put into practice: a building in which a single level with multiple folds replaces the traditional stacking of storeys.

In order to implement this concept, first of all a self-sufficient outer shell is needed. And to integrate this shell into the block of buildings, as required by the city authorities, Koolhaas used a trick: with a narrow block containing the apartments of the embassy personnel on only one side of the corridor, the glass cube with sides of 27 metres just touches its neighbours, but on the water side a raised garden is left free. An interior road winds it way through the eight storeys of the cube from the entrance to the roof. From the second to the third floor, the promenade rises like a bay window above Klosterstrasse and extends the length of the building. Traditional building categories – building structure and space, solitary building and block, interior and exterior, public and private world – are intermingled. And this unconventionality in itself is typical of the Netherlands.
(hwh)

Botschaft Vatikanstadt / Vatican State Embassy

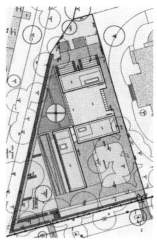

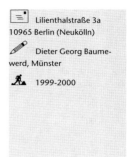

Lilienthalstraße 3a
10965 Berlin (Neukölln)

Dieter Georg Baume-
werd, Münster

1999-2000

links/left: Ansicht Lilienthal-
straße/View from Lilienthal-
strasse
rechts/right: Lageplan/Site plan

Die Botschaft des Papstes entschied sich für ein Grund-stück auf dem Gelände der Johannes-Basilika am Rand des Volksparks Hasenheide in Neukölln. Bei einem Wettbewerb mit sieben Teilnehmern konnte sich 1998 der Münsteraner Architekt Dieter Georg Baumewerd durchsetzen. Sein Entwurf, bestehend aus drei gleich hohen Baukörpern, muß neben der mächtigen neo-romanischen Basilika bestehen. Die orthogonal und parallel zum Querschiff der Kirche angeordneten Gebäude werden auf dem dreieckigen Grundstück miteinander kombiniert. Die Gebäude stehen im Abstand von mindestens zehn Metern zur Johannes-Basilika, dem größten katholischen Gotteshaus in Berlin.

Zwei Quader wurden rechtwinklig zum Kirchenschiff plaziert. In ihnen ist die Kanzlei mit Repräsentations- und Arbeitsräumen untergebracht. Dazwischen liegt in der Achse des Querschiffs eine zweigeschossige Halle. Auf der Rückseite befindet sich der dritte Quader, in dem der Nuntius mit seinen Mitarbeitern in einer klosterähnlichen Gemeinschaft lebt. Ein Andachtsraum nimmt das erste und zweite Stockwerk ein. Die Nuntiatur wird von einem hohen Zaun und einer Hecke umschlossen. Der Entwurf wurde 1998 auch auf Wunsch des Nuntius überarbeitet, das Haus auf vier Stockwerke beschränkt und das Bauvolumen damit um zehn Prozent reduziert. Die beiden in der Eingangshalle vorgesehenen Treppen kamen jetzt in separate Bereiche. Erhalten blieb die große Glaswand mit Blick auf die Rosette der Basilika.

The papal embassy decided on a plot on the land of the St. John Basilica on the edge of Hasenheide park in Neukölln. A competition with seven participants in 1998 was won by the Münster architect Dieter Georg Baumewerd. His design, which consists of three structures of equal height, needs to hold its own alongside the towering neo-Romanesque basilica. The buildings are aligned orthogonally and parallel to the transept of the church and are combined with each other on the triangular plot. The buildings are at least ten metres from the St. John Basilica, the largest Catholic church in Berlin.

Two blocks are placed at right angles to the church nave. They contain the embassy itself, with representation and working rooms. Between them and the same axis as the transept is a two-storey hall. On the rear is the third block in which the nuncio and his staff live in an almost monastic community. There is a room for devotions and meditations on the first and second floor. The nunciature is enclosed by a high fence and a hedge. In 1999 the design was revised with the support of the nuncio, the building limited to four storeys and the volume thus reduced by ten per cent. The two staircases which were planned to be in the entrance hall were now placed in separate areas. The large glass wall with a view of the basilica rosette was retained.

Botschaft der Republik Ungarn / Embassy of Hungaria

Unter den Linden 76
10117 Berlin (Mitte)

Adam Sylvester,
Budapest

1999-2001

Blick Unter den Linden/
Ecke Wilhelmstraße/
View from the corner Unter den
Linden and Wilhelmstrasse

Im „Architekturführer der Hauptstadt der DDR" tauchte die alte ungarische Botschaft als zweites Gebäude auf – gleich nach dem Brandenburger Tor. Sie entstammte der kurzen Epoche, in der die osteuropäische Baukunst Anschluß an die Weltarchitektur gefunden hatte. Ihre 1965 von Karl-Ernst Swora und Rainer Henslik in Kooperation mit den ungarischen Architekten Endre Koltai und Laszlo Kovácy im International Style entworfene Aluminium-Glas-Fassade stand für alles, nur nicht für lokale Besonderheiten. Erhalten davon bleibt nur der prominente Standort, der dem mitteleuropäischen Land Bedeutung verschafft. Mit der Begründung, das Gebäude sei „zu groß" und entspräche nicht mehr „dem Geist der ungarischen Baukunst", beantragte seine Regierung 1998 den Abriß. Weil „das Interesse, eine neue Botschaft zu errichten, höher einzustufen" sei „als die Wiederaufbauarchitektur zu erhalten," genehmigte ihn der Berliner Senat trotz des seit der Wende bestehenden Denkmalschutzes.

Die neue Botschaft wird nurmehr die Hälfte des Grundstücks einnehmen. Das Haus an der Ecke Unter den Linden/Wilhelmstraße wird vom Budapester Architekten Adam Sylvester errichtet, der sich in einer nationalen Konkurrenz durchsetzte. In seinem Entwurf liegen die Gesellschaftsräume in den beiden Geschossen unterhalb der Büroetagen. Die mit graugelblichem Polygranit verkleideten und mit von Hand gefertigten, grün lasierten Keramikplatten verzierten Fassaden unterwerfen sich der örtlichen Gestaltungssatzung. Die Architektur nimmt Anleihen bei der Sezessions-Baukunst, die zu Beginn dieses Jahrhunderts en vogue war, als Ungarn noch im Vielvölkerstaat der k.u.k. Monarchie nach Unabhängigkeit strebte. (hwh)

In the architectural guide to the capital city of the GDR, the old Hungarian embassy was listed as the second building – after the Brandenburg Gate. It dated from the short period when Eastern European architecture was in step with world architecture. The aluminium and glass facade designed in 1965 in the international style by Karl-Ernst Swora and Rainer Henslik in cooperation with the Hungarian architects Endre Koltai and Laszlo Kovácy represented many things, but not local traditions. But all that now remains is the prominent location which gives significance to the Central European state. On the grounds that the building was "too big" and no longer in harmony with "the spirit of Hungarian architecture", the Hungarian government applied for demolition in 1998. And because "the interest in building a new embassy" was "greater than the interest in preserving restoration architecture", the Berlin Senate gave demolition permission in spite of the monument protection which had been in force since the fall of the Berlin Wall.

The new embassy will now occupy only half of the land. The building on the corner of Unter den Linden and Wilhelmstrasse is being built by the Budapest architect Adam Sylvester who won the national competition. In his design, the social rooms are situated in the two storeys below the office storeys. The facades, which are clad with grey-yellow polygranite and adorned with hand-made, green varnished ceramic tiles, comply with the local design regulations. The architecture borrows elements from secessionist architecture which was in fashion at the beginning of the century when Hungary was still in the multi-ethnic state of the "royal and imperial monarchy" and striving for independence. (hwh)

Botschaft der Republik Polen / Embassy of Poland

Unter den Linden 72
10117 Berlin (Mitte)

Emil Leibold und Christian Seyfarth (Altbau/old building); Budzynski, Badowski und Kowalewski, Warschau (Neubau/new building)

1964, ab 2000

Altbau / Old building

Polen verfügte, wie das Nachbarland Ungarn, in Berlin bereits zu DDR-Zeiten über eine beachtliche Botschaft. Unmittelbar nebeneinander lagen, beide am repräsentativen Standort Unter den Linden und zeigten auch gestalterische Parallelen. Den Stahlskelettbau, den die deutschen Architekten Emil Leibold und Christian Seyfarth 1964 fertigstellten, bedeckte eine für die Entstehungszeit innovative, aber nicht eben landestypische Vorhangfassade mit Brüstungsfeldern aus farbigem Glas in den oberen Etagen und Naturstein über dem Erdgeschoß.

Wie Ungarn konnte sich auch Polen nach der Wende mit dieser Architektur nicht mehr identifizieren. Doch im Gegensatz zur Neubauplanung des Nachbarlands fand der Entwurf der Architekten Budzynski, Badowski und Kowalewski beim Berliner Senat keinen Gefallen. Gelobt wurde allein der hofseitige Garten, der sich über drei Ebenen ziehen, für die Öffentlichkeit zugänglich sein und auch dem Polnischen Kulturinstitut dienen soll. Gestritten wurde indes über die Fassade: Kritisiert wurde zum einen das zum Boulevard fast geschlossene, mit Skulpturen versehene Sockelgeschoß. Zum anderen standen die quadratische Befensterung, die Rankgitter sowie die Kupferverkleidung im Widerspruch zur örtlichen Gestaltungssatzung, die stehende Fenster, den Verzicht auf Vorbauten sowie Fronten in hellen Naturtönen verlangte. Die polnischen Baumeister machten sich daraufhin an eine Überarbeitung, in deren Verlauf das Pflanzgerüst verschwand und die metallene Verkleidung auf Dach und Erdgeschoß reduziert wurde. Da die Kompromißsuche noch nicht abgeschlossen ist, wird man noch länger mit der alten polnischen Botschaft eines der letzten Exemplare der International-Style-Architektur Unter den Linden bewundern können. (hwh)

Like its neighbour Hungary, Poland already had a substantial embassy in Berlin in the GDR period. The two embassies were next to each other in the major location of Unter den Linden and also had parallels in their design. The steel framework structure which the German architects Emil Leibold and Christian Seyfarth completed in 1964 had a curtain facade which was innovative at the time but not typical of the country, with parapet panels of coloured glass in the upper storeys and natural stone above the ground floor.

And like Hungary, Poland was also no longer able to identify with this architecture after the fall of Communism. But by contrast with the new building plans of its neighbour, the design by the architects Budzynski, Badowski and Kowalewski did not find the favour of the Berlin Senate. The only element to be praised was the courtyard garden which was designed to extend over three levels, be open to the public and also serve the Polish cultural institute. The facade caused controversy; one point that was criticised was the almost closed pedestal storey facing the boulevard with its sculptures. And the square windows, climbing trellises and copper cladding were in contradiction to the local design regulations which demand upright windows, no structures in front of the wall and facades in light natural colours. The Polish architects then revised their design, removed the trellis and reduced the metal cladding to the roof and the ground floor. As the search for a compromise has not yet ended, we will still be able to admire the old Polish embassy for some time – one of the last examples of international style architecture on Unter den Linden.

(hwh)

Botschaft der Schweizerischen Eidgenossenschaft / Embassy of Switzerland

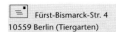 Fürst-Bismarck-Str. 4
10559 Berlin (Tiergarten)

 Friedrich Hitzig (Altbau/old building); Diener & Diener, Basel (Umbau und Erweiterung/extension)

 1870, 1998-1999

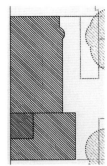

Links/left: Alt- und Neubau (rechts im Bild)/Old and new building (on the right)
rechts/right: Lageplan/Site plan

Kein Land ist dem Bundeskanzler näher als die Schweiz. An ihrer Gesandtschaft richtet sich das „Band des Bundes" aus, in dem sich auch der Dienstsitz des deutschen Regierungschefs befindet. Die Eidgenossenschaft erwarb das Stadtpalais, das Friedrich Hitzig 1870 errichtet hatte, bereits 1919. Während der Rest des noblen Alsenviertels erst den Speer-Planungen für die Nord-Süd-Achse zum Opfer fiel, blieb die Botschaft von den Umzugsaufforderungen der Nazis wie von dem Bombenhagel verschont. Sogar die Repräsentations- und Residenzräume im Erdgeschoß und dem ersten Obergeschoß sind erhalten, wenngleich ihre Pracht in der Nachkriegszeit weitgehend unbeachtet blieb. Von daher war klar, daß die Schweiz sich auch im wiedervereinigten Deutschland in ihnen präsentieren würde. Allein ließen sich Mission und Kanzlei darin nicht getrennt erschließen, so daß man sich für eine Erweiterung entschied. Den ausgelobten Wettbewerb unter acht Schweizer Architekten konnte 1995 das Büro Diener & Diener für sich entscheiden. Ihr Entwurf sieht einen Anbau in der Höhe des Altbaus, aber mit fünf statt drei Geschossen vor, in denen die diplomatischen und konsularischen Dienste untergebracht sind. Zusätzliche Eigenständigkeit gewinnt er durch seine äußerst reduzierte, von Sichtbeton dominierte Gestalt, die genau jene Schlichtheit und Materialverliebtheit zeigt, die für die moderne Architektur der Alpenrepublik charakteristisch ist. Die Fenster der an den Altbau anschließenden Front wurden so gesetzt, daß sie den Besucher zum neuen Atrium lenken. Die Fertigstellung verzögerte sich, weil mit dem Bau erst nach Deckelung des Tiergartentunnels, der genau unter der Botschaft verläuft, begonnen werden konnte. (hwh)

No country is closer to the German Chancellor than Switzerland. Its embassy is right next to the ribbon of new government buildings which includes the official residence of the German head of state. The Swiss Confederacy purchased the city palace, which Friedrich Hitzig had built in 1870, in 1919. The rest of the noble Alsen district was lost to Speer's plans for a north-to-south axis, but the embassy survived the attempts at forced relocation and the bombs. Even the representation and residence rooms on the ground floor and first floor are preserved, although their splendour was largely unnoticed in the post-war period. Therefore it was clear that Switzerland would again use this building for its embassy in the reunified Germany. But it was not possible to create separate entrances for the delegation premises and the embassy offices, so it was decided to build an extension. The 1995 competition among eight Swiss architects was won by the office of Diener & Diener. Their design envisages an extension of equal total height, but with five storeys instead of three, for the diplomatic and consular services. The separate identity of this extension is heightened by its extremely plain concrete facade which celebrates simplicity and a love of materials in a way that is characteristic of modern Swiss architecture. The windows in the frontage adjoining the old building are arranged so that they guide the visitor to the new atrium. Completion was delayed because the construction work could only begin after the roof had been fitted on the Tiergarten tunnel which runs exactly under the embassy. (hwh)

Kanadische Botschaft / Embassy of Canada

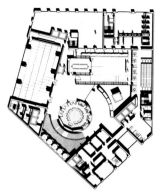

Leipziger Platz 16-17, Voßstraße 20-21 10117 Berlin (Mitte)

Kuwabara Payne McKenna Blumenberg Architects, Toronto mit Smith Carter Architects, Winnipeg und Gagnon, Letellier, Cyr Architects, Quebec City

1999-2001

links/left: Blick von Norden, Voss-/Ecke Ebertstraße/View from the north, Vossstrasse and corner of Ebertstrasse
rechts/right: Grundriß EG/ Ground plan, ground floor

Geographisch sind Kanada und die USA Nachbarn, und in Berlin errichten sie ihre Repräsentanzen in vergleichbarer städtebaulicher Situation. Doch ihr Auftreten unterscheidet sich diametral: Während die USA bei der Wiedererrichtung ihrer Gesandtschaft wegen gewachsener Sicherheitsbedürfnisse in Konflikt mit der Stadt gerät, präsentiert sich Kanada als erster Botschaftsbau in Berlin so offen wie sonst kaum ein Diplomatenhaus: Von dem neunstöckigen Gebäude am Leipziger Platz wird das Land nur die Hälfte selbst nutzen, den Rest nehmen Wohnungen und Geschäfte ein. Die Öffentlichkeit soll zu den Läden, dem Café und dem Ausstellungsbereich im Erdgeschoß jederzeit Zutritt haben.

Der Entwurf dafür setzte sich 1999 gegen zwei Konkurrenten durch. Er stammt von einer Arbeitsgemeinschaft, deren beteiligten Büros aus Toronto, Winnipeg und Quebec die kulturelle Vielfalt des Staates auf geradezu mustergültige Weise repräsentieren. Landestypisch sind vor allem Bautypologie und Material. Eine „Mall" – seit jeher das Standardelement kanadischer Gesellschaftsbauten – bildet auch das Herzstück der Berliner Botschaft. Im Zentrum ist die kegelstumpfförmige „Timber Hall", die ein Konferenzzentrum erschließt. Nahezu haushoch ist sie einem der wichtigsten Exportgüter des Landes gewidmet: Holz von Douglasfichten aus British Columbia belegt ihre Wände, Quebecer Ahorn ihren Boden. Um die Offenheit nach außen zu transportieren, ignorierten die Kanadier an der Fassade die in Berlin üblichen gestalterischen Gepflogenheiten: An der Ebertstraße entmaterialisiert sich die mit poliertem Tyndall-Kalkstein aus Manitoba verkleidete Lochfassade zu einem überdimensionalen Schauregal. Deutlicher kann ein Willkommensgruß kaum ausfallen. (hwh)

Canada and the USA are neighbours geographically, and in Berlin they are building their diplomatic buildings in comparable urban settings. But the way they set about it is diamatrically opposite. Whereas the USA is caught up in conflict with the city in the reconstruction of its embassy because of an increase in its security requirements, Canada's first embassy in Berlin is one of the most open embassies. The nine-storey building on Leipziger Platz will only use half of the land itself, the rest will be taken up by apartments and shops. The public is planned to have access to the shops, the café and the ground floor exhibition area at any time.

The design was successful in 1999 against two competitors. It originates from a working group made up of offices from Toronto, Winnipeg and Quebec which represents the cultural variety of the country in an exemplary manner. The type of building and the material are typical of the country. A "mall" – which has long been the standard element in Canadian public buildings – is also the heart of the building in Berlin. At the centre is the truncated cone of the "timber hall" which leads to a conference centre. It is almost as tall as the building itself and devoted to one of the most important export goods of the country: its walls are faced with Douglas fir from British Columbia, and the floor with Quebec maple. To transport the public character to the outside, the Canadians ignored the normal design customs of Berlin in their facade design. On Ebertstrasse, the perforated facade faced with Tyndal limestone from Manitoba opens up to form an over-sized showcase. The welcome could hardly be more clearly expressed. (hwh)

Botschaft der Republik Österreich / Embassy of Austria

  Tiergartenstraße 12-14
Ecke Stauffenbergstraße 1-4
10785 Berlin (Tiergarten)

Hans Hollein, Wien

1999-2000

Blick von der Tiergartenstraße/
View from Tiergartenstrasse

Unter den Auslandsvertretungen Österreichs ist jene in der deutschen Hauptstadt die wichtigste. Der Neubau stellt für das Land eine Art Heimkehr dar, denn bereits seit dem Ende des k.u.k.-Imperiums residierte man in derselben Straße, nur zehn Hausnummern weiter südlich. Seit 1938 lag das Stadtpalais infolge des „Anschlusses" der Alpenrepublik brach und wurde dann im Zweiten Weltkrieg von Bomben zerstört.

Ähnlich bedeutsam ist der Bau für den Wiener Architekten Hans Hollein, der bisher keinen seiner öffentlichen Bauvorschläge für Berlin realisieren konnte. Den Zuschlag für die Botschaft bekam er 1998 in einer europaweiten Konkurrenz, weil sein Entwurf den städtebaulichen und funktionalen Anforderungen am besten gerecht wurde. Den Übergang zwischen Kulturforum und Villen bewältigte der Architekt durch Aufteilung der Botschaft in drei Baukörper: Ein Kubus, der mit dreigeschossiger Putzfassade, engem Fensterraster sowie zurückgesetztem Geschoß unter flachem Dach ganz im Stil der Klassischen Moderne gehalten ist und die Konsularabteilung aufnimmt, schließt an Traufhöhe und Bauflucht der vorhandenen Bebauung an. Auf der Rückseite wendet sich eine Villa dem Diplomatenviertel zu, in der die Wohn- und Gästeräume des Botschafters unterkommen. Aus beiden erwächst ein mit Kupfer verkleidetes Gebilde, das an der Tiergartenstraße das spektakuläre Entree des Quartiers bildet. Aus seiner tropfenförmigen Baumasse sind die Räume in eigener Logik herausgeschnitten: Im Erdgeschoß liegt der Empfangssaal, darüber der Amtsbereich des Botschafters, der durch ein fast ganz umlaufendes Panoramafenster in den Tiergarten blickt. Übrig bleiben Vorfahrten, Säle und Galerien, die protokollarischen Anläßen optimal Raum geben. (hwh)

The embassy of Austria in the German capital is the most important of its foreign embassies. The new building is a sort of homecoming: since the end of the Imperial and Royal Empire, Austria had its residence in the same street, but ten door numbers further south. The building became redundant in 1938 when Austria was incorporated into the Reich, and it was destroyed by bombs in the Second World War.

The building is equally significant for the Viennese architect Hans Hollein, who has not previously been able to implement any of his publicbuilding proposals for Berlin. He was awarded the commission against competitors from all over Europe because his design best fulfilled the urban development and functional requirements. Hollein achieved a transition between the Kulturforum and villas by dividing the embassy into three structures. A cube with a three-storey rendered facade, a tight window grid and a receding storey under a flat roof which is in a classical modernist style and contains the consular department creates a link to the eaves height and alignment line of the existing buildings. To the rear of this building is a villa oriented towards the diplomatic district which contains the residential and guest areas for the ambassador. Out of these two buildings arises a copperclad structure which forms the spectacular entrance to the complex on Tiergartenstrasse. The representation rooms are cut out of its droplet-like shape and have a logic of their own: the ground floor contains the reception hall, above that are the official rooms of the ambassador who has a view of the Tiergarten through a panoramic window that goes almost around the entire building. There are also access drives, rooms and galleries which offer ample space for protocol occasions.

Botschaft von Indien / Embassy of India

Tiergartenstr. 16-17
10785 Berlin (Tiergarten)

Léon Wohlhage Wernik
Architekten, Berlin

1999-2000

Längsansicht von Osten/
Long side from the east

Für die indische Botschaft wurde ein großer Neubau auf einem 1996 erworbenen Grundstück an der Tiergartenstraße errichtet. Er liegt zwischen der Botschaft von Südafrika und der Landesvertretung von Baden-Württemberg. Das Architekturbüro Léon Wohlhage Wernik konnte sich bei einem beschränkten Architekturwettbewerb 1998 mit einem archaischen Entwurf durchsetzen, der „die indische Baukunst abstrakt" interpretiert. Das schmale Grundstück wurde fast maximal bebaut. Von Norden aus wird das Gebäude abwechslungsreich gegliedert, in den Verwaltungstrakt, die öffentlichen Ausstellungs- und Konferenzräume, die Privaträume des Botschafters und den großen Wohntrakt im Süden.

Das zentrale Motiv ist das Spiel mit plastischen Formen und Positiv- und Negativräumen: Während im fünfgeschossigen Gebäude an der Straße ein rundes Atrium als Eingang aus der Baumasse ausgeschnitten wurde, findet sich diese Form im Garten an der Südseite als Zylinder wieder, in dem das Büro des Botschafters liegt.

Vom Hohlraum am Eingang gelangt man über das Foyer mit Ausstellungsräumen zum Gartenhof im Zentrum der Anlage. Dieser wird südlich von einem Querbau begrenzt, in dem sich Wohnungen und die Residenz des Botschafters befinden. Eine große Freitreppe führt seitlich an den hängenden Gärten vorbei zum Dachgarten mit Blick über die Stadt. Sie bildet sich in der Fassade ab, die aus großen Betonpaneelen besteht. Darin wurden Bruchsteine aus indischem Sandstein eingegossen, die die Fassaden eindrucksvoll rot schimmern lassen. Eine Wasserfläche, die vom Eingang durch das Erdgeschoß über die Gartenterrassen bis zur Residenz führt, ist nur eines der vielen liebevollen Details der indischen Botschaft.

A large new building has been built for the Indian Embassy on a plot of land in Tiergartenstrasse which was purchased in 1996. It is situated between the federal state offices of Baden-Württemberg and the South African embassy. The architectural office of Léon Wohlhage Wernik was successful in a restricted architectural competition in 1998 with an archaic design which interprets "Indian architecture in an abstract way". The narrow plot is built on almost to the maximum possible extent. From the north, the building is dynamically subdivided into the administrative section, the public exhibition and conference rooms, the ambassador's private rooms and the large residential wing to the south.

The central motif is the interplay of structures, forms and positive and negative space. In the five-storey building facing the road, a round atrium is cut out of the structure as an entrance, and this form is also reflected in the garden in the south of the plot as a cylinder containing the office of the ambassador.

From the hollow space in the entrance, the visitor passes through the foyer with its exhibition rooms to the garden courtyard in the centre of the complex. To the south of the garden is a transverse building containing apartments and the ambassador's residence. A large outdoor flight of stairs leads past the hanging gardens to the roof garden with a view of the city. It is reflected in the facade which consists of large concrete panels and contains inset fragments of Indian sandstone which give the facade an impressive red tone. A stretch of water leading from the entrance through the ground floor and over the garden terraces to the residence is just one of the many attractive details in the Indian Embassy.

Botschaft der Republik Estland / Embassy of Estonia

Hildebrandstraße 5
10785 Berlin (Tiergarten)

Kayser und Großheim
(Umbau/alterations 1883);
Olavi Nömmik, Tallinn (Sanie-
rung/renovation)

1880, 1883, 1999-2000

Ansicht Hildebrandstraße/
View from Hildebrandstrasse

Die Botschaft von Estland befindet sich in einem Altbau in der Hildebrandstraße im Diplomatenviertel. Das dreigeschossige Wohnhaus von 1880 wurde Ende des 19. Jahrhunderts mehrfach umgebaut und diente seit 1923 als Vertretung von Estland. Es hat zwei ungleich hohe Seitenflügel, eine Sandsteinfassade und ein bewegtes, schiefergedecktes Mansarddach. Das Dach auf dem um ein Geschoß höheren rechten Flügel verspringt auf die Höhe der benachbarten griechischen Botschaft.

Weil das Haus im Zweiten Weltkrieg weitgehend unbeschädigt blieb, war es – anders als die meisten Gebäude am Tiergartenrand – durchgehend bewohnt. Estland gehört zu den wenigen Ländern, deren Grundstücksbesitz samt Gebäude kontinuierlich erhalten blieb. Das bedeutete aber auch, daß die Vertretung entmietet werden mußte, ehe mit den Umbauten begonnen werden konnte. Dennoch ist Estland der erste der drei baltischen Staaten, der seine Botschaft in Berlin in Betrieb nimmt. Der Architekt Olavi Nömmik aus Tallinn wurde mit der Sanierung beauftragt. Er hatte sich bei einem beschränkten nationalen Architekturwettbewerb durchsetzen können. Obwohl von außen keine Veränderungen am Haus sichtbar sind, wurde es innen erheblich umgebaut. Man betritt das Haus vom rückwärtigen Flachbau aus. Im herrschaftlichen Hochparterre des Hauptgebäudes wurde eine Bibliothek eingerichtet und im Souterrain das Konsulat. Im zweiten Obergeschoß liegen die Büros der Botschaft. Zur Erschließung dienen zwei neue Aufzüge und eine neue Treppe. Das Dachgeschoß wurde zur Wohnung des Botschafters ausgebaut. Das Dach des rechten Flügels wurde aufgestockt und nimmt ein Gästeappartement auf.

The Estonian Embassy is situated in an old building in Hildebrandstrasse in the diplomatic district. The three-storey residential building dating from 1870 was altered several times at the end of the 19th century and served as the Estonian Embassy from 1923. It has two side wings of unequal height, a sandstone facade and a lively, slate-covered mansard roof. The roof on the right hand wing, which is one storey higher, jumps to the height of the adjacent Greek embassy.

Because the building was largely undamaged in the Second World War it was constantly lived in – by contrast with most other buildings on the edge of Tiergarten. Estonia is one of the few countries whose land and buildings were continuously preserved. But that also means that the embassy had to terminate the tenancy of the occupants before alteration work could begin. Estonia is nevertheless the first of the three Baltic states to open its embassy in Berlin. The architect Olavi Nömmik from Tallinn was commissioned with the renovation and reconstruction after he won a restricted national architectural competition. Although no changes to the building are visible from the exterior, considerable alterations were made on the inside. The entrance to the building is via the flat building at the rear. A library was placed in the magnificent upper ground floor of the main building, and the consulate is on the lower ground floor. The offices are on the second floor and are reached via two new lifts and a new staircase. The attic was made into an apartment for the ambassador. The roof of the right hand wing was raised and includes a guest apartment.

Botschaft der Griechischen Republik / Greek Embassy

Hiroshimastraße 11
Hildebrandstraße 4
10785 Berlin (Tiergarten)

G. und C. Krause (Altbau/old building); Dimitris G. Papaioannou, Athen (Um- und Neubau/alterations and new building,)

1911, 1999 - 2001

Ansicht Hiroshima- /Ecke Tiergartenstraße/View from the corner of Hiroshimastrasse and Tiergartenstrasse

Weil „Griechenland als Hort der Kultur erfahren im Umgang mit Baudenkmälern" ist, wollte es seine alte dreistöckige Botschaft am Tiergartenrand erhalten. Sie bestand aus zwei Altbauten: einem Doppel-Wohngebäude (1911) an der heutigen Hiroshimastraße, das mit einem zweiten an der Hildebrandstraße durch ein Quergebäude verbunden ist, und einem Nachbargrundstück. Die repräsentative Jugendstilvilla wurde von G. und C. Krause entworfen. In den zwanziger Jahren übernahm Griechenland das Haus als Gesandtschaft. Der im Krieg beschädigte Bau wurde danach dem Verfall anheimgegeben. Die reich dekorierte Steinfassade ist dennoch gut erhalten, während die Inneneinrichtung bei einem Brand zerstört wurde.

1997 wurde Dimitris Papaioannou von der griechischen Regierung mit der Restaurierung und dem Entwurf für einen Anbau beauftragt. Residenz und repräsentative Empfangssäle befinden sich im restaurierten Altbau an der Hildebrandstraße. Das Innere wurde in Anlehnung an den ursprünglichen Zustand aufwendig saniert. Der zweite Altbau nimmt den größeren Teil der Botschaft auf.

Auf dem Nachbargrundstück an der Hiroshimastraße entsteht ein fünfgeschossiger Neubau mit eigenem Zugang. Der Entwurf übernimmt Formensprache und Konstruktion des Altbaus und nimmt in seiner Materialwahl auf den Bestand Bezug. „Einheit und Harmonie von Tradition und Moderne", das Hauptanliegen des Architekten, werden verstärkt durch ähnliche Fassadengestaltung und -proportion. Ein Glasstreifen bildet die Fuge zwischen beiden Gebäuden. Beide Gebäude stehen in einer Flucht, sind gleich hoch und haben eine ähnliche Dachform. Im Neubau werden Büros, das Generalkonsulat und das Informationsbüro untergebracht.

Because Greece is a "home of culture with experience in dealing with architectural monuments", it wanted to preserve its three-storey embassy on the edge of the Tiergarten.

It consisted of two old buildings: a double residential building (1911) on what is now Hiroshimastrasse, which is connected with a second building by a connecting wing, and an adjacent plot. The splendid villa in the Art Nouveau style was designed by G. and C. Krause. In the 1920s, Greece took over the building as its embassy. But the building was damaged during the war and left to deteriorate. The richly decorated stone facade is still well preserved, but the interior was destroyed in a fire.

In 1997, Dimitris Papaioannou was commissioned by the Greek government with the restoration work and the task of designing an extension. The residence and the splendid reception rooms are in the restored old building on Hildebrandstraße. The interior was extensively renovated in keeping with its original condition. The second old building contains the major part of the embassy.

On the neighbouring plot on Hiroshimastraße, a five-storey new building with its own entrance is being built. The design takes up the formal language and structure of the old building and uses materials in keeping with the existing buildings. "Unity and harmony of tradition and the modern style", the main concern of the architect, are underlined by the similar design and proportions of the facades. A glass strip forms the joint between the two buildings. Both buildings stand on one alignment line and have the same height and a similar roof form. The new building will be used for office accommodation, the general consulate and the information office.

Botschaft der Italienischen Republik / Embassy of Italy

 Tiergartenstr 21a-23
Hiroshimastraße 1
10785 Berlin (Tiergarten)

Friedrich Hetzelt (Altbau/
old building); Vittorio De Feo,
Rom und Stefan Dietrich, Berlin
(Renovierung/renovation)

1943, 1999-2000

Zustand 1940/
The building in 1940

Friedrich Hetzelt entwarf 1939 den Bau im Stil eines italienischen Palazzos der Hochrenaissance, nachdem ein italienischer Entwurf von den deutschen Behörden abgelehnt worden war. Die kostbare Innenausstattung mit Türen und Friesen aus dem Palazzo Ducale in Gubbio (1495) sollte die Bedeutung der „Achsenmacht" betonen. Der Komplex umfaßt über 300 Räume. Ein viertes Geschoß versteckt sich hinter dem Dachgesims. An der monumentalen Straßenfassade hat das Haus einen fünfachsigen Mittelrisalit. Der Sockel ist mit römischem Travertin verkleidet und das Piano Nobile rotbraun verputzt.

Nachdem die Botschaft im Zweiten Weltkrieg beschädigt wurde, diente der weitgehend unversehrte Kanzleiflügel an der Hiroshimastraße bis 1950 wieder als Botschaft, danach als Generalkonsulat, während die übrigen Teile des Hauses verfielen.

Bei einem nationalen Wettbewerb zur Sanierung konnte sich 1995 der römische Architekt Vittorio De Feo durchsetzen. Sein Konzept sah vor, die Teilruine „respektvoll zu restaurieren und möglichst originalgetreu wieder herzurichten". Im zweiten Stock ist die Residenz des Botschafters untergebracht. Im Westflügel liegen Konsulat und Verwaltung.

Die Spuren der Geschichte sollen nicht verwischt werden. Schäden an der Fassade werden nicht beseitigt, und die faschistischen Reliefs an der Tür des Botschafterbüros werden zwar entfernt, aber denkmalgerecht konserviert und im Haus ausgestellt. Im Hof wird eine große Freitreppe gebaut. Dem pragmatischen Umgang der Italiener mit ihrem Gebäude liegt die Auffassung zugrunde, daß die Akzeptanz der Geschichte gleichzeitig vor ihrem Vergessen schützen soll.

The building was designed in 1939 by Friedrich Hetzelt in the style of a high Renaissance Italian palazzo after an Italian design had been rejected by the German authorities. The valuable interior with doors and friezes from the Palazzo Ducale in Gubbio (1495) aimed to underline the importance of the "axis power". The complex contains over 300 rooms. Although the building appears to have three storeys, a fourth storey is concealed behind the eaves. In the monumental street facade the building has a central projection spanning five axes. The pedestal is clad with Roman travertine and the "piano nobile" is rendered in a reddish brown.

After the embassy was damaged in the Second World War, the largely undamaged embassy wing in Hiroshimastrasse was again used as the embassy until 1950, and then as the consulate general, but the other parts of the building were left to decay.

A national competition for the renovation in 1995 was won by the Roman architect Vittorio De Feo. His concept was that the partial ruin should be "respectfully restored and rebuilt as faithfully as possible to the original". The ambassador's residence is on the second floor. The west wing contains the consulate and administration.

The traces of history are to be preserved. The damage to the facade was not removed, and the Fascist reliefs on the door of the ambassador's office were taken away, but expertly conserved as artistic monuments and displayed in the building. An outdoor flight of stairs is being built in the courtyard. The pragmatic treatment of the building by the Italians is based on the view that an acceptance of history will at the same time help us not to forget.

Botschaft von Japan/ Embassy of Japan

Tiergartenstr. 24-25
10785 Berlin (Tiergarten)

Ludwig Moshamer (Altbau/old building); Kisho Kurokawa und Tajii Yamaguchi (Umbau/alterations); Ryohel Amemiya, Tokio mit HPP, Berlin (Neubau/new building)

1940, 1988, 1998-2000

Ansicht Hiroshimastraße/
View from Hiroshimastrasse

Die Japanische Botschaft wurde 1940 nach Plänen von Ludwig Moshamer erbaut. In dem Monumentalbau wurden Repräsentationsräume, Wohnungen und Büros vereinigt. Das kalksteinverblendete Gebäude hat einen zurückspringenden Mittelteil. Die kostbare Innenausstattung von Caesar Pinnau sollte die politische Bedeutung des Tennos als Verbündetem illustrieren. Nach dem Zweiten Weltkrieg blieb das ruinöse Haus, nur notdürftig gesichert, größtenteils verwaist. Erst 1988 wurde aus dem nach Plänen der japanischen Architekten Kisho Kurokawa und Tajii Yamaguchi rekonstruierten Gebäude eine wissenschaftliche Begegnungsstätte. Da die Bausubstanz in schlechtem Zustand war, riß man den Altbau bis auf den Seitenflügel ab und schuf eine Replik. Die Vorderfront wurde originalgetreu wiederaufgebaut und das Innere neu gestaltet. Hinter dem Hauptgebäude wurden moderne Anbauten angefügt und ein japanischer Garten angelegt.

Das Japanisch-Deutsche Zentrum war bis 1998 Mieter des Hauses. Mit der deutschen Wiedervereinigung beschloß Japan, seine Botschaft von Bonn nach Berlin zu verlegen und dafür seine alte Repräsentanz erneut um- und auszubauen. Nach Plänen von Ryohel Amemiya wurde die Kanzlei an der Hiroshimastraße umgebaut und durch einen Neubau für das Konsulat erweitert. Er gliedert sich in einen kubischen viergeschossigen Bürotrakt und einen einstöckigen Bau mit einer aufgesetzten, zweigeschossigen Ellipse mit der Visaabteilung. Der Entwurf paßt sich an den Altbau in Form und Materialien an. Der Kopfbau wird zu Repräsentationszwecken und für die renovierte Residenz genutzt.

The Japanese Embassy was built in 1940 to plans by Ludwig Moshamer. The monumental building combined representation rooms, apartments and offices. The sandstone-faced building has a receding central section. The splendid interior by Caesar Pinnau was designed to illustrate the political importance of the Japanes head of state as an ally. After the Second Word War the ruins of the building were provisionally secured and largely left to decay. It was only in 1988 that the building was reconstructed to plans by the Japanese architects Kisho Kurokawa and Tajii Yamaguchi and made into a scientific meeting place. Because the structure was in a poor condition, the old building was demolished except the side wing and a replica was built. The front facade was rebuilt as a faithful copy of the original, and the interior was redesigned. Behind the main building, modern extensions were added and a Japanese garden was created.

Until 1998, the building was rented by the Japanese-German centre. When Germany was re-unified, Japan decided to move its embassy from Bonn to Berlin and to alter and extend its old embassy building. The building on Hiroshimastrasse was altered to plans by Ryohel Amemiya and extended by the addition of a new consulate building. It is sub-divided into a cube-like four-storey office wing and a single-storey building with an added two-storey ellipse containing the visa department. The form and materials of the design match the old building. The building at the end of the complex is used for representation purposes and the renovated residence.

oben/above: Ansicht Kupferband Klingelhöferstraße/
View of the ribbon of copper
from Klingelhöfersstrasse
rechts oben/right above:
Lageplan/Site plan
rechts unten/right below:
Gemeinschaftshaus/Building for
mutual use

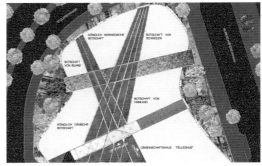

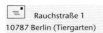 Rauchstraße 1
10787 Berlin (Tiergarten)

Gesamtentwurf und Ge-
meinschaftshaus/Masterplan
and Building for mutual use:
Berger + Parkkinen Architekten,
Wien/Helsinki
Dänische Botschaft/Embassy of
Denmark: Nielsen, Nielsen &
Nielsen A/S, Arhus
Finnische Botschaft/Embassy of
Finland: VIIVA Arkkitehtuuri Oy,
Helsinki
Isländische Botschaft/Embassy
of Iceland: Pälmar Kristmund-
son, Reykjavik
Norwegische Botschaft/Embassy
of Norway: Snøhetta as, Oslo
Schwedische Botschaft/Embassy
of Sweden: Wingårdh Arkitekt-
kontor AB, Göteborg
Koordinierende Architekten und
Bauleitung/Coordinating archi-
tects and supervision of building
works: Pysall Ruge Architekten,
Berlin

 1996-1999

Botschaften der Nordischen Länder / The Embassies of the Nordic Countries

Dänische Botschaft/
Embassy of Denmark

Mit rund 300.000 Einwohnern ist Island nicht gerade eine Supermacht. Und doch hat das Land nicht nur eine Gesandtschaft in Berlin gebaut, sondern es verfügt auch noch über ein Veranstaltungshaus. Möglich wird das, weil sich die fünf nordischen Staaten Dänemark, Finnland, Norwegen, Schweden und eben Island wider Konkurrenzdenken und Eifersüchteleien für einen gemeinsamen Botschaftskomplex entschlossen haben. Obgleich eine solche Entscheidung ob der kulturellen Gemeinsamkeiten und der effizienteren Vertretung zweifellos Sinn macht, stellt sie doch einen gänzlich neuen Schritt auf dem diplomatischen Parkett dar.

Vorbildlich ist auch, wie hier die Architektur zum Botschafter wird. Das zeigt sich bereits beim Blick auf den Stadtplan: Die Länder, die selbst von Landschaft dominiert werden, wählten ein Grundstück, das diese Eigenschaft soweit widerspiegelt, wie das im Hauptstadtbezirk einer Millionenmetropole möglich ist. Die Nordspitze des Tiergarten-Dreiecks reckt sich in den größten Park der Stadt, den Tiergarten. Auch die Baufigur, mit der sich die Architekten Alfred Berger und Tiina Parkkinen Ende 1995 in einem offenen Wettbewerb, der in allen EU-Staaten sowie in Norwegen und Island ausgelobt wurde, gegen über 200 Konkurrenten durchsetzten, unterstreicht, daß sich urbanes Leben in Nordeuropa gegenüber der Natur stets behaupten muß: Die Anlage wird durch ein frei geschwungenes, 16 Meter hohes Band aus Kupferlamellen gegenüber der wildromantischen Spontanvegetation abgegrenzt, die sich im ehemaligen Diplomatenviertel aussamte, nachdem es infolge von Krieg und Teilung brachgefallen war. An die leuchtend grüne Wand schmiegen sich innenseitig die einzelnen Botschaftsbauten, die durch schmale Straßen aus der kom-

With about 300,000 inhabitants, Iceland is not exactly a superpower. But the country has not only built an embassy in Berlin, it even has its own separate building for official events. That is possible because the five Nordic states of Denmark, Finland, Norway, Sweden and Iceland decided against competitive thinking and jealousy and in favour of a joint embassy complex. Although such a decision is undoubtedly sensible in view of the common elements of their culture and the increased efficiency, it is nevertheless a completely new departure in the diplomatic realm.

The way architecture itself becomes an ambassador is also exemplary. This can be seen by just looking at the city map: the countries which themselves have wide expanses of landscape selected a plot which reflects this characteristic as far as that is possible in a metropolitan capital city with millions of inhabitants. The northern tip of the old Tiergarten Triangle stretches into the largest park in the city, the Tiergarten. And even the design with which the architects Alfred Berger and Tiina Parkkinen won the open competition at the end of 1995 – a competition held in all EU states, Norway and Iceland in which there were over 200 entries – underlines that urban life in Northern Europe must always assert itself against nature. A 16 metre high ribbon of copper shutters separates the complex from the wildly romantic spontaneous vegetation which spread in the former diplomatic district after it became wasteland as a result of war and the division of the city. The individual embassy buildings, which are cut out of the compact structure by narrow dividing alleys, are nestled against the inside of the bright green wall. The dividing alleys place the "solitary" buildings in relationship to each other: in

Finnische Botschaft/
Embassy of Finland

pakten Baumasse herausgeschnitten sind. Die Straßen sind so plaziert, daß sie die „Solitäre" in Beziehung zueinander setzen: In Dimension und Plazierung bilden sie ein grobes Abbild der realen Größenverhältnisse und der geographischen Lage der Länder, die sie repräsentieren. Sie sind also Landmarken im besten Sinne.

Da die Straßen zwar einen Gemeinschaftsraum bilden, aber nicht allen Aktivitäten, die die fünf Länder gemeinsam unternehmen wollen, optimale Entfaltungsmöglichkeiten geben, liegt gleich links des Platzes, mit dem sich dieses Botschaftscamp zur Stadt öffnet, das **Felleshus**, das gleichfalls von dem finnisch-österreichischen Büro entworfen wurde. Hier kommen alle Konsularabteilungen, das Restaurant, Bankett- und Veranstaltungssäle unter. Seine Fassade entfaltet ein ähnliches Vexierspiel wie die Gesamtkomposition: In das mit Holz ausgefachte Betonrahmenwerk sind schmale Glasbänder eingeschnitten. Sie sind so plaziert, daß nicht durch die Umgebung abgelenkt wird, wer sich schon in dem Gebäude befindet, und dem Außenstehenden gerade soviel Einblick gewähren, daß seine Neugier an dem im Innern stattfindenden Kulturprogramm geweckt wird. Die Aktivitäten bündelt ein Atrium, das durch Stege, Treppen und die eingestellte Ebene des kaum abgeteilten Veranstaltungssaals architektonisch ebenso spannend ist wie funktional. Es durchtrennt die „Erlebnislandschaft" des Felleshus' mittig und formt dort, wo es die Fassade zum Platz durchstößt, ein Tor, das Passanten geradezu einlädt, nordische Kultur kennenzulernen.

Ihm gegenüber liegt die **Dänische Botschaft** von Nielsen, Nielsen & Nielsen, die in ihrer Heimat zu den erfolg-

their dimensions and position they form a rough representation of the sizes and geographical positions of the countries they represent. They are thus landmarks in the best sense.

As these alleys form a shared spatial context but do not create the ideal setting for all activities that the five countries want to share, there is a **"Felleshus"** 1 to the left of the open space which opens the embassies out to the city, a building that was also designed by the Finish-Austrian architectural office and contains all consular departments, the restaurant and the banquet and festive hall. Its facade is as enigmatic as the overall composition. Small bands of glass are inserted into the wooden panels in the concrete frame. They are placed in such a way that anyone in the building is not distracted by the surrounds, and that a person outside sees just enough to arouse curiosity about the cultural programme in the interior. The activities are gathered in an atrium which is architecturally both exciting and functional with its walkways, stairs and the inserted festive hall, which is only partly enclosed by walls. This hall divides the "experience landscape" of the "Felleshus", and where it protrudes through the facade to the square outside it forms a gate which invites passers-by to get to known Nordic culture.

Opposite this building is the **Danish Embassy** by Nielsen, Nielsen + Nielsen, who are among the most successful architectural offices in Denmark. It consists of a gently curved block which exactly follows the outer contours of the copper ribbon with another straight block in front of it. This contrast gives the long, glass-

Botschaften der Nordischen Länder / The Embassies of the Nordic Countries

reichsten Architekturbüros zählen. Sie besteht aus einem sanft geschwungenen, die äußere Kontur des Kupferbandes exakt nachzeichnenden Riegel, vor den ein geradliniger gesetzt ist. Durch diesen Kontrast bekommt der langgestreckte, glasgedeckte Raum dazwischen eine Spannung, die mit dem Atrium des Felleshus' konkurrieren kann. Die Wand des geschwungenen Riegels, die den überdachten Weg begleitet, ist wie in Alvar Aaltos Finnischem Pavillon auf der Weltausstellung 1939 in New York mit feinen Holzlamellen bekleidet und als Panoptikum ausgebildet. Darüber hinaus besticht das mit Lochblechen aus Edelstahl verkleidete Haus durch Details von Schlichtheit und Eleganz, wie sie seit Jahrzehnten Markenzeichen dänischen Designs sind.

Auch die **Isländische Botschaft** des jungen Pälmar Kristmundson besteht aus zwei Blöcken, die freilich keinen Innenraum formen, sondern die Randlage und bescheidenen Ausmaße der Botschaft mit einer starken Geste kompensieren wollen. Sie bestehen außen aus den elementaren Materialien Beton bzw. rotem isländischen Ryolith-Stein, das Lärchenholz ist in jedem Funktionsbereich unterschiedlich behandelt. Die jeweils vier Geschosse werden alle im wesentlichen über die verglasten Dächer erhellt, wodurch dramatische Lichteffekte erzielt werden. Nicht zuletzt verleiht Kristmundson durch die Art, wie die beiden Körper verkeilt sind, den Naturgewalten seiner Heimat kraftvoll Ausdruck.

Um Inszenierung geht es auch dem Osloer Architekturbüro Snøhetta, das zur Zeit mit der Weltbibliothek in Alexandria eine der prestigeträchtigsten Bauaufgaben überhaupt fertigstellt. Seine **Norwegische Botschaft** –

covered space between them a tension which can compete with the atrium in the "Felleshus". The wall of the curved block along the covered path is clad with wooden slats and formed as a collection of curios like Alvar Aalto's Finnish Pavilion at the 1939 world exhibition in New York. The building is faced with perforated stainless steel sheeting and is impressive in its details of simplicity and elegance, features that have been typical of Danish design for decades.

The **Icelandic Embassy** by the young Pälmar Kristmundson also consists of two blocks, although they do not form an inner space, rather they aim to compensate for the peripheral position and modest size of the embassy with a strong gesture. On the outside they consist of the elementary materials of concrete and red Icelandic Ryolith stone; the larchwood is treated differently in each functional area. The four storeys in each block mainly receive their light through the glazed roofs, which creates dramatic lighting effects. Not least, Kristmundson aims to lend powerful expression to the powers of nature in his home country by the way in which the two structures are interlinked.

Dramatic effect is also the concern of the Oslo architectural office of Snøhetta which is currently completing one of the most prestigious of all construction projects, the world library in Alexandria. Their **Norwegian Embassy** – a simple structure with a metal grid suspended in front of the facade – recedes completely, focusing all the attention on the granite slab at its end which is as tall as the building, 5 metres wide, 70 centimetres thick and weighs 120 tonnes and which conceals the entrance

Norwegische Botschaft/
Embassy of Norway

ein simpler Baukörper mit vor die Fassade gehängtem Metallgitter – nimmt sich vollkommen zurück, alle Aufmerksamkeit konzentriert sich auf die gebäudehohe, fünf Meter breite, 70 Zentimeter dicke und 120 Tonnen schwere Granittafel an seiner Stirnseite, die den Eingang verbirgt und die in einem Stück aus dem norwegischen Gebirge geschnitten wurde, um ebenso monolithisch nach Berlin transportiert zu werden. Als einziges stehendes Element steht sie im Blickpunkt der gesamten Anlage und setzt die Vertikalität der Fjordlandschaft, die Norwegen von allen anderen skandinavischen Staaten unterscheidet, dramatisch in Szene.

Eine horizontale Fassadengliederung war für alle Botschaften vorgegeben. Sie ist zugleich eines der wenigen Merkmale, die die **Schwedische Gesandtschaft** mit seinen Nachbarn verbindet, die mit dem unliebsamen Bauplatz in der nordöstlichen Ecke des Komplexes vorlieb nehmen muß. Während ihre Nachbarn in sich konsistente Architekturkonzepte verfolgen, kombiniert der Göteborger Gerd Wingårdh verschiedenste Elemente, was durchaus ein Grundcharakterzug der schwedischen Architektur ist. Das Gebäude zerfällt in eine helle, leichte mit gotländischem Kalkstein sowie transparentem und opalisiertem Glas verkleidete Südfront, hinter der fast alle Empfangsräume der Botschaft liegen, und eine dunkle Westfassade, aus der sich überschneidende, zickzack-artige Platten aus schwarzem Diabas-Stein herausklappen und hinter der sich mehrheitlich Verwaltungstrakte befinden. Dem Inneren merkt man an, daß der Architekt vor allem Bürohäuser für Bauherren mit ausgeprägtem Repräsentationsbedürfnis, aber wenig Profil entwirft. Die Materialien – vor allem gebeiztes Birken-

and was cut in one piece out of a Norwegian mountain and transported to Berlin as a monolith. As the only standing element, it can be seen throughout the complex and dramatically symbolises the vertical character of the fjords which distinguish Norway from all other Scandinavian states.

Horizontal sub-division of the facade was prescribed for all embassies. And it is one of the few characteristics that the **Swedish Embassy**, which occupies the unrewarding site at the north-eastern corner of the complex, has in common with its neighbours. Whereas the neighbours follow architectural concepts that are consistent in themselves, the Göteborg architect Gerd Wingårdh combines different elements, which is a basic feature of Swedish architecture. The building consists of a light and bright south facade faced with Gotland limestone and transparent and opaque glass behind which almost all reception rooms in the embassy are situated and a dark western facade from which overlapping zigzag panels of black diabase stone project and behind which there are mainly administrative offices. The interior reflects the fact that the architect mainly designs office buildings for clients with a great need of impressive representation but a moderate aesthetic profile. The materials – mainly stained birchwood – are extremely intricate in their treatment, but without logic. Whereas all the other embassies create a design contrast to the copper ribbon, strips of this metal on the staircase in the Swedish light courtyard setting obscure the clear separation of the exterior and the interior, the multilateral and the national.

Botschaften der Nordischen Länder / The Embassies of the Nordic Countries

Schwedische Botschaft/
Embassy of Sweden

holz – sind äußerst aufwendig, aber ohne Logik verarbeitet: Während alle anderen Botschaften gestalterisch auf Distanz zum Kupferband gehen, verwischen in der schwedischen Lichthoflandschaft Streifen dieses Metalls an der Treppe die klare Trennung von innen und außen, von multilateral und national.

Ein Musterbeispiel an Stringenz ist dagegen die **Finnische Gesandtschaft** von Rauno Lehtinen, Pekka Mäki und Toni Peltola, was sich insbesondere an der – natürlich horizontal gegliederten – Fassade zeigt: Schmale Lärchenholzstäbe, die schon nach kurzer Zeit eine silbrige Patina ansetzen werden, legen sich in kaum handbreitem Abstand vor eine Glashaut. Konsequenter als die übrigen Botschaften behält sich die Finnische Vertretung ihre eigentlichen Reize – die seltsam geknickte Erschließung aus Eingang, Foyer, Treppe und mit Birkenholz ausgekleidetem Konferenzsaal – für das Innere vor, genau wie es im rauhen Klima Skandinaviens Tradition ist.

Insgesamt erzählt die Gemeinschaftsgesandtschaft der Nordischen Staaten weit mehr über die Länder, die sie vertritt, als jede andere Botschaft in Berlin. Architektonisch wie von der geplanten Nutzung ist sie das beste Beispiel der Festivalisierung von Politik, die das gesamte Hauptstadtprojekt kennzeichnet.

The **Finnish Embassy** by Rauno Lehtinen, Pekka Mäki and Toni Peltola, on the other hand, is a model of stringency, which is particularly apparent in the facade – which is of course horizontally sub-divided. Narrow larchwood rods, which will have a silvery patina before long, are mounted hardly a hand's width away from a glass shell. More consistently than the other embassies, the Finnish embassy restricts the charms of its design – the strangely folded access with the entrance, foyer and stairs and the conference hall clad with birchwood – to the interior, in keeping with the tradition in the rough climate of Scandinavia

On the whole, the joint embassy complex of the Nordic states shows much more about the countries it represents than any other embassy in Berlin. Architecturally and in its planned utilisation it is the best example of festive politics in the whole capital city project.

Tiergarten–Dreieck: Botschaften von Malaysia/Jemen/Luxemburg / Tiergarten Triangle: Embassies of Malaysia, Yemen, Luxembourg

 Rauchstraße, Klingelhöferstraße, Stülerstraße, Corneliuspromenade

Städtebauliche Planung: Machleidt und Partner mit Walter Stepp; Pysall Stahrenberg & Partner (Malaysia); Sayed Mohammad Oreyzi, Köln (Luxemburg)

ab 1998

Gesamtareal/General view

Das Tiergarten-Dreieck markiert den wichtigsten stadtstrukturellen Gewinn, den Berlin im Zuge des Hauptstadtprojekts verbuchen konnte. Erstaunlich ist bereits, daß hier überhaupt etwas gebaut wird, nachdem das Areal in der Nachkriegszeit lediglich als Rummelplatz genutzt wurde und alle früheren Bauvorhaben scheiterten. Wichtiger ist, daß das neue Quartier das Zentrum am Zoo mit dem Diplomatenviertel verbindet, wodurch zumindest eine der Sollbruchstellen überwunden wäre, die bisher zwischen City-West und alter Mitte lagen.

Die Verbindung gelingt zum einen im Städtebau: 1995 gewannen Hildebrand Machleidt und Walter Stepp den entsprechenden Wettbewerb mit einem Entwurf, der die traditionelle Haustypologie des westlichen Zentrums – Bauwerke mit Vorderhaus, Seitenflügel und Quergebäude – so freistellte, wie es für das Diplomatenviertels charakteristisch ist. Die 13 Bausteine sollten mit einer Höhe von 18 Metern und einer Orientierung an der Straßenflucht so einheitlich wie ein innenstädtischer Block sein, gestalterisch aber so solitär wie die nahegelegen Villen dastehen, weshalb sie von mehr als einem halben Dutzend Architekten entworfen werden.

Zum zweiten kommt es funktional zur Synthese. Einerseits nimmt das Tiergarten-Dreieck Repräsentanzen auf, die auch im Diplomatenviertel dominieren: Neben der Botschaft Malaysias an der Klingelhöferstraße, die ein Gebäude von Pysall Stahrenberg & Partner bezieht, hat Luxemburg eine Etage in einem Bauwerk gekauft, das der Kölner Architekt Sayed Mohammad Oreyzi entworfen hat. Jemen hat die Nordwest-Ecke erworben, wo ein Wettbewerb die Botschaftsgestalt klären soll. Zugleich entstehen innenstädtische Nutzungen wie eine Galerie, ein Health-Club und 160 Wohnungen. (hwh)

The Tiergarten Triangle is the most important urban structure gain which Berlin has made in the course of the capital city project. The very fact that the land is being developed is surprising in itself: since the war the land has been used as a fairground and all previous building projects failed. But it is more important that the new development links the Zoo district with the diplomatic district, thus bridging at least one of the gaps that have so far existed between the western city and the old centre. Firstly, the link is successful in its urban design. In 1995, Hildebrand Machleidt and Walter Stepp won the competition with a design which modified the traditional building typology of the western centre – buildings with a front section, side wing and transverse structure – to create detached units characteristic of the diplomatic district. The 13 modules were to have a uniform height of 18 metres and to be oriented towards the road alignment line and to be as uniform in type as an inner city block, but to be separate in their design like the nearby villas, which is why they were designed by more than half a dozen architects.

Secondly, there is a functional synthesis. On the one hand, the Tiergarten Triangle includes embassies, which are also predominant in the diplomatic district: apart from the embassy of Malaysia on Klingelhöferstrasse, which occupies a building by Pysall Stahrenberg & Partner, Luxembourg has purchased a storey in a building designed by the Cologne architect Sayed Mohammad Oreyzi. Yemen has purchased the north-west corner, where a competition will decide on the design of the embassy. But at the same time, inner city facilities are being included such as a gallery, a health club and 160 apartments. (hwh)

Botschaft der Vereinigten Staaten von Mexiko / Embassy of Mexico

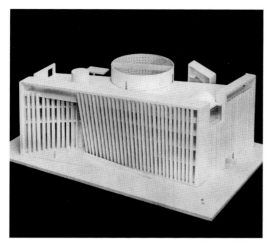

Klingelhöferstraße 3,
Rauchstraße 27
10787 Berlin (Tiergarten)

Teodoro González de
León, Francisco Serrano,
Mexico-City

1999-2000

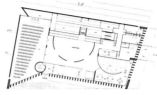

links/left: Eingangssituation/
Entrance area
rechts/right: Grundriß EG/
Ground plan, ground floor

Auf dem Tiergarten-Dreieck bestimmte 1995 ein städtebaulicher Wettbewerb, den Hildebrand Machleidt und Walter Stepp gewannen, den Rahmen, in dem sich die Botschaften zu bewegen hatten. Die Repräsentanzen durften zwar frei stehen, mußten sich aber in die Bauflucht einreihen. Das Höhenstreben hatte auf 18 Meter sein Ende zu finden. Gleichwohl wünschte sich Mexiko, daß sein erster Botschaftsneubau in Europa „die Reichtümer seiner Kultur" und die „Erwartungen des Landes für das nächste Jahrtausend" widerspiegeln sollte. Teodoro González de León und Francisco Serrano, die bereits die Gesandtschaften in Brasilien und Guatemala bauten, gelang dieser Spagat. Ihr Kubus ist regelgerecht und huldigt doch der Sprache und dem Optimismus der in der Stadt gegenwärtig verpönten Moderne. In der Fassade, die aus vom Bürgersteig bis zur Traufe durchlaufenden weißen Betonlamellen besteht, trifft sich die Schlichtheit, die man in Berlin von einem städtischen Haus erwartet, mit der kaum zu überbietenden Monumentalität, die mexikanische Architektur seit präkolonialer Zeit prägte. Der Lamellenvorhang ist sanft nach hinten zusammengenommen, so daß ein gebäudehohes Portal entsteht. Schon wie Freitreppe und Behindertenrampe ineinandergreifen, verrät die Meisterschaft der Architekten. Das Innere folgt dem Typus des traditionellen mexikanischen Hofhauses. Der erweiterbare Mehrzwecksaal im Parterre, das Konsulat im ersten Obergeschoß, die darüberliegenden Empfangsräume des Botschafters oder der terrassierte Garten: Alles konzentriert sich auf einen großen Zylinder aus perforiertem Beton. Das Licht wird diesem Raum eine ebenso repräsentative wie meditative Atmosphäre verleihen. (hwh)

On the Tiergarten Triangle an urban design competition in 1995, which was won by Hildebrand Machleidt and Walter Stepp, defined the framework within which the embassies had to move. The embassies could be detached, but they had to adhere to the alignment line. Their vertical dimension had to end at 18 metres. Mexico nevertheless wanted its first new embassy building in Europe to reflect "the riches of its culture" and the "expectations of the country for the next millennium". Teodoro Gonzaléz de León and Francisco Serrano, who had already built the embassies in Brazil and Guatemala, achieved this combination. Their cubic structure complies with the regulations and nevertheless makes use of the modernist formal language and optimism which are currently out of favour in Berlin. The facade consists of white concrete slats from the pavement to the eaves, thus combining the austerity which the city expects of an urban building with the almost unsurpassable monumentality which has dominated Mexican architecture since pre-colonial times. The curtain of louvered slats recedes slightly, creating a portal that is as high the building itself. The way this portal joins with the outdoor steps and the ramp for the disabled shows the mastery of the architects. The interior is like a traditional Mexican courtyard house. The extending multi-purpose hall on the ground floor, the consulate on the ground floor, the ambassador's reception rooms above that and the terraced garden: all are concentrated on a large cylinder of perforated concrete. In this spatial context, light will create an atmosphere that is both impressive and meditative. (hwh)

Botschaft des Königreichs Spanien / Embassy of the Kingdom of Spain

 Lichtensteinallee 1
10787 Berlin (Tiergarten)

Walter und Johannes Krüger; Pedro Muguruza Otaño (Altbau/old building); José Luis Iñiguez de Onzoño und Jesús Velasco Ruiz (TYPSA), Madrid (Umbau/alterations)

1943, 1999-2001

Hauptportal/Main entrance

Die Botschaft Spaniens residiert seit 1943 auf einem Eckgrundstück am Tiergartenrand. Das Gebäude, 1938 entworfen (Architekten: Walter und Johannes Krüger sowie Pedro Muguruza Otaño), war Teil des neuen Botschaftsviertels im Tiergarten, das nach Speers Plänen eine „einheitliche Baugesinnung widerspiegeln" sollte.

Die beiden spitzwinkligen Flügel dienen der Verwaltung und der Residenz. Ein repräsentativer Haupteingang erschließt die große Halle. In den letzten Kriegsmonaten machten Bomben aus der Botschaft eine Teilruine. In den fünfziger Jahren erfolgte, abermals durch Johannes Krüger, die Instandsetzung des Kanzleiflügels, der lange der einzige genutzte Teil des monumentalen Gebäudes blieb. Als in den achtziger Jahren der expandierende Berliner Zoo ein Tiergehege auf dem Grundstück bauen wollte, verhinderte nur der Denkmalschutz den Abriß.

1991 entschied sich Spaniens Vertretung zur Rückkehr in ihre Berliner Botschaft und zur grundlegenden Sanierung des Altbaus. Bei einem Wettbewerb entschied man sich für das Büro TYPSA aus Madrid. Das Haus wurde entkernt und innen neu errichtet. Man sah einen „Neubau mit ähnlichen Materialien wie beim Original hinter alter Fassade" vor. Spanien erlaubte erhebliche Eingriffe in die Bausubstanz, denn das Haus wurde „historisch entrümpelt" und die Reliefs entfernt. Nur der Denkmalschutz garantierte den Erhalt eines Großteils der „faschistischen" Fassaden. Die Anpassung an den Altbau versucht, den weitgehenden Abriß zu mildern. Der Kanzleiflügel wurde dennoch abgebrochen, und nur die Fassade des Repräsentationsflügels und der Kopfbau blieben erhalten. Dahinter wird ein neuer Bürotrakt gebaut.

From 1943 the Spanish embassy was situated on a corner plot on the edge of the Tiergarten. The building was designed in 1938 (architects: Walter and Johannes Krüger/ Pedro Muguruza Otaño) and was part of the new embassy district in Tiergarten which, according to the plans of Speer, was to "reflect a uniform architectural taste".

The two pointed wings are used for administration and the residence. A splendid main entrance leads into the great hall. In the last few months of the war, bombs partly destroyed the embassy. In the 1950s the embassy wing was restored, again by Johannes Krüger, and for a long time this wing was the only part of the monumental building that was actually in use.

In the 1980s, when the expanding Berlin zoo wanted to build an animal enclosure on the plot, demolition was only prevented by the monument conservation authority.

The Spanish embassy decided in 1991 to return to its embassy building in Berlin and to carry out thorough renovation of the old building. In a competition, the commission was awarded to the TYPSA office from Madrid. The building was hollowed out and completely rebuilt on the inside. It was planned to be a "new building with similar materials to the original behind an old facade". Spain permitted considerable alterations to the structural substance because the building was "historically purified" and the reliefs removed. A major proportion of the "Fascist" facades were only preserved because of monument conservation. The adaptation to fit in with the old architecture endeavours to alleviate the excessive demolition work. But the embassy wing was still demolished, and the facade of the representation wing and the end building are all that remains. Behind them, a new office wing is being built.

Botschaft von Kuwait / Embassy of Kuwait

Griegstraße 5-7
14193 Berlin (Zehlendorf)

Breslauer & Salinger (Alt-
bau/old building); Kroos & Zittlau-Kroos, Berlin (Umbau/altera-
tions)

1929, 1999 - 2000

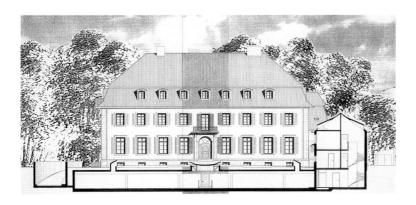

Schnitt durch Neubau/Cross
section of the new building

Die Botschaft des Emirats Kuwait residiert in einer Villa im Grunewald, die zuletzt als Sitz des Wissenschaftszentrums diente. Haus und Garten stehen unter Denkmalschutz. Der Golfstaat hatte das Areal mit dem Altbau 1995 gekauft und ein Nachbargrundstück dazugekauft. Das ehemalige Wohnhaus mit herrschaftlicher Auffahrt und Park, der einmal bis zur Regerstraße gereicht hatte, wurde 1929 für den Fabrikanten Heidemann von den Architekten Breslauer & Salinger erbaut und erinnert an einen märkischen Landsitz. Um den Botschaftsbetrieb mitten im umgebenden Wohngebiet zu ermöglichen, mußte der Bebauungsplan geändert werden.

Das Architekturbüro Kroos & Zittlau-Kroos ging 1997 aus einem Wettbewerb als Sieger hervor. Sein Konzept sieht vor, mit möglichst wenigen Eingriffen die repräsentativen Räume des Hauses umzubauen. Veränderungen aus der Nachkriegszeit (zwischenzeitlich war das Gebäude als Altersheim genutzt worden) werden zum größten Teil rückgängig gemacht.

Das große Haus wird restauriert und zur Botschaft umgebaut. Anstelle des ehemaligen Chauffeurhauses wird das neue Konsulat errichtet. In der Nähe der zweigeschossigen Villa sind zwei Neubauten mit je drei Wohnungen geplant. Um die Vorfahrt nicht als Wagenstellfläche nutzen zu müssen, entsteht eine Tiefgarage. Der Bauherr respektiert die Architektur einer konservativen, deutschen Villa mit gediegener Innenausstattung und hält sich mit eigenen Gestaltungswünschen vornehm zurück. Notwendige moderne Ergänzungen werden sensibel eingefügt.

The embassy of the Emirate of Kuwait is located in a villa in Grunewald which was recently used as the headquarters of the Science Centre. The building and garden are listed monuments. The Gulf State purchased the land with the old building in 1995 and an adjoining plot, too. The former residential house with its estate-style drive and park, which once extended to Regerstrasse, was built in 1929 for the factory-owner Heidemann by the architects Breslauer & Salinger and is reminiscent of the country mansions in the March of Brandenburg. The zoning plans had to be revised to enable the embassy to open in the middle of a residential district.

The architectural office of Kroos & Zittlau-Kroos was the winner in a competition in 1997. The concept envisages converting the impressive rooms in the building with as few changes as possible. Alterations from the post-war period (including the time when the building was used as an old people's home) are largely being restored to their former state.

The large mansion is being restored and converted for use as the embassy. The new consulate is being built in place of the former chauffeur's house. Near the two-storey villa, two new buildings with three apartments each are planned. An underground car park is being built to avoid the necessity of using the drive for parking. The client respects the architecture of a conservative German villa with luxurious interior fittings and refrains from expressing excessive design wishes of its own. The necessary modern additions are being added sensitively.

Botschaft von Israel / Embassy of Israel

Auguste-Viktoria-Straße 74-78/Reinerzstraße 46-48 14193 Berlin (Zehlendorf)

Philipp Schaefer (Altbau/old building); Orit Willenberg-Giladi, Tel Aviv (Neubau/new building)

1930, 1999 - 2000

rechts im Bild: Villa Schlöndorff/on the right: Villa Schlöndorff

Einen angestammten Sitz hat der junge Staat Israel in Berlin naturgemäß nicht. Aus Sicherheitsgründen baut er seine Botschaft in Schmargendorf auf einem Gelände, auf dem alle Gebäude bis auf eine denkmalgeschützte Villa, die als Residenz dient, abgerissen wurden. Der freistehende Neubau wird im Park errichtet. Der Entwurf stammt von Orit Willenberg-Giladi. Die junge Architektin aus Tel Aviv hat auch die israelischen Botschaften in Bangkok, Manila und Canberra entworfen. Die zweigeschossige Villa (Architekt: Philipp Schaefer/Karstadt-Baubüro, 1930) wird rekonstruiert und im Erdgeschoß ein Ort für repräsentative Empfänge geschaffen. Im Obergeschoß liegt die Wohnung des Botschafters.

Ursprünglich sollte die Botschaft im Altbau eingerichtet und die Residenz im Park gebaut werden. Dann entschied man sich anders und widmete den vierstöckigen Neubau, der im stumpfen Winkel zur Villa steht, der Botschaft. Wegen der günstigen Grundstückskosten fällt das Haus besonders großzügig aus. Alt- und Neubau haben einen gemeinsamen Eingang von einem Wegerondell zwischen den Gebäuden aus. Wie beim Altbau ist die Fassade aus Muschelkalk und das Dach aus Kupfer. Dennoch ist der Entwurf sehr eigen. Sechs Steinreliefs in der betont graphischen Fassade sollen die sechs Millionen ermordete Juden symbolisieren. Die Ornamente auf beiden Seiten des Eingang stehen hingegen für die mosaischen Gebotstafeln. Dahinter befindet sich ein schlichter Glaskörper mit Flugdach. Eine asymmetrische Natursteinmauer setzt sich im gebäudehohen Atrium fort und bildet den Hintergrund für diplomatische Empfänge. In seinem Bestreben, „Komplexität und Symbolik" Israels in Deutschland zu vermitteln, wirkt der Entwurf etwas bemüht.

The relatively new state of Israel naturally does not have a traditional embassy site in Berlin. For safety reasons, it is building its embassy in Schmargendorf on a plot on which all buildings, apart from a listed villa which serves as the residence, have been demolished. The detached new building is being built in a park to a design by Orit Willenberg-Giladi. The young female architect from Tel Aviv also designed Israel's embassies in Bangkok, Manila, Geneva and Canberra. The two-storey villa (architect: Philipp Schaefer/Karstadt construction office, 1930) is being reconstructed, and accommodation for splendid receptions is being created on the ground floor. The ambassador's residence is on the first floor.

Originally, the embassy was to be integrated into the old building and the residence to be built in the park. Then the plans were changed and the four-story new building, which is at an angle to the villa, was devoted to the embassy. Because of the moderate land costs, the building is particularly generous in its design. The old and new buildings have a joint entrance from a round access area between the buildings. Like the old building, the new building has a facade of shell limestone and a roof of copper. The design is nevertheless eccentric. Six stone reliefs in the decidedly graphic facade are intended to symbolise the six million exterminated Jews. But the ornaments on the two sides of the entrance stand for the Mosaic stone tablets bearing the commandments. Behind them is a simple glass structure with a single-pitch roof. An asymmetrical natural stone wall continues into the atrium, which is as tall as the building, and forms the background for diplomatic receptions. The design appears rather contrived in its effort to mediate the "complexity and symbolic character" of Israel in Germany.

Botschaft des Staates Katar / Embassy of the State of Qatar

Hagenstraße 56
14193 Berlin (Grunewald)

ab 2000

links/left: Ansicht Hagenstraße/
View from Hagenstrasse
rechts/right: Lageplan/Site plan

Katar ist das einzige Land, daß sich mit ausgesprochen folkloristischer Botschaftsarchitektur in Berlin präsentiert. Der exotische Entwurfsimport wirkt wie ein Märchenschloß aus Tausendundeiner Nacht im Grunewald. Das Gebäude in der Hagenstraße hat vier Stockwerke und ist reich mit Säulen, zinnenbekrönten Türmen und Ornamenten verziert, die Architekturmotive der arabischen Baukunst auffällig zitieren. Besonders liebevoll ist das gebäudehohe Hauptportal mit bunten Fliesenmustern geschmückt. Das Gebäudevolumen ist stark gegliedert und wirkt dadurch wie eine kleine, geheimnisvolle „Stadt in der Stadt". Dahinter verbergen sich allerdings die gewöhnlichen Büroräume einer Botschaft. Der Emir von Katar legte 1999 den Grundstein, bevor eine Baugenehmigung vorlag. Er war auf Staatsbesuch in Berlin und überraschte den Bezirk mit seinen Plänen für das prächtige orientalische Gebäude, der jedoch „begeistert war". Einen „Architekturzoo" wollte man nicht verhindern. In die Architektur mische man sich nur ein, „wenn sie völlig unverträglich" erscheine. Der Baubeginn verzögerte sich jedoch danach noch. Katar gehört dank seiner Erdgas- und Ölvorkommen zu den reichsten Ländern der Welt.

Qatar is the only country to present itself in Berlin with embassy architecture drawn expressly from its own folk lore. The exotic imported design appears like a fairy tale castle from the Arabian Nights in Grunewald. The building in Hagenstrasse has four storeys and is richly adorned with columns, battlements towers and ornaments which show striking motifs from Arabian architecture. The portal, which is as high as the building, is particularly lovingly decorated with colourful tile patterns. The building is intricately sub-divided and thus appears like a small and mysterious "city in the city". Behind this facade, however, are the normal rooms of an embassy. The Emir of Qatar laid the foundation stone in 1999 before building permission had been given. He was on a state visit to Berlin and surprised the district authorities with his plans for the majestic oriental building, but the authorities "were delighted". They did not want to prevent an "architectural zoo". They would only interfere in the architecture if it "appears completely unsuitable". But the beginning of construction work was nevertheless delayed. With its mineral gas and oil resources, Qatar is one of the richest countries in the world.

Botschaft der Republik Makedonien / Embassy of Macedonia

Hubertusallee 5,
Koenigsallee 2
14193 Berlin (Zehlendorf)

Hannes Sauer, Berlin

1996-1997

Ansicht Hubertusallee/
View from Hubertusallee

Das erst seit 1990 unabhängige Makedonien eröffnete 1997 den ersten fertigen Neubau unter den Berliner Botschaften. Das Land war damit schneller als die Bundesregierung in der Hauptstadt. Der vierstöckige Bau im Grunewald wurde offiziell zunächst nur als Residenz und Kanzlei genutzt. Eine Außenstelle der Botschaft verblieb vorläufig in Bonn als diplomatische Vertretung. Es ist kein Zufall, daß die ehemals zu Jugoslawien oder der Sowjetunion gehörenden jungen Staaten gleich in Berlin ihre Botschaften bauten, da die ehemaligen Teilstaaten keine eigenen Vertretungen besaßen. Das Gebäude liegt an der Hubertus- / Ecke Koenigsallee. 1999 wurde ein Anbau begonnen, der bis zum Umzug der Botschaft fertiggestellt wurde. Der Entwurf stammt von dem Berliner Architekten Hannes Sauer. Er versucht, auf dezente Weise Elemente der charakteristischen, traditionellen Architektur Makedoniens aufzunehmen: Die im Grundriß punktsymmetrisch-quadratische Stadtvilla hat einen typisch weiten Dachüberstand und rote Ziegeldeckung. Alle Ecken sind in verglaste Erker aufgelöst. Die Villa ist weißverputzt und hat ein rotes Zeltdach aus Holz. Die dunkelbraunen Fenster treten vor die Fassade. Der Entwurf genügt dennoch den städtebaulichen Vorgaben für den Grunewald. Das Haus paßt sich den benachbarten Villen an. Der Bau war umstritten, weil der Stadtteil Grunewald eigentlich dem Wohnen vorbehalten werden soll. Es wurde berücksichtigt, daß das Grundstück einigem Verkehrslärm ausgesetzt ist. Das Gebäude beinhaltet alle für eine Botschaft notwendigen Funktionen wie Konsulat, Büros und Festsaal. Die Residenz des Botschafters und die diplomatische Vertretung befinden sich unter einem Dach.

Macedonia, which has only been independent since 1990, was the first country to open a new embassy building in Berlin in 1997. The country thus moved to the German capital before the German government. The four-storey building in Grunewald was initially only used as a residence and offices. An auxiliary embassy office initially remained in Bonn as a diplomatic representation. It is no accident that the new states which formerly belonged to Yugoslavia and the Soviet Union built their embassies in Berlin from the outset because the former regions did not previously have their own premises in Germany. The building is on the corner of Hubertusallee and Koenigsallee in Wilmersdorf. An extension was begun in 1999 and completed by the time the embassy moved in. The design was by the Berlin architect Hannes Sauer. He tried to include elements of the characteristic, traditional Macedonian architecture in a restrained way: The city villa has a square symmetric-point ground layout with a typical wide roof overhang with tiles. All corners are visually softened by glazed bay windows. The villa has white rendering and a red wooden tent-type roof. The dark brown windows protrude in front of the facade, but the design nevertheless complied with the urban planning regulations for Grunewald and fits in with the neighbouring villas. The building was controversial because Grunewald is meant to be reserved for residential buildings. It was taken into account that the land is exposed to a certain amount of traffic noise. The building contains all functions necessary for an embassy such as consulate, office and festive hall. The ambassador's residence and the diplomatic quarters are situated under the same roof.

Botschaft der Königreichs Thailand / Embassy of the Kingdom of Thailand

Lepsiusstraße 64-66
12163 Berlin (Steglitz)

J.S.K Berlin (Um- und Neubau/alterations and new building)

1994-1995

Ansicht Lepsiusstraße mit Durchfahrt/
View from Lepsiusstraße with vehicle entrance

Das fünfgeschossige Büro- und Wohngebäude der thailändischen Botschaft in der Lepsiusstraße im Berliner Bezirk Steglitz schließt eine Baulücke. Durch eine drei Stockwerke hohe Öffnung wird der Blick auf eine dahinterliegende Altbauvilla freigegeben. Der Durchgang trennt den linken Wohnungsteil mit fünf Appartements von den Büros auf der rechten Seite und ist ebenso groß wie die Villa selbst. Im dritten und vierten Obergeschoß über der „Brücke" liegen weitere Büros. Zur Lepsiusstraße hat das Haus eine horizontal gestreifte Lochfassade aus blauen und weißen Metallpaneelen und ein steil geneigtes Zinkblechdach. Ein gläserner Erker und ein Balkonturm treten als Sonderelemente aus der flachen Fassade hervor. Ebenso wie im Durchgang ist die Rückfassade an den Treppenhäusern mit großen Glasflächen aufgerissen. Sie hat eine weißverputzte Lochfassade, gläserne Erker und ein Flachdach.

Die zweigeschossige klassizistische Villa wurde zum Verwaltungsgebäude des Konsulats umgebaut. Lediglich zwei Fassaden blieben stehen, der Rest wurde neu gebaut. Sie steht als weißverputzter Würfel im Garten. Der rote Klinkersockel des Altbaus wurde fortgeführt. Motive oder Prinzipien der thailändischen Baukunst haben keinen Eingang in die Architektur des Hauses gefunden.

The five-storey office and residential building of the embassy of Thailand in Lepsiusstrasse in the district of Steglitz closes a gap in the row of buildings. A three storey high opening provides a view of a villa which is a listed monument behind the new building. The entrance separates the residential section on the left with five apartments from the offices on the right and is just as large as the villa itself. Further offices are situated in the third and fourth storey over the "bridge". On the side facing Lepsiusstrasse, the building has a horizontally striped perforated facade of blue and white metal panels and a steeply sloping zinc metal roof. A glass bay and a balcony tower protrude from the flat facade as special elements. In the passage and on the rear facade, the staircase facade has large areas of glass. The rear facade has a white rendered perforated facade, glass bays and a flat roof.

The two-storey classical style villa has been altered for use as the administration building of the consulate. Only two facades were left intact, the rest was rebuilt. The villa is like a white rendered cube in the garden. The red brick pedestal of the old building was continued. Motifs and principles of Thai architecture had no influence on the design of the building.

Botschaften/Embassies

Ägypten/Egypt
Botschaft der Arabischen Republik
Ägypten/Embassy of the Arab Repu-
blic of Egypt
Stauffenbergstraße 5-7
10785 Berlin (Tiergarten)

Äthiopien/Ethiopia
Botschaft der Demokrat. Bundesrep.
Äthiopien/Embassy of the Democratic
Republic of Ethiopia
Boothstraße 20a
12207 Berlin (Lichterfelde)

Afghanistan/Afghanistan
Botschaft des Isl. Staates Afghani-
stan/Embassy of the Isl. State of Afgha-
nistan
Wilhelmstraße 65
10117 Berlin (Mitte)

Algerien/Algeria
Botschaft der Demokrat. Volksrepu-
blik Algerien/Embassy of the Democratic and Popular Republic of Algeria
Görschstraße 45-46
13187 Berlin (Pankow)

Bolivien/Bolivia
Botschaft der Republik Bolivien/
Embassy of the Republic of Bolivia
Bismarckstraße 91
13467 Berlin (Charlottenburg)

Bosnien und Herzegowina/
Bosnia and Hercegovina
Botschaft der Republik Bosnien und
Herzegowina/Embassy of the Repu-
blic of Bosnia and Hercegovina
Albertinenstraße
14165 Berlin (Zehlendorf)

Bulgarien/Bulgaria
Botschaft der Republik Bulgarien/Em-
bassy of the Republic of Bulgaria
Leipziger Straße 20-21
10117 Berlin (Mitte)

Chile/Chile
Botschaft der Republik Chile/
Embassy of the Republic of Chile
Mohrenstraße 42
10117 Berlin (Mitte)

China/China
Botschaft der VR China/Embassy of
the People's Republic of China
Arnold-Zweig-/Ecke Neumannstraße
13189 Berlin (Pankow)

Eritrea/Eritrea
Botschaft von Eritrea/Embassy of Eritrea
Stavanger Straße 18
10439 Berlin (Prenzlauer Berg)

Ghana/Ghana
Botschaft der Republik Ghana/
Embassy of the Republic of Ghana
Stavanger Straße 19
10439 Berlin (Prenzlauer Berg)

Indonesien/Indonesia
Botschaft der Republik
Indonesien/Embassy of the Republic
of Indonesia
Hermann-Hesse-Straße 38
13156 Berlin (Pankow)

Irak/Iraq
Botschaft der Republik Irak/
Embassy of the Republic of Iraq
Tschaikowskistraße 51
13156 Berlin (Pankow)

Iran/Iran
Botschaft der Islamischen Rep.
Iran/Embassy of the Islamic Rep. of
Iran
Podbielskiallee 67
14195 Berlin (Zehlendorf)

Irland/Ireland
Botschaft der Republik Irland/
Embassy of the Republic of Ireland
Friedrichstraße 200
10117 Berlin (Mitte)

Jugoslawien/Yugoslavia
Botschaft der Bundesrep.
Jugoslawien/Embassy of the Fed. Rep.
of Yugoslavia
Taubertstraße 18
14193 Berlin (Zehlendorf)

Kambodscha/Kampuchea
Botschaft des Königreichs Kambod-
scha/Embassy of the Kingdom of
Kampuchea
Benjamin-Vogelsdorff-Straße 2
13178 Berlin (Pankow)

Kap Verde/Cape Verde
Botschaft der Republik Kap
Verde/Embassy of the Republic of
Cape Verde
Stavanger Straße 16
10439 Berlin (Prenzlauer Berg)

Kasachstan/Kazakhstan
Botschaft der Republik
Kasachstan/Embassy of the Republic
of Kazakhstan
Nordendstraße 14-15
13156 Berlin (Pankow)

Süd-Korea/South Korea
Botschaft der Republik Korea/
Embassy of the Republic of Korea
Schöneberger Ufer 81
10785 Berlin (Tiergarten)

Kirgisien/Kyrgyzstan
Botschaft der Republik Kirgisien/
Embassy of the Republic of Kyrgyzstan
Otto-Suhr-Allee 146
10585 Berlin (Charlottenburg)

Kroatien/Croatia
Botschaft der Republik Kroatien/
Embassy of the Republic of Croatia
Ahornstraße 4
10787 Berlin (Schöneberg)

Kuba/Cuba
Botschaft der Republik Kuba/
Embassy of the Republic of Cuba
Stavanger Straße 20, Ibsenstraße 12
10439 Berlin (Pankow)

Lettland/Latvia
Botschaft der Republik Lettland/
Embassy of the Republic of Latvia
Reinerzstraße 40-41
14193 Berlin (Wilmersdorf)

Libanon/Lebanon
Botschaft der Libanesischen Republik/
Embassy of the Republic of Lebanon
Esplanade 8-10
13187 Berlin (Pankow)

Litauen/Lithuania
Botschaft der Republik Litauen/
Embassy of the Republic of Lithuania
Kurfürstenstraße 134
10785 Berlin (Tiergarten)

Moldawien/Moldavia
Botschaft der Republik Moldau/
Embassy of the Republic of Moldavia
Gotlandstraße 16
10439 Berlin (Prenzlauer Berg)

Mongolei/Mongolia
Botschaft der Mongolei/
Embassy of Mongolia
Gotlandstraße 12
10439 Berlin (Prenzlauer Berg)

Namibia/Namibia
Botschaft der Republik Namibia/
Embassy of the Republic of Namibia
Wichmannstraße 5
10787 Berlin (Tiergarten)

Neuseeland/New Zealand
Botschaft von Neuseeland/
Embassy of New Zealand
Friedrichstraße 60
10117 Berlin (Mitte)

Nigeria/Nigeria
Botschaft der Bundesrepublik Nigeria/
Embassy of the Fed. Rep. of Nigeria
Platanenstraße 98 a
13156 Berlin (Pankow)

Pakistan/Pakistan
Botschaft der Isl. Republik Pakistan/
Embassy of the Isl. Republic of Pakistan
Schaperstraße 29
10719 Berlin (Wilmersdorf)

Philippinen/Philippines
Botschaft der Republik der Philippinen/
Embassy of the Rep. of the Philippines
Hohenzollerndamm 196
10717 Berlin (Wilmersdorf)

Portugal/Portugal
Botschaft der Portugiesischen
Republik/Embassy of the Republic of
Portugal
Hiroshimastraße 23-25
10785 Berlin (Tiergarten)

Rumänien/Romania
Botschaft von Rumänien/
Embassy of Romania
Dorotheenstraße 55/56
10117 Berlin (Mitte)

Russische Föderation/
Russian Federation
Botschaft der Russischen Föderation/
Embassy of the Russian Federation
Unter den Linden 63-65
10117 Berlin (Mitte)

Saudi-Arabien/Saudi Arabia
Botschaft d. KönigreichsSaudi-Arabien
/Embassy of the Kingdom of Saudi Arabia
Tiergartenstraße 34
10785 Berlin (Tiergarten)

Singapur/Singapore
Botschaft der Republik Singapur/
Embassy of the Republic of Singapore
Friedrichstraße 200
10117 Berlin (Mitte)

Slowakei/Slovakia
Botschaft der Slowakischen Republik/
Embassy of the Republic of Slovakia
Leipziger Straße 36
10117 Berlin (Mitte)

Slowenien/Slovenia
Botschaft der Republik Slowenien/
Embassy of the Republic of Slovenia
Hausvogteiplatz 3-4
10117 Berlin (Mitte)

Sri Lanka/Sri Lanka
Botschaft der Republik Sri Lanka/
Embassy of the Republic of Sri Lanka
Niklasstraße 19
14129 Berlin (Zehlendorf)

Südafrika/South Africa
Botschaft der Republik Südafrika/
Embassy of the Republic of South Africa
Tiergartenstraße 17a/18
10785 Berlin (Tiergarten)

Taiwan/Taiwan
Botschaft der Republik Taiwan/
Embassy of the Republic of Taiwan
Markgrafenstraße 35
10117 Berlin (Mitte)

Tschechien/Czech Republic
Botschaft der Tschechischen Republik/
Embassy of the Czech Republic
Wilhelmstraße 44
10117 Berlin (Mitte)

Tunesien/Tunesia
Botschaft der Tunesischen Republik/
Embassy of the Republic of Tunesia
Lindenallee 16
14050 Berlin (Charlottenburg)

Türkei/Turkey
Botschaft der Republik Türkei/
Embassy of the Republic of Turkey
Tiergartenstraße 19-21
10785 Berlin (Tiergarten)

Turkmenistan/Turkmenistan
Botschaft der Republik Turkmenistan/
Embassy of the Republic of Turkmenistan
Langobardenallee 14
14052 Berlin (Charlottenburg)

Ukraine/Ukraine
Botschaft der Ukraine/
Embassy of the Ukraine
Albrechtstraße 26
10177 Berlin (Mitte)

Usbekistan/Uzbekistan
Botschaft der Republik Usbekistan/
Embassy of the Republic of Uzbekistan
Mauerstraße 83-84
10117 Berlin (Mitte)

Venezuela/Venezuela
Botschaft der Republik Venezuela/
Embassy of the Republic of Venezuela
Große Weinmeisterstraße 53
14482 Potsdam

Vereinigte Arabische Emirate/
United Arab Emirates
Botschaft der Vereinigten Arabischen
Emirate/Embassy of the United Arab
Emirates
Hiroshimastraße 16-20
10785 Berlin (Tiergarten)

Vietnam/Vietnam
Botschaft der Sozialistischen Republik
Vietnam/Embassy of the Socialist Re-
public of Vietnam
Elsenstraße 3-4
12435 Berlin (Treptow)

Weißrußland/Belorussia
Botschaft der Republik Belarus/
Embassy of the Republic of Belarussia
Unter den Linden 55-61
10117 Berlin (Mitte)

Zypern/Cyprus
Botschaft der Republik Zypern/
Embassy of the Republic of Cyprus
Wallstraße 27
10179 Berlin (Mitte)

Parlamentsbauten/
Parliament Buildings

Bürogebäude/Office Building
Unter den Linden 44-60
(Ehemaliges DDR-Ministerium für
Außenhandel/Former GDR Ministry
of Foreign Trade)
10117 Berlin (Mitte)

Bürogebäude/Office Building
Unter den Linden 69-73
(Ehemaliges DDR-Ministerium für
Volksbildung/Former GDR Ministry
for Education)
10117 Berlin (Mitte)

Stiftungen/Foundations

Friedrich-Naumann-Stiftung/
Friedrich Naumann Foundation
Büro Berlin
Tempelhofer Ufer 23-24
10963 Berlin (Kreuzberg)

Heinrich-Böll-Stiftung/
Heinrich Böll Foundation
Rosenthaler Straße 40-41
10178 Berlin (Mitte)

Ländervertretungen/
Federal State Offices

Freie und Hansestadt Hamburg
/Hanseatic city of Hamburg
Jägerstraße 1-3
10117 Berlin (Mitte)

Sachsen/Saxony
Brüderstraße 11/12
10117 Berlin (Mitte)

Sachsen-Anhalt/Saxony-Anhalt
Luisenstraße 18
10117 Berlin (Mitte)

Parteizentralen/
Party Headquarters

Bündnis 90/Die Grünen
Platz vor dem Neuen Tor 1
10115 Berlin (Mitte)

FDP
Reinhardtstraße 20-21
10117 Berlin (Mitte)

PDS
Kleine Alexanderstraße 28
10178 Berlin (Prenzlauer Berg)